TOFU

Isa Does it

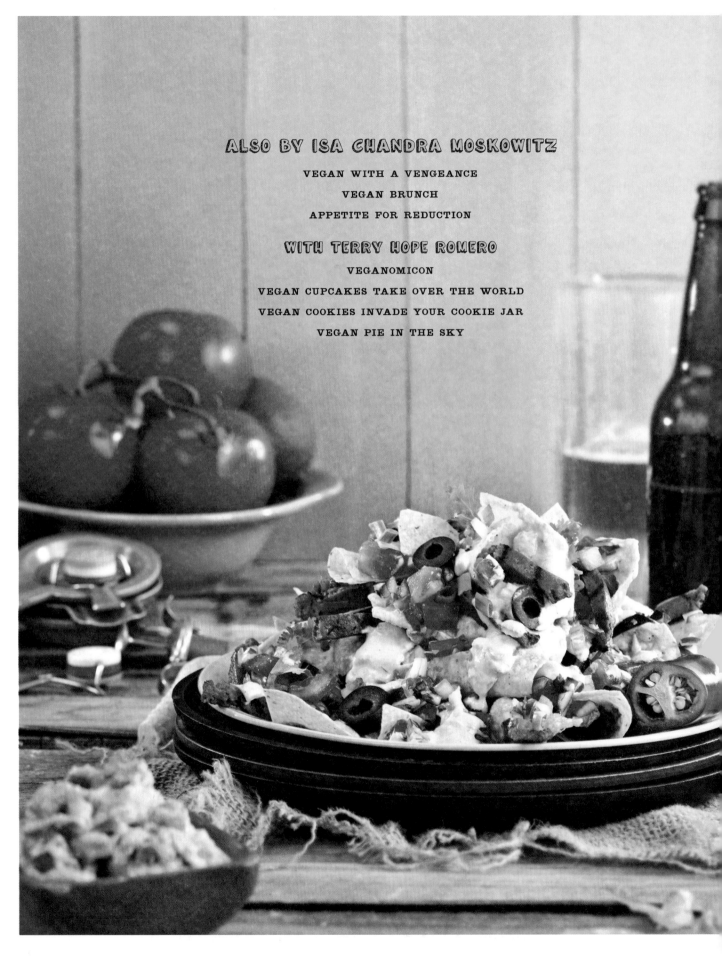

Isa Does it

AMAZINGLY EASY, WILDLY *delicious* VEGAN RECIPES FOR EVERY DAY of the WEEK

Isa Chandra Moskowitz

PHOTOGRAPHY BY VANESSA REES

L B

LITTLE, BROWN AND COMPANY
NEW YORK | BOSTON | LONDON

Opposite title page: Nacho Night, pages 232–33

Opposite contents page: Tempeh Orzilla, page 137

COPYRIGHT © 2013 by Isa Moskowitz

PHOTOGRAPHS © 2013 by Vanessa Rees

Little, Brown and Company
Hachette Book Group
237 Park Avenue, New York, NY 10017
littlebrown.com

First Edition: October 2013

Little, Brown and Company is a division of Hachette Book Group, Inc. The Little, Brown name and logo are trademarks of Hachette Book Group, Inc.

The publisher is not responsible for websites (or their content) that are not owned by the publisher.

The Hachette Speakers Bureau provides a wide range of authors for speaking events. To find out more, go to hachettespeakersbureau.com or call (866) 376-6591.

Design by Laura Palese

Drawings on endpapers and inside the book by Erica Rose Levine

ISBN 978-0-316-22190-0
LCCN 2013935098

10 9 8 7 6 5 4 3 2 1

IM

Printed in Thailand

TO NORAH & MAX,
the next generation of tofu lovers

CONTENTS

Isa Does it

introduction

WHAT DOES ISA DO?

From-Scratch Vegan Meals Made Easy!

WELCOME TO *Isa Does It!* This book has a mission: to get you in the kitchen, cooking satisfying meals with fresh ingredients any day of the week.

Cooking doesn't come second nature to everyone. In fact, I'd go so far as to say that in this age of convenience food, it hardly comes naturally to *anyone*, except maybe bloggers and reality show contestants.

But what I'm proposing isn't a diatribe against convenience food; my fingers have known the pleasures of keying up a microwave burrito. Maybe you already cook, but not as much as you would like. Maybe you're a proficient cook but new to the vegan pantry. Or maybe you're familiar with vegan cooking and simply looking to breathe new life into your repertoire? What I'm offering are recipes, tips, strategies, and even some philosophy to make your time in the kitchen as productive, easy, and hopefully even as fun as possible! Of course, fun isn't a *requirement.* I've spent many a night angrily sautéing rainbow chard, but it should be at least somewhat enjoyable most of the time.

MY COOKING JOURNEY

I burn with jealousy when cookbook authors recount their love of apple pie, developed while sitting on the kitchen counters of their granny, or the curry paste created by their mother with ingredients from her garden, or how they awoke every morning to the wafting scent of Dad's French toast.

Nope. For my family it was Hamburger Helper and powdered mashed potatoes all the way. Sure, we had the occasional home-cooked meal here and there, but for the most part cooking was as unfamiliar to teenage me as astrophysics. I was as likely to make a lasagna as I was to vote for Reagan, teach my mom how to use the VCR, or discover the Higgs boson. That is to say, not very.

And then I went vegetarian.

A few weeks and several cheeseless pizzas later, I was ready to branch out. Luckily for me, my mom and sis decided to come along for the journey. One day my mom came home from work with a small stack of vegetarian cookbooks, and the adventure began.

I suppose fearlessness is just a by-product of youth; the same way I never thought twice about riding the subway between cars or swimming way too far out at Coney Island, I never looked at how long a recipe took, how many ingredients were needed, or how many dishes were required. That was the spirit in which I dove into cookbooks like Louise Hagler's *Tofu Cookery*—with total abandon. Which is kind of funny, because even with all that chutzpah, tofu scared the hell out of me.

But what I love about that time, too, is that people didn't assume that tofu was somehow reprehensible. American cooking titles like *That Was TOFU? You Bastard!* and *I Can't Believe You Served Me Tofu!* had not yet appeared. Instead, the recipes in *Tofu Cookery* were written as though tofu were something delicious and wondrous and, most important, loved. This is what it became for me, and this is what it had been in China and Japan for hundreds of years.

Hi! I'm Isa.

Maybe you have a few of my cookbooks, or maybe this is your first. Before we get down to business, I think it's important that we know how to pronounce my name. Not my middle or my last (I can't even pronounce those) but my first. It's *EE*-sa, like "Lisa" but with no "L."

I don't know why my mom decided to name me Isa. My sister and brother were simply named "Michelle" and "Aaron." In fact, my sister didn't even receive the honor of a middle name. So we were always giving her new ones, like "Sponge" and "Squishy" and "Spoon."

But in any case, if the title of this book was lost on you, you should be all up to speed now!

So this is where my love of cooking began—in 1989, in a small kitchen in Sheepshead Bay, Brooklyn, with linoleum floors and fluorescent lighting, alongside my mom and my sis and even my brother, who hated vegetarians but would soon have to admit that he loved our cooking. My best friend would come over and we'd get out all the pots and pans, blast the music, crank up the burners, and have at it. For almost any occasion. I can recall a gigantic Thanksgiving spread with ten different kinds of tofu for every course and strawberries way out of season. A Chinese-inspired Christmas buffet with spring rolls that needed ten layers of brown paper shopping bags to absorb the oil. Everything wasn't always a success, but most of it was, and even if we failed we had fun.

This marks the time in my life when the kitchen went from smelling vaguely of microwaved frozen dinners to becoming the heart of our home. You'd open the front door downstairs, leave the cold air and the sound of the Q train overhead, and enter a downright enchanting bouquet: garlic, olive oil, and cinnamon, all mingling and cozy.

Of course, things from then on weren't always smooth sailing on almond milk seas.

Enter adulthood. My free time became more and more precious. I worked full-time, often at more than one job, and was always being asked out on dates. Okay, the second part isn't true, but I was pretty busy, and cooking wasn't always a top priority. Especially in a city where you could dial a number and have a delicious, steamy pad thai delivered to your front door before you even hung up.

But still, I cooked. In tiny kitchens, with not the best equipment, and now with a different focus, on nourishing myself, saving money, and also taking time to do something good for myself. The recipes in this book are designed with that period of my life in mind.

And now, even as a cookbook author, or perhaps *especially* as a cookbook author, I don't always feel like creating extravagant spreads, amuse-bouches, and five-course dinners. I want dinner on the table. But I want it to be relatively painless. If you do, too, I hope this book will help you get there. Easily.

xo ISA

How Does
ISA DO IT?

PANTRY AND SUPERMARKET FRIENDLY

It's not even necessarily only the cooking that stands between you and dinner; sometimes it's the shopping and the planning, too. So I've tried to use pantry ingredients, and fruits and veggies that are, or can easily enough become, staples in the fridge. This isn't the book to show you how to experiment with molecular gastronomy or heirloom vegetables passed down from the Byzantine era; it's about using what you have around. The pantry ingredients can easily be obtained in most large supermarkets these days, without a trip to a specialty market or health food store.

FAST COOKING TIMES

This one speaks for itself! Many of the recipes here have cooking times of 30 minutes or less.

DOWNTIME

Yes, some of the recipes have suspiciously longish-looking cooking times. But don't raise your eyebrows at recipes that take an hour or so to cook; the active time will be much, much shorter. The simple fact is that, well, some foods take time to cook! But I've designed the recipes in this book to be full of luxurious downtime. It's not all about speed: Sometimes the "easy" part comes while something roasts away in the oven or simmers along on the stovetop and you are free to do whatever else in the world you feel like doing.

PLANNING AHEAD

This is such an important part of weeknight cooking. I'm not talking about extensive planning. Rather, these are simple things you can do that take less than a minute of work but will save you hours of time in the kitchen. Soaking cashews, soaking beans and grains, cooking and freezing grains—these are but a few steps that will make getting dinner on the table a breeze!

TECHNIQUE BUILDING

We all have a skill of some sort, or at least something we're good at and can do quickly. Chances are you didn't pick up that guitar and just start noodling out tunes. Even skills we're used to doing on automatic—say, riding a bike—had to be learned at some point. And so it is with cooking. It takes me less than a minute to dice an onion, and the more *you* do it, the easier it will get. But beyond onions, I approached writing the recipes in this book as if they were mini cooking lessons. What I'm hoping is that the more you use the recipes and the common techniques, the further you'll be on the road to becoming a better and better home cook. I'm not talking flambés or soufflés here! Once you get down a few prep skills and everyday cooking practices, like sautéing and roasting, you'll be slinging hash like a pro (or slinging lasagna, or soup . . . wait, don't sling soup!).

FEWER DISHES

If you're like me, you've got great bone structure, you have terrible taste in movies, *and* you hate cleaning up. I hear you! I worked really hard to come up with recipes that involve the fewest number of dishes possible. Cooking is work enough; you don't need to spend an hour afterward washing up.

DO IT SATISFYING

Perhaps the most important thing to get right with home cooking is to make it satisfying. I don't want any deprived vegans running around. If you're making dinner most nights, it should be worth your while, not just nutritionally but gastronomically as well. Here are my keys to ultra-tasty vegan cooking:

Char

There is something that speaks to the caveman (or caveperson, if you prefer) in all of us. The part of us that says *"fire good."* Giving up meat doesn't mean giving up on satisfying smokiness. To achieve char, equipment is your top priority. Cast-iron skillets, grilling, and roasting are all ways to get your char on. Whether you're cooking meaty things like homemade seitan or unsuspecting innocents like Brussels sprouts, charring brings out surprising flavor and appeals to our most primitive senses.

Creaminess

Perhaps the biggest hankering I got when I went vegan was for something truly creamy. Something that hit my tongue just right and filled up all my senses. After a few failed cream of spinach soups made with soy milk, I knew that something had to change. Now I think I've got a handle on it. Creaminess can come from cashews, which mimic heavy cream when puréed. Coconut milk is an obvious option. A simple purée of root vegetables can get the job done. And yes, sometimes they got things right in the '80s—puréed silken tofu makes a great creamy replacement for sour cream and sauces!

Complexity

Ah, simple, simple complexity! What exactly does it mean? I suppose the easiest way to understand it is to think about when you take a bite of something delicious and wonder, "How did they do that?" It's something we often experience in restaurant-quality cooking, and it's the reason we return again and again to, say, that pizza joint with the addictive sauce or that Thai place with the *"OMG WTF IS IN THAT PAD THAI?"*

Complex flavors can be tricky to achieve at home, but there are easy ways to get there. For one thing, contrasting flavors, like sweet and sour. For another, herbs and spices, especially ones like star anise and bay leaf, which permeate sauces and stews with what can only be described as sorcery. Other ingredients with lots of umami flavor, like miso or nutritional yeast flakes, prove to be godsends in the weeknight vegan kitchen. Caramelizing onions, reducing white wine, proper seasoning . . . all of these add to the complexity of a dish, and the recipes in this book capitalize on simple techniques like these to get you complex flavors.

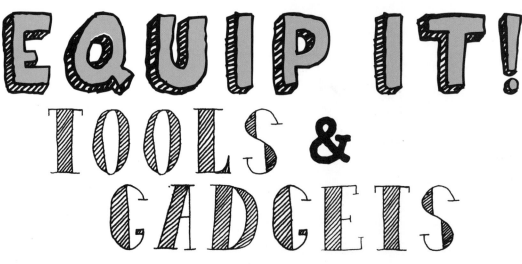

EQUIP IT!
TOOLS & GADGETS
that every kitchen needs

You don't need to spend a lot (or get married just for the presents) in order to have a kitchen that can handle most anything you throw at it. The recipes in this book require a few items, but none are too pricey, and you can build your arsenal as you go.

STUFF THAT PLUGS IN

Blender

For creamy sauces, you'll definitely need a blender. I don't have one of those high-tech $400 ones; just a nice solid one that costs less than $100 and gets good online reviews should do. Although if you do have a Vitamix or the like, congratulations Queen of France! You can make all the cashew sauces in this book without having to soak the nuts first.

Immersion blender

This is one of those "How did I ever live without it?" gadgets for me. Instead of transferring a soup back and forth from pot to blender, you just stick this magic wand in and get perfectly puréed soup, exactly the texture you want it, in under a minute!

Food processor

You can make about 95 percent of the recipes in this book without it, but a big ol' food processor with a metal blade and a shredding attachment can be a lifesaver.

PRIMITIVE TOOLS

Wooden cutting board

A chunky, solid wooden cutting board. One that takes muscle to pick up. One that could knock out a burglar. A wooden cutting board that means business. Forget your plastic, your silicone; don't even say the word *glass*. Invest in a cutting board that will last a lifetime, preferably one with rubber grips on the bottom so that it stays put while you chop up your masterpieces. The more scuffed up and worn the cutting board gets, the better and better a cook you will become.

Chef's knife

What kind of chef's knife are you using? Are you even using a chef's knife? Because if you're using a steak knife and your cutting board is a paper towel (hello, my boyfriend), then that (literally) isn't going to cut it. Get yourself a chef's knife. If you don't have the resources to make an investment (a $100 one that will last you a lifetime), then at least Google "best chef's knife for $20" and get something adequate.

Of course, go to the kitchen supply store and play around for a bit, see what feels best for you, and check the reviews on it (either at Consumer Reports or Amazon). Don't fall for whatever is prettiest and trendiest, unless that really is the best. Pretend you're buying a car or picking out a school for your child or a sweater for your dog. *It's that important!* Once you get your dream knife, take it to get professionally sharpened twice a year. Don't do it yourself and don't let your cousin do it. Once again, pretend you're taking care of your car or your bike. *It's that important!*

Thin metal spatula

In soooo many recipes I say to use a thin metal spatula. You might start thinking, "Shut up about the thin metal spatula already." Or worse yet, you might ignore me completely. But listen. Those big plasticky rubbery spatulas are only good for playing spatula tennis. If you use them to flip food that requires browning, unless you're using a ton of oil, all they will manage to do is separate the bulk of your food from its lovely browned surface. A thin metal spatula gets under the food, preserving all that browning or breading, thus keeping the flavor intact. It's such an important tool and so often overlooked. And for pennies you can acquire one at a thrift store, with an adorable granny-reminiscent handle. Or for a few bucks more, you can purchase one new. But the handle won't be nearly as cute.

Angled wooden spatula

For stirring soups and stews. Do round pots and pans have corners? I don't know what else to call the crevice of the soup pot where the side meets the bottom. In any case, an angled (or slanted) wooden spatula gets into hard-to-reach places and ensures even cooking and perfectly unburned stovetop delights. What's more, if you accidentally leave a wooden spatula in the pot while something is cooking, it won't melt or burn you. Thanks, wood!

Potato masher (big and small)

You'll need a mama potato masher for exactly what the name implies: mashing potatoes! But pick up a baby one, too, often called an avocado masher, because vegan cooking requires lots of mashing of the smaller varieties of food, like beans. Oh, and yes, avocados.

Tongs

You'll need some of these for flipping around greens and for reaching stuff high up on shelves, and you can also use them like a hand puppet and make them say "Get out of the kitchen" in a funny voice whenever someone comes in to bug you.

Peeler

You'll see many vintage peelers in the food photography in this book, and those are wonderful for photos but not so wonderful for your hands. To avoid third-degree blisters, a good solid vegetable peeler, with a big comfortable handle that looks like it could double as a guided missile, is a necessity. And if it's brightly colored, so much the better.

Other stuff that should be stuffed into a kitchen crock and kept on your counter at all times

Serving spoon, slotted spoon, ladle, Microplane grater, pasta spoon.

POTS & PANS

Large cast-iron pan

I'm not going to do such a huge song and dance about any other pot or pan. But I am going to make a big show of trying to get you to cook with cast iron. Why? Well, it's affordable and will last, quite literally, forever. But honestly, even if I had to buy a brand-new one every year, I would still cook with cast iron because *it makes food taste better*. Well-seasoned cast iron is naturally nonstick, so less oil is needed. In fact, with cast iron, sometimes less oil makes for better browning. Food cooks evenly in cast iron. And the pan can easily go from stovetop to oven, which is great for casseroles.

Don't be worried that cast iron is hard to care for. Always hand wash with a bristle brush. Dry completely with a clean kitchen towel, never a paper towel, as it can leave a papery film. Rubbing with a little oil keeps it in tip-top shape; just apply a very thin coat of olive or flaxseed oil and rub all over with your hands, make sure to get the handle and the bottom of the pan, too. And if it ever does rust up, simply scour the rust away. If that doesn't do the job, bake your pan in the oven at 350°F for an hour to get the rust off.

4-quart stainless-steel soup pot

All of the soup and stew recipes in this book can be made in a 4-quart pot. No need to break out the cauldron! Mashed potatoes, pasta, and large amounts of grains all come together in a 4-quart pot.

2-quart saucepan
For sauces and smaller amounts of grains.

Lids
It has come to my attention that not everyone has secure-fitting lids for their pots and pans. You need lids.

Steamer
I use a stovetop steamer, but whether you prefer stovetop or electric, make sure you have a convenient way to steam your kale.

Cast-iron grill pan
If you like to do some indoor grilling (and you do).

For the oven
Two rimmed baking sheets.
Large (9 x 13–inch) ceramic casserole dish.

BAKING EQUIPMENT

Most of the dessert recipes in this book require just one bowl! *I know!* You're welcome. So you don't need too much in the baking department, but here are the necessities:

- A MIXING BOWL, MAYBE WITH A HANDLE
- A GOOD, STURDY FORK—YES, A FORK—THAT WON'T BEND WHEN YOU MIX
- DRY MEASURING CUPS, STAINLESS STEEL, WITH STRONG HANDLES
- A 4 X 8-INCH LOAF PAN
- MUFFIN TINS
- AN 8-INCH SQUARE OR A 9-INCH SQUARE METAL BAKING PAN
- BUNDT PAN, AS FANCY OR SIMPLE AS YOU LIKE
- LARGE WOODEN SPOON FOR MIXING BATTERS
- MEASURING SPOONS THAT FIT INTO SPICE JARS
- BAKING SHEETS
- MESH SIFTER
- ICE CREAM SCOOPER FOR DOLING OUT MUFFIN BATTER
- COOLING RACKS

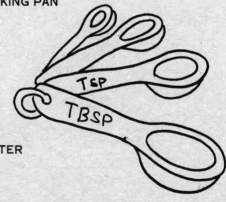

STOCK IT!
MAKE YOUR
pantry complete

If someone asked for my best kitchen advice, it might be, "Keep your pantry stocked and never run out of garlic and onions." If you've got these ingredients around, then a good meal is never more than a cabinet door away. You don't need to rush out and get everything on this list today, but once you make a few of the recipes, you'll see a common thread forming. And before you know it, your pantry will be complete!

HERBS, SPICES & BLENDS THAT I USE, LIKE, ALL THE TIME

Dried thyme, dried oregano, ground cumin, sweet paprika, crushed red pepper flakes, ground cinnamon (Vietnamese is my favorite), mild chili powder, mild curry powder, fennel seeds, coriander seeds, and, of course, black peppercorns in a pepper mill.

HERBS, SPICES & BLENDS THAT I USE ONLY SOME OF THE TIME

Ground fennel, dried rosemary, dry rubbed sage, powdered sage, star anise, bay leaves, onion powder, granulated garlic, cumin seeds, dried tarragon, ground mustard, whole yellow mustard, smoked paprika, ground cloves, ground allspice, ground nutmeg, ground ancho chile powder, pizza seasoning, garam masala, and saffron if I'm feeling rich. I also have a curry powder addiction and love to have several other varieties around besides basic mild, including oriental curry powder and Jamaican curry powder. I do, however, give alternatives for those items in the recipes that call for them.

A Few Words about Herbs & Spices

Those little tins of spices from the '70s are really great for looking absolutely adorable on your tchotchke shelf, but please do not use old spices! I'm talking, replace those spices every six months or so. They lose their potency and can end up making your precious cooking taste dull or, worse, dusty. I suggest purchasing herbs and spices from the bulk bins in amounts according to how often you use them. So, for instance, I buy a big package of dried thyme from my favorite spice shop because I know I'll go through it in a matter of months. Meanwhile, I only need a scoop of smoked paprika. Your needs may differ, but you get the idea. And ignore those gigantic jugs of 99-cent spices. You're not going to use it all anyway, so what's the value in that? Going for high-quality herbs and spices in the quantities you need will actually save you money in the long run. And your food will thank you for it.

PANTRY ESSENTIALS

- **BEANS, CANNED AND/OR DRY:** chickpeas, black beans, pinto beans, white beans (great northern or navy), black-eyed peas, kidney beans, lentils

- **QUICK-COOKING LEGUMES:** brown lentils, red lentils, yellow split peas

- **GRAINS AND THE LIKE:** quinoa, brown rice, brown basmati and/or white basmati rice, wild rice blend, whole-wheat couscous, polenta, sturdy grains like wheat berries or spelt berries

- **PASTA AND NOODLES:** linguine, small pasta (like macaroni or shells), rice noodles, orzo, fusilli, penne. Use whole-wheat or whole-grain varieties for the best nutrition. Unless you're gluten-free, of course, in which case, I suggest brown rice pasta.

- **NUTS AND SEEDS:** unroasted cashews, roasted peanuts, shelled walnuts, sliced almonds, pine nuts, sunflower seeds, toasted sesame seeds

- **CANNED GOODS:** coconut milk (regular and/or lite), chipotles in adobo sauce, 28-ounce cans crushed tomatoes (with basil, if available), 28-ounce cans whole tomatoes. Choose organic and fire-roasted tomato varieties when you can afford to.

- **OILS:** olive, canola, refined coconut, toasted sesame; plus a spray bottle of oil, either an organic can from the supermarket or the kind you fill yourself, such as Misto

- **VINEGARS:** balsamic, apple cider (for baking), red wine, rice wine

- **CONDIMENTS:** Dijon mustard, ketchup, vegan mayo (Vegenaise brand is the best, low-fat or grapeseed varieties)

- **SAUCES:** sriracha, Frank's RedHot, tamari (gluten-free) or soy sauce, hoisin sauce, liquid smoke

- **JARS:** roasted red peppers, capers, kalamata olives, almond butter, peanut butter, tahini, concentrated vegetable broth. About that vegetable broth: Because this is a weeknight cookbook, I'm recommending concentrated vegetable broth, for its ease and affordability. You can use whichever brand you like best, whether in powdered or jarred form. I use broth in such large amounts that it would be impossible to keep up with the homemade stuff, and I prefer the concentrated kind that comes in a jar. My favorite brand right now is Better Than Bouillon, either the No-Chicken or Vegetable flavors.

- **VEGAN MILKS:** I'm ridiculous and have about five different kinds of milks. My favorite is unsweetened almond milk. A few others I love are soy milk, hemp milk, and rice milk. You should discover your favorite; just make sure that it's unsweetened so that it works in savory cooking as well as sweet.

- **WINE:** Keep sale-rack bottles of dry white in the fridge and red at room temperature. Chardonnay and Merlot, respectively, are my go-to cooking wines. Keep mirin (Japanese cooking wine) in the pantry.

- **BREAD CRUMBS:** I use dry bread crumbs in all of my recipes, both panko and American-style bread crumbs, be they seasoned, whole wheat, or plain.

Freeze Frame!

As I mentioned, there may be a few microwave burritos in my freezer. But there's also lots of other cool stuff that makes from-scratch weeknight cooking a whole lot easier. You can purchase rice and quinoa in frozen packages, but it's easy (and way less expensive) to freeze your own grains. Just cook up a huge batch of rice or quinoa, let cool completely, then store in freezer bags in whatever amounts you prefer. They will keep for up to a month. Microwave in a bowl when ready to use, or gently reheat on the stovetop.

FRIDGE STAPLES

Tofu (extra-firm), tempeh, light miso (mellow white or chickpea), prepared red curry paste (check to see that it has no fishy ingredients, like bonito flakes or fish sauce).

FREEZER STAPLES

Berries, corn, peas.

BAKING STUFF

All-purpose flour (unbleached organic, if you can), whole-wheat pastry flour, rolled oats, ground flaxseed, semisweet chocolate chips, unsweetened cocoa powder, unsweetened applesauce in single-serving containers, refined coconut oil, organic cornstarch (if you're avoiding GMOs), baking soda, and baking powder.

SWEETENERS

Granulated sugar (evaporated cane juice), light brown sugar, agave nectar (I use whatever is cheapest), grade B maple syrup, and, very occasionally, brown rice syrup and molasses.

WEIRDO INGREDIENTS

I have really tried to keep the weirdo ingredients to a minimum in this book. For these ingredients, you'll probably need to take a trip to your friendly neighborhood food co-op or Whole Foods. If neither is realistic, then order online. If you're already vegan, you probably have these around anyway. If not, read on.

ORGANIZE IT

Whether you live in a studio apartment, a hippie commune, or a suburban ranch house, you should always keep your pantry organized. And this is laughable coming from me, the most unorganized person in the world (I have a dresser drawer that contains socks, capris, *and* pajamas, to give you an idea). But organize it in a way that makes sense to you, always making sure that the stuff you use most often (hello, sriracha!) is not buried behind anything and remembering to throw out anything that you haven't used in recent memory (hello, pomegranate vinegar!).

I keep all of my regularly used spice jars on two lazy Susans in a cabinet. My other, less used spices go into a shoe box that is easy to pull in and out of the cabinet.

All of my baking stuff is together in one cabinet. I even keep my apple cider vinegar away from all the other vinegars because I know that I use it mostly in baking. So I'm never running around the kitchen like a tofu with its head cut off looking for the baking powder. I know it's there, in the baking cabinet.

Maybe it's not the neatest pantry in the world, maybe everything isn't brightly labeled, but for the most part, I've got it under control. Would someone else ever be able to figure out where the rolled oats are? I bet it would be an epic journey for them. But so long as I know, then everything is okay.

Vital wheat gluten

This is the magical flour-like substance that makes delicious seitan, also known as wheat meat. When vital wheat gluten is combined with a few wet ingredients, and maybe some beans, you'll have a fabulous array of homemade vegan meats to choose from.

Nutritional yeast flakes

Affectionately dubbed "nooch," this is the go-to ingredient for adding creamy texture and cheezy, nutty flavor to seitan, sauces, and other yummy stuff.

Chickpea flour

This is what it sounds like: ground-up dried chickpeas! It has a fabulous toasty eggy flavor and so I love to use it in savory cooking every now and again. Namely, as the flour for my roux and in tofu omelets. It's also sold in Indian markets as "besan" flour.

Cashews

I know what you're thinking: "Why are cashews in a list of weirdo ingredients? I know what a cashew is!" Maybe a cashew used to be simply the nut you snacked on in the car when you forgot to eat breakfast. But in this book, most of the time, we're turning them into cashew cream. When soaked for a few hours and blended with liquid, cashews become a thick and creamy concoction

ABS:
ALWAYS BE SOAKING

I don't want you to be intimidated by recipes that call for soaking cashews. There is no reason in the world that you shouldn't be able to whip up something creamy any night of the week. If you follow my mantra and always have a cup of cashews soaking, then you'll never have to turn a creamy sauce away.

It's easy! To soak, place cashews in a bowl and cover with water by an inch or two. Cashews expand a bit when soaked. Cover the bowl with plastic wrap (or with the lid, if you're using Tupperware) and let soak for at least 2 hours, overnight, or up to 3 days in the refrigerator. Drain before using.

If a recipe calls for soaked cashews, I make sure that I begin making the cashew cream first thing. I leave the blender running for a minute with the cashews in it and go about my business making everything else. I don't just stand there and blend for 5 minutes. I also prep stuff, get all my other ingredients out, and then, from time to time, I check on the cashews and give my blender motor a break. Rub the cream between your fingers to test for smoothness. A little graininess is okay, but you want it to be as smooth as possible. If they're not ready, just let them sit there for a minute to rest, and then restart the blender and begin again. The amount of time it takes really depends on the strength of your machine.

Oh, and if you are the lucky owner of a high-tech blender, like a Vitamix or a Blendtec, then the soaking step is not even necessary.

And if you totally forget to soak them, you can boil for 15 minutes and then let them soak as long as you can. That will soften them up!

similar to heavy cream. We will use it to make creamy tomato sauces, mac and cheese, and really, anything where you might expect to find heavy cream. Purchase unroasted cashews. They don't have to say "raw" on the label, just so long as they don't say "roasted." If you're allergic to cashews, you can use sunflower seeds instead. They don't get *as* creamy, but they work!

Dried mushrooms

Dried mushrooms are great to have on hand for soups and stews, and ground-up mushrooms, especially porcini, make an excellent flavoring element as well. They're much cheaper and more widely available than fresh. I don't use them that often in these recipes, but dried wood-ear, porcini, shiitakes, and mixed wild mushrooms make brief appearances.

Refined coconut oil

For use in baking, in place of butter/margarine things, and also for some savory cooking, I absolutely adore coconut oil. It's solid when cool but liquid when warm, so always pay attention to the recipe. If it calls for melted coconut oil, measure first and then a few seconds in a microwave or gently heated on the stovetop should do it. If it calls for solid coconut oil and yours is liquid, then a brief stint in the freezer will get it where you want it to be. I prefer expeller-pressed refined coconut oil to "virgin" because the coconut flavor is less pronounced. So long as the label reads "expeller-pressed," it means that it hasn't been chemically treated.

VEGGIES & A FEW FRUITS: THE HEART & SOUL OF VEGAN COOKING

This isn't an exhaustive list of the fruits and veggies used in the book, but I bet if you have these items stocked, you can make 95 percent of the savory recipes herein.

Countertop veggies (& fruits)

I always have these veggies out in a big vintage bowl on my countertop: yellow onions (buy 5-pound bags); red onions, garlic, potatoes (russets, Yukon Gold, or red), sweet potatoes (or yams), beets, limes, lemons, bananas, avocados (which I transfer to the fridge when ripe).

Greens in the crisper

Kale (try pretty varieties, like Red Russian), Swiss chard, baby spinach, baby arugula, romaine, bok choy, sprouts.

Cruciferous

Cauliflower, broccoli, Brussels sprouts, cabbage (red and green).

Squash

Zucchini in the fridge, winter squashes like butternut and acorn out on the counter.

Other fridge staples

Fresh ginger, red and green bell peppers, celery, cucumbers, carrots (and baby carrots for super-lazy times), tomatoes (which I grow all summer, too!), mushrooms (cremini, portobello, and shiitake).

Once-in-a-while veggies

Eggplant, shallots, string beans, asparagus, shallots, leeks, fresh corn.

Fresh herbs & the like

Thyme, cilantro, scallions, mint, basil, dill.

Also

Fresh, edible flowers are really essential for most recipes. Especially purple ones! (Just kidding.)

VEGAN BUTCHERY

I didn't invent the concept of "vegan butchery," but I sure love it!
It's so important to know how to handle vegan proteins and to have
fun while doing it. Creating perfect cubes is definitely a skill to
master, but no one wants to eat cubes all the time, so try a few of
the other shapes, too. And once you get the hang of it, you may be
creating cuts of your own. Heart-shaped tofu, anyone?

A few tips for the new butcher:

1. **USE A SHARP 8- OR 9-INCH CHEF'S KNIFE.** A serrated knife will give you funny lines (or maybe you like that?) and a paring knife isn't long enough to make even cuts.

2. **SLICE IN ONE MOTION.** Don't saw or hack.

3. **USE A LARGE CUTTING BOARD** so that you have room to maneuver your knife and your food.

TOFU BUTCHERY

CUBES

Let's start with the most common cut—the cube! This is what you'll throw into stir-fries and on top of bowls.

1. START BY TURNING THE BLOCK OF TOFU ON ITS SIDE, THEN SLICE LENGTHWISE.

2. KEEPING THE BLOCK INTACT, FLIP IT OVER FLAT ON THE CUTTING BOARD. SLICE DOWN THE MIDDLE SO THAT YOU HAVE TWO EVEN HALVES.

3. NOW SLICE EACH HALF IN HALF, SO THAT YOU HAVE FOUR EQUAL PIECES. **NOTE:** if you desire smaller cubes, you can instead slice each half into thirds.

4. TURN THE KNIFE SIDEWAYS AND MAKE A LENGTHWISE CUT.

5. NOW TWO MORE LENGTHWISE CUTS ABOVE AND BELOW THE FIRST ONE.

6. AND OMG, WILL YOU LOOK AT THAT? YOU'VE GOT CUBES!

BABY TRIANGLES

Once you have cubes, you can slice them corner to corner for little tiny triangles. Use baby triangles where you would use cubes.

SLABS

Slabs are what you want for grilling or baking. You can stuff 'em into sandwiches or slice them into strips once cooked. Or, just, ya know…eat 'em!

1. LAY TOFU FLAT AND SLICE RIGHT DOWN THE MIDDLE, MAKING TWO EVEN HALVES.

2. SLICE A HALF IN HALF.

3. NOW SLICE THOSE HALVES IN HALF! SO MANY HALVES.

4. REPEAT ON THE OTHER SIDE. NOW YOU HAVE PERFECTLY EVEN SLABS! OR CLOSE ENOUGH TO PERFECT, ANYWAY.

SQUARES & LONG TRIANGLES

Sometimes slabs get tiring. Guess what? You can butcher them even further into more cute shapes. These are both great on the grill, as well.

TRY SLICING A SLAB IN HALF FOR SQUARES.

OR, SLICE CORNER TO CORNER FOR LONG TRIANGLES.

TEMPEH BUTCHERY

Tempeh comes in different shapes and forms, but the most common is this rectangle. If yours isn't in a rectangle but instead is a fat square, you can often slice that square across the center like opening a clam shell, then place the squares side by side to approximate a rectangle.

PLANKS

These long rectangles are great for sandwiches or grilled and placed on top of salads.

1. SLICE TEMPEH RIGHT ACROSS THE MIDDLE, WIDTHWISE.

2. SLICE EACH OF THOSE HALVES IN HALF TO FORM QUARTERS.

3. SLICE EACH OF THOSE QUARTERS INTO THIRDS. YOU'LL NOW HAVE TWELVE BEAUTIFUL PLANKS.

LITTLE RECTANGLES

Sometimes you want little rectangles, to break up the monotony. I use these in the Tempeh Giardino (page 186), but you can use rectangles in place of cubes anywhere, at any time.

1. FOLLOW STEPS 1 THROUGH 3 FOR PLANKS.

2. NOW GRAB A SECTION OF PLANKS AND SLICE THEM WIDTHWISE.

3. THERE ARE YOUR LITTLE RECTANGLES!

CUBES

More fun with cubes! Now you'll have perfect squares for stir-fries, to top off soups, or to mix into pastas and salads.

1. FOLLOW STEPS 1 AND 2 FOR PLANK TEMPEH SO THAT YOUR SLAB OF TEMPEH IS IN QUARTERS.

2. SLICE EACH QUARTER IN HALF.

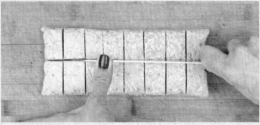

3. TURN YOUR KNIFE SIDEWAYS AND SLICE THE TEMPEH DOWN THE MIDDLE LENGTHWISE.

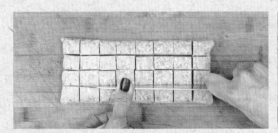

4. NOW MAKE TWO CUTS, ONE ON THE TOP HALF, ONE ON THE BOTTOM HALF.

5. YOU NOW HAVE THE BEST TEMPEH CUBES EVER!

BIG TRIANGLES

I usually use these big triangles in an entrée or to magically turn a salad into an entrée.

1. SLICE TEMPEH ACROSS THE MIDDLE WIDTHWISE.

2. NOW SLICE EACH HALF CORNER TO CORNER.

3. YOU NOW HAVE FANCY TRIANGLES OF TEMPEH!

4. YOU MAY WANT TO SLICE THEM FURTHER IF YOU PREFER THINNER PIECES. I CALL THIS CLAM TEMPEH. SIMPLY STAND A TRIANGLE UP AND SLICE IT IN HALF, LIKE SPLITTING OPEN A CLAMSHELL, VEGAN-STYLE.

7 TIPS for COOKING your heart out WITH EASE

The number one tool in the kitchen is . . . you! Wait, I'm not calling you a tool; I'm just saying, get yourself in there. If cooking isn't second nature to you, the more and more you do it, the easier and easier it will get. That said, here are a few (well, seven) bits of wisdom that I think will prove priceless.

1. **MISE EN PLACE:** I'm sure you've all heard that phrase by now. It simply means "putting in place." In French. So gather all of your ingredients before preparing your feast and place them on the counter. But don't stop there; gather all of your equipment as well. Not just the pots and pans, but make sure you scan the recipe for absolutely anything you might need, including measuring utensils, colanders, can openers, and so on. This also gives you a great opportunity to . . .

2. **PLAN AND SCAN:** Scan the recipe! Give it a read through so you know what's coming up. Like a good Boy or Girl Scout, you have to be prepared.

3. TIME MANAGEMENT: While scanning the recipe, you might see pockets of downtime. Use some of that time to prep instead of prepping everything before starting the recipe. For instance, if a recipe calls for sliced onions, sliced mushrooms, minced garlic, and diced potato, chances are those ingredients aren't all going in at once. So sauté the onion and, while that is working in the pan, prep the mushrooms and garlic. While those are cooking, prep the potato. Of course, that is just an example, but many recipes are set up to give you some time to prep while other items cook. Use it wisely!

4. KEEP IT WITHIN REACH: Storage is really important. If your cutting board is in a pain-in-the-butt place to reach under a bunch of pots and pans, you will be less inclined to use it. Keep your most frequently used items easily accessible; that is, your essential pots, pans, and utensils. As soon as I arrive home, I pull out my cutting board and knife and put them on the counter, because I know that at the very least I will need those.

5. COUNTER CULTURE, NOT COUNTER CLUTTER: Speaking of counters, always keep your work space as uncluttered as possible. This might sound impossible, especially if you live in a city and have a tiny kitchen, but it makes cooking (and thus life) so much easier. Again, if you come home and first have to clear your kitchen counter by removing a stack of bills from two months ago, your oatmeal from the morning, and your gym bag, you'll be burned out before you even begin. I have a mantra: "If the kitchen is clean, everything is okay." I'm not saying to tie your hair back with a *schmatte* and lug out the mop every day. Just keep your cooking area inviting. Oh, and don't let the dirty dishes get too out of control, either.

6. TIMING IS ALMOST EVERYTHING: Use a timer to remind yourself that something is roasting or boiling. Can I tell you a secret? I get really frustrated with those multi-timers, so I use two separate wind-up timers; or I just use the one on my microwave and the one on the stove. But it gives peace of mind! You don't have to stress about burning stuff or to keep repeating to yourself, "Remember the lentils. Remember the lentils." Because by the fifth time it sounds like "Lememba da lentrils" anyway, and you won't even know what you're talking about.

7. LIST LUST: Could this be the most mundane tip ever? Possibly. But keeping a list of items that you're running low on can save many a dinner that needed soy sauce, but oops, you were out of it. A dry-erase board hanging right on my freezer door is my solution. When it's time to shop, I just use my phone to take a pic of the list, and off I go.

SWAP MEET:

my favorite modifications for common allergens

SWAP MEET! I want everyone to be able to enjoy these recipes, but I know that sometimes dietary restrictions make that dream impossible. Here are a few of my favorite swaps when cooking for my wonderful (but tragically allergic) buddies.

GLUTEN

Gluten can be found in the darndest places! Always check labeling for hidden ingredients. These are some of the most common gluten hangouts and what I do to replace them.

SOY SAUCE: Use gluten-free tamari. San-J is my favorite brand, and it's also widely available. In fact, I never even use soy sauce now since it's easy and delicious to simply keep tamari on hand.

BREAD CRUMBS: For fine, dry, bread crumbs, unsalted gluten-free pretzels work wonders, but they can also be expensive. An affordable alternative is Chex-type cereals in either rice or corn varieties. To make the bread crumbs, finely grind the cereal or pretzel pieces in a blender until they're in tiny, almost powdery, crumbs.

ROUX: To thicken curries, stews, and even mac and cheese, I love to use chickpea flour in place of all-purpose. It works wonderfully and gives a nice toasty flavor, too!

PASTA: Easy enough! There are zillions of gluten-free pastas on the market. Sometimes I use it just because I like it. My favorite varieties are quinoa and rice pastas.

COOKIES AND SCONES: Other baked goods can get more complicated, but for cookies and scones it's pretty simple. I use certified gluten-free oats. Grind the oats into a flour and then measure. I usually need a bit more flour than the recipe calls for; say, a tablespoon or two extra per cup of flour. For everything else, just read online reviews for the best baking mixes and purchase them that way.

NUTS

OK, so we've got tree-nut allergies, and we've got nut and seed allergies, and we've got peanut allergies. Life for cookbook authors can get complicated fast when trying to accommodate! Here are a few of my favorite swaps for all different sorts of no-nuts-allowed occasions.

PEANUTS: If the diner doesn't have a tree-nut allergy, use cashews. If the diner does, then sesame seeds make a nice treat in savory dishes, even if the texture will be different.

PEANUT BUTTER: Sunbutter (which is sunflower seed butter) makes a great replacement. Although, in baked goods, it sometimes turns the dough green. Maybe that would be fun? If the diner doesn't have a tree-nut allergy, then almond butter is a great alternative.

CASHEWS: As far as the recipes in this book go, cashews are probably the biggest bummer because of all of the cashew cream recipes. My heart bleeds for you, it truly does! But listen, a few of my testers had cashew allergies and they had happy results using sunflower seeds instead. In Thai and Indian dishes, coconut milk is a fantastic alternative as well.

SOY

I hope that I've provided enough soy-free recipes to keep you entertained for years. But if you're looking to replace soy sauce, there are soy-free miso pastes that you can blend with water. Just make sure that it's still good, thick, and salty and not too watered down. You can then use it anywhere in place of soy sauce, even in seitan!

SOUPS

Let's BEGIN at the BEGINNING,

shall we? Soup is one of the first meals I learned how to prepare and one of the most forgiving. Sauté some aromatics to build flavor, add your broth, your veggies, and your proteins—it truly is the ideal one-pot meal! Perfect for seasoned cooks who like to put their own spin on things, and a low-key way for newbs to learn the ropes. Zen out and chop some onions and experiment with all of the textures and methods that you pick up from soup making. Perhaps most important, soup is very, very difficult to screw up. All that is really required is a pot, a spoon for stirring, a ladle for serving, and a desire for something delicious bubbling away on your stovetop. Many of the soups here make a fabulous and complete main course, like the Wild Rice Soup with Browned Seitan Strips. To turn others into a main event, you can serve them with a crusty loaf of bread from the bakery; or, if you're feeling ambitious, I even provide a recipe for my favorite soup bread from scratch. Soup and salad are classic buds, and you can also serve soup alongside a sandwich or burger. It's easy enough to pull together any day of the week, and most offer ample amounts of downtime. There is not a single culture in the world that doesn't have its signature soup. Indeed, the variety is endless. Well, in the case of this chapter, it is sixteen recipes, but you can really take these soups and run with them. (No, silly, not literally!)

ALPHABET SOUP

serves 6 · total time: 30 mins · active time: 20 mins

2 teaspoons olive oil

1 small yellow onion, diced

2 ribs celery, thinly sliced

½ teaspoon salt, plus a pinch

2 cloves garlic, minced

1 cup diced carrots (½-inch dice)

12 ounces Yukon Gold potatoes, diced into ¾-inch pieces

1 teaspoon dried thyme

¼ teaspoon dried tarragon

6 cups vegetable broth

1 cup dried small pasta

1 teaspoon agave syrup

1 (16-ounce) can tomato sauce

1 cup frozen peas

NOTES:

• I love using Yukon Gold potatoes here since they don't need to be peeled, but if you're using russets, peel them first—the texture will be better. Also, if you can't find any alphabet pasta, don't let that stop you. You can use tiny shells, wheels, orzo, or elbow macaroni. Any bite-size pasta will do!

• To take the frozen flavor off the frozen peas, simply place them in a colander and run lukewarm water over them until all of the icy bits are washed away.

This is everyone's favorite—homemade alphabet soup! The kind Andy Warhol might make a painting of. The kind that you used to spell out your name and the name of your cats with when you were a kid. The kind my mom used to put in an omelet! Although I still haven't found anyone else who grew up on *that* particular delicacy.

It's a really, really, really, really, *really, really* simple tomato-based vegetable soup. It's not here to be innovative, but it does exactly what alphabet soup was born to do—it hits the spot! Everyone needs a basic recipe like this.

Preheat a 4-quart soup pot over medium heat and add the oil. Sauté the onion and celery in the oil with a pinch of salt until soft, about 5 minutes. Add the garlic and cook until fragrant, 30 seconds or so.

Add the carrots, potatoes, thyme, tarragon, remaining ½ teaspoon salt, and broth. Cover and bring to a boil. Once boiling, lower the heat to a simmer, add the pasta, and cook until the pasta and vegetables are soft, about 10 more minutes.

Add the agave, tomato sauce, and frozen peas and heat through (5 minutes or so). Remove from the heat. It tastes better the longer you let it sit, so give it at least 10 minutes or so before digging in, if you can. Taste for seasoning, and serve.

PURÉED SPLIT PEA & RUTABAGA SOUP

serves 6 to 8 · total time: 1 hour · active time: 15 mins

This soup is smooth and creamy without an ounce of cream (vegan or otherwise), *and* it's full of protein thanks to the beautiful yellow split peas, which melt into the broth and makes the soup thick and velvety. Rutabaga and star anise have a natural affinity for each other because they share a compound called anethole, which makes 'em taste licorice-y. But you don't need to know that. All you need to know is that the wacky flower-shaped alien spice pod brings out the earthy fragrance of the rutabaga, which is my favorite root veggie. (Don't tell beets.) If you don't have sherry, white wine will do.

1 tablespoon olive oil

1 medium yellow onion, diced

2 ribs celery, coarsely chopped

1 teaspoon salt, plus a pinch

3 cloves garlic, chopped

2 teaspoons dried rosemary

½ cup cooking sherry

1½ cups yellow split peas

1 pound rutabagas, peeled and cut into 1-inch chunks

8 cups vegetable broth

Several pinches of fresh black pepper

2 whole star anise pods

Celery leaves, for garnish (optional)

Preheat a 4-quart soup pot over medium-high heat and add the oil. Sauté the onion and celery in the oil with a pinch of salt until soft and translucent, about 5 minutes. Add the garlic and rosemary and sauté for 15 seconds or so. Add the sherry and scrape the bottom of the pan with a spatula to deglaze. Bring the heat up to a boil and let the liquid reduce for about 3 minutes.

Add the split peas, rutabagas, broth, the remaining 1 teaspoon salt, and pepper. Cover and bring to a boil. Once boiling, turn the heat to medium and cook until the split peas are tender, stirring occasionally. (This could take anywhere from 20 minutes to 45 minutes depending on your split peas.) About 15 minutes into the boiling time, add the star anise.

Once the split peas are tender (like, really tender, almost mushy), remove the star anise. Use an immersion blender to purée the soup until smooth and creamy. If you don't have an immersion blender and need to use a food processor or blender, remember to lift the lid every few seconds to let steam escape. Thin with a little water if desired, taste for salt and pepper, and serve! Top each bowl with finely chopped celery leaves, if desired.

NOTE:

The cooking time for split peas can vary depending on how old they are. The longer they've been sitting around, the longer they take to cook. So, if your split peas aren't cooking down in the time the recipe states, simply cook them a little longer. And if you know you're going to be getting your soup on and you'd like to ensure a super-fast cooking time, you can even soak them for a few hours in advance and drain before adding them to the recipe.

CHICKPEA-RICE SOUP
with Cabbage

serves 8 · total time: 40 mins · active time: 15 mins

1 tablespoon olive oil

1 medium yellow onion, thinly sliced

1 teaspoon salt, plus a pinch

2 cloves garlic, minced

1 teaspoon dried thyme

Freshly ground black pepper

½ cup jasmine rice, rinsed

1½ cups carrots in ½-inch chunks

1 pound green cabbage, thinly sliced

6 cups vegetable broth

1 (24-ounce) can chickpeas, rinsed and drained (about 3 cups)

3 tablespoons chopped fresh dill, plus extra for garnish

There's something seductively subtle about Eastern European flavors. No one is going to knock you over the head with cumin or turn the garlic up to eleven on the dial. Instead, here's some sautéed onion and a little dill. I think of these sorts of brothy soups as "babushka soups," or grandma soups. You should be able to experience each ingredient: the sweet earthiness of the carrot, the toothsome bites of cabbage, the succulence of the chickpea, the substance of the rice. Simple, comforting flavors that are easy to love. I dig the floral notes from jasmine or basmati rice here, but you can use whatever rice you like. Just note that brown rice will take twice as long to cook.

Preheat a 4-quart pot over medium heat and add the oil. Sauté the onion in the oil with a pinch of salt for about 5 minutes, until translucent. Add the garlic, thyme, the remaining 1 teaspoon salt, and pepper and sauté for 1 more minute.

Add the rice, carrots, and cabbage and then pour in the broth. Cover and bring to a boil. Once boiling, bring down to a simmer, add the chickpeas, and cook for about 15 minutes more, until the rice is cooked and the carrots are tender.

Stir in the dill and taste for salt and pepper. This definitely tastes better the longer you let it sit, but it can be enjoyed right away, too. Garnish with extra fresh dill.

CREAMY POTATO-LEEK SOUP

serves 8 · total time: 35 mins (plus time for soaking the cashews) · active time: 15 mins

Those gray winter months demand comfort food. Comfort isn't just about warmth and flavor (although those things don't hurt); it's about texture, too. I crave creaminess in the winter. The kind of food I can curl up on the couch with in my footie pajamas and feel soothed with every spoonful. This soup does the job! The recipe is very minimalist; no twists are needed when serving a classic like potato-leek soup. It's a classic for a reason—because it's pretty much perfect as is. The Roasted Vegetable Romesco Sandwiches (page 106) make a great accompaniment.

2 tablespoons olive oil

1 large leek (about 1 pound), white and light green parts, thinly sliced

1 small yellow onion, finely diced

1 teaspoon salt, plus a pinch

½ cup cashews, soaked for at least 2 hours (see "ABS: Always Be Soaking," page 14)

1½ cups water

2 pounds russet potatoes (about 4), peeled and cut into 1-inch chunks

Several pinches of freshly ground black pepper

1 tablespoon fresh thyme leaves, finely chopped, plus extra leaves for garnish

4 cups vegetable broth

Preheat a 4-quart pot over medium heat and add the oil. Sauté the leeks and onion in the olive oil with a pinch of salt for about 10 minutes, until the leeks are completely softened.

In the meantime, we'll make the cashew cream. Drain the cashews and place in a food processor. Add the water and blend like crazy, until smooth. This can take anywhere from 1 to 5 minutes depending on your machine. Scrape down the sides with a rubber spatula every now and again to make sure you get everything.

Back to the soup. Add the potatoes, black pepper, the remaining 1 teaspoon salt, thyme, and broth. Cover and bring to a boil. Once boiling, lower the heat to a simmer. Cook for about 15 minutes, until the potatoes are very tender.

With the soup on low heat, use a potato masher to mash the potatoes in the pot until they are pretty creamy. Add the cashew cream, stir, and heat through. Taste for salt and pepper and serve.

NOTE:

Leeks can be really sneaky about hiding dirt, so make sure to wash them *after* slicing them, to get out any of the dirt that may be camping out in the rings.

SWEET POTATO & RED CURRY SOUP

with Rice & Purple Kale

serves 8 · total time: 40 mins · active time: 15 mins

1 teaspoon olive oil

1 small yellow onion, diced

1 teaspoon salt, plus a pinch

3 cloves garlic, minced

1 tablespoon minced fresh ginger

¾ cup basmati or jasmine rice, rinsed

6 cups vegetable broth

2 to 3 tablespoons red curry paste

1 pound purple kale, leaves torn into bite-size pieces

1 large sweet potato, peeled and cut into ½-inch chunks

1 15-ounce can lite coconut milk

3 tablespoons fresh lime juice

1 tablespoon agave syrup

Chopped fresh cilantro, for garnish (optional)

Sriracha, for serving

NOTES:

- Since curry pastes vary from brand to brand, start with 2 tablespoons and add more from there. I don't make this very spicy, but I definitely serve it with plenty of sriracha.

- If you would like to use brown rice, that's fine! Just let it simmer for 20 minutes more before adding the curry paste, sweet potatoes, and kale.

This soup is a grab bag of texture. The kale is rugged and chewy, the rice is fluffed up and soaked through with flavor, and the sweet potatoes are tender but not mushy, just the perfect sweet bite. All of this in a creamy coconut base bursting with sensuous red curry flavors. The gingery aroma will waft through your entire mansion. So stop spending money on scented candles; soup is the best aromatherapy. This is the perfect soup to serve alongside the Shiitake *Banh Mi* (page 105).

Preheat a 4-quart soup pot over medium heat and add the oil. Sauté the onion in the oil with a pinch of salt for 5 minutes or so, until translucent. Add the garlic and ginger and sauté for 1 more minute.

Add the rice, broth, and remaining 1 teaspoon salt, cover the pot, and bring to a boil.

Once boiling, lower the heat to simmer. Mix in 2 tablespoons of the curry paste. Add the kale and sweet potatoes. Cover the pot and let simmer for about 15 minutes, until the sweet potatoes are tender.

Add the coconut milk, lime juice, and agave. Taste for seasoning. Add more curry paste if you think it needs it. Serve garnished with fresh chopped cilantro, if you like, and sriracha.

SHROOMY HOT & SOUR SOUP

serves 6 to 8 · total time: 50 mins · active time: 15 mins

1 ounce dried wood ear mushrooms

2 cups boiling water

2 teaspoons toasted sesame oil

2 cloves garlic

1 tablespoon minced fresh ginger

4 cups vegetable broth

¼ cup rice vinegar

3 tablespoons soy sauce

2 teaspoons sriracha

2 teaspoons granulated sugar

1 (8-ounce) can bamboo shoots, drained

5 ounces cabbage, thinly sliced (about 3 cups)

14 ounces tofu, diced into ½-inch pieces

½ cup water

1 tablespoon organic cornstarch

4 ounces small button or cremini mushrooms, sliced in half

1 cup chopped scallions

Chow mein noodles (optional)

When I left Brooklyn, it became impossible for me to get the kind of hot-and-sour soup I was used to, and oh, how I crave it! With springy wood ear mushrooms, spicy vinegary broth, and lots of cabbage. This one is great for weeknights and uses ingredients that are fairly easy to get in the international aisle of any supermarket. I've always loved my H&S a bit spicy, so if you're like me, up the sriracha a bit.

And here's permission to be super lazy: Instead of slicing cabbage, you can totally use a bag of coleslaw mix (the kind without carrots). Or, if instead you're feeling an urge to be somewhat authentic, you can use napa cabbage. You can also just use regular old green cabbage. It gets cooked down so much that ultimately it doesn't really matter; so long as you get that wonderful stringy texture that sops up lots of flavor, you're good to go. If you can't find dried wood ear mushrooms, then dried shiitakes would make a good sub.

Place the wood ears in a small bowl and pour over the boiling water. Cover the bowl (a little plate works well to cover) and let sit for 30 minutes to soften. Remove the wood ears and chop into bite-size pieces. Reserve the soaking water.

Preheat a 4-quart soup pot over low heat and add the oil. Sauté the garlic and ginger in the oil for 30 seconds or so, being careful not to burn. Add the broth, wood ears, reserved soaking water, vinegar, soy sauce, sriracha, sugar, bamboo shoots, and cabbage. Cover the pot and bring to a full boil.

Once boiling, lower the heat to medium so that it's at a simmer. Add the tofu, cover, and let cook for about 5 minutes.

In the meantime, in a measuring cup, stir together the water and cornstarch until dissolved. Mix into the soup and add the button mushrooms as well. Cook to thicken for about 5 more minutes.

Taste for spiciness/saltiness/sourness and adjust as necessary. Serve garnished with scallions and chow mein noodles, if desired.

CHUNKY MISO VEGETABLE SOUP

serves 6 to 8 • total time: 30 mins • active time: 15 mins

If chicken soup is Jewish penicillin, then this soup is vegan penicillin: lots of veggies in a deeply delicious, salty, and nourishing miso soup. I like to throw in some big chunky kidney beans, but white beans or chickpeas would represent well here. And don't wait for your next sniffly cold to enjoy it; a big bowlful is welcome all year round!

1 tablespoon olive oil

1 large yellow onion, diced

Pinch of salt

2 cloves garlic, minced

1 cup peeled carrots in ¼-inch slices

2 ribs celery, cut into ¼-inch slices

4 cups cauliflower florets

1 cup green beans trimmed and cut into 1-inch pieces

6 cups vegetable broth

Several pinches of freshly ground black pepper

1 (15-ounce) can kidney beans, rinsed and drained (1½ cups)

½ cup mellow white miso

1 cup thinly sliced scallions

Preheat a 4-quart pot over medium-high heat and add the oil. Sauté the onion in the oil with a pinch of salt until softened, about 3 minutes. Add the garlic and sauté for about 30 seconds, until fragrant. Add the carrots and celery and sauté for 3 minutes or so. Add the cauliflower and green beans, along with the broth and pepper. Cover the pot and bring to a boil. Once boiling, reduce the heat to a simmer and cook with the lid slightly ajar so steam can escape for about 10 minutes, or until the cauliflower is tender.

Add the kidney beans and miso and stir to dissolve the miso. Once dissolved, taste for seasoning. Add the scallions and serve.

HARIRA

with Eggplant & Chickpeas

serves 8 to 10 · total time: about 45 mins · active time: 20 mins

2 tablespoons olive oil

1 medium yellow onion, thinly sliced

1 teaspoon salt, plus a pinch

4 cloves garlic, minced

2 tablespoons minced fresh ginger

½ teaspoon crushed red pepper flakes

8 cups vegetable broth

1 medium eggplant (about 1 pound), peeled and cut into ½-inch chunks

½ cup brown or green lentils

2 teaspoons sweet paprika

¼ teaspoon ground cinnamon

1 teaspoon saffron threads, crushed (optional)

1 (24-ounce) can crushed tomatoes (fire-roasted are great)

1 (15-ounce) can chickpeas, rinsed and drained (1½ cups)

¼ cup chopped fresh mint, plus extra for garnish

¼ cup chopped fresh cilantro, plus extra for garnish

4 ounces angel hair pasta

Harira is a Moroccan noodle soup, served during Ramadan to break the fast. It's aromatic and slightly spicy, and this version is made thick with eggplant and lentils and studded with a few chickpeas swimming about. Now, if I just invented this soup out of the blue, and someone told me to put noodles in it, I would think we were on a cooking reality show and that someone was trying to sabotage me. But the noodles make it. This soup is a meal on its own. As you can imagine, you might not have the energy to cook a million dishes after fasting. This gets the deed done in one pot. The eggplant really just disintegrates into the soup, to give it a meaty thickness. In traditional *harira,* lamb is used for that purpose, but, you know. . . .

I had an existential crisis trying to figure out if this recipe should go in the soup or the stew section, and so I went on a spiritual journey and decided, soup. My spiritual journey basically involved looking at fifty other cookbooks to see how they classified it. The soup thickens *a lot* as it's left to sit, what with the noodles, so thin it out with water when reheating. The saffron is expensive and thus optional.

Preheat a 4-quart soup pot over medium-high heat and add the oil. Sauté the onion in the oil with a pinch of salt until translucent, 3 to 4 minutes. Add the garlic, ginger, and red pepper flakes and sauté for 1 more minute.

Deglaze the pot with a splash of broth. Add the eggplant, lentils, paprika, cinnamon, remaining 1 teaspoon salt, and saffron threads (if desired), along with about 4 cups of the broth. If you add all of the broth it will take a longer time to come to a boil and break down the lentils and eggplant, which is why we're not adding it all at once.

Cover the pot and bring to a boil. Keep it at a boil, but lower the heat a bit if it's boiling too violently. Leave the lid slightly ajar so that steam can escape, and boil for about 20 minutes, checking and stirring occasionally. The eggplant should be mostly disintegrated and the lentils should be soft.

Add the tomatoes, chickpeas, mint, and cilantro and at least 2 more cups of vegetable broth, and more if needed to make it soup-like and not too thick. Bring to a boil, then break the pasta strands into thirds and add to the pot, gently coaxing with a spatula to submerge and separate the strands. Cook until the pasta is soft, then thin out the soup with the remaining broth, if needed. Serve in big bowls, with extra herbs for garnish.

BABUSHKA BORSCHT

serves 6 to 8 · total time: about 45 mins · active time: 20 mins

I love a classic borscht. It automatically brings to mind my ancestors in Mother Russia, hovered over a wood-burning stove making beet soup. Or maybe that was a scene from *Fiddler on the Roof*? In any case, I have no desire whatsoever to update that mental image. Borscht speaks to my soul, and I like mine chunky with beets (obviously), cabbage, and potatoes. Some fresh dill and a little cashew cream completes heaven on earth.

1 tablespoon olive oil

1 medium yellow onion, diced

½ teaspoon salt, plus a pinch

3 cloves garlic, minced

1 pound red beets, peeled and cut into ½-inch chunks

2 large russet potatoes, peeled and cut into ½-inch chunks

½ of a small head of green cabbage, thinly sliced

6 cups vegetable broth

Several pinches of freshly ground black pepper

2 tablespoons fresh lemon juice

Cashew cream (see Note; optional)

Fresh dill fronds, for garnish

Preheat a 4-quart pot over medium heat and add the oil. Sauté the onion in the oil with a pinch of salt for 5 to 7 minutes, until translucent. Add the garlic and sauté until fragrant, about 30 seconds.

Add the beets, potatoes, cabbage, broth, remaining ½ teaspoon salt, and pepper. Cover the pot and bring to a rolling boil. Once boiling, lower the heat a bit so that it's at a simmer, leave the lid slightly ajar, and let cook for about 35 minutes, until the beets are tender.

Add the lemon juice, taste for seasoning, and serve, topped with cashew cream, if desired, and garnished with dill.

NOTE:

To make a very simple cashew cream that's perfect for swirling into soups, simply soak 1 cup cashews in water for at least 2 hours to soften. Drain the cashews, place in a blender, and combine with 1½ cups fresh water. Blend until totally smooth. Feel free to add a pinch of salt or a touch of lemon juice, but it's not wholly necessary since you'll be adding the cashew cream to a flavorful soup. The cashew cream thickens when refrigerated. Use a little water to thin it, if necessary.

WILD RICE SOUP

with Browned Seitan Strips

serves 4 to 6 · total time: 40 mins · active time: 20 mins

For the soup:

1 tablespoon olive oil

1 medium yellow onion, thinly sliced

½ teaspoon salt, plus a pinch

4 cloves garlic, minced

1 cup peeled and thinly sliced carrots

2 ribs celery, thinly sliced

1 teaspoon dried thyme

½ teaspoon dried tarragon

2 teaspoons sweet paprika

1 cup wild rice, rinsed

½ cup red lentils

6 cups vegetable broth

For the seitan:

2 teaspoons olive oil

1 pound seitan, sliced into thin strips

1 (15-ounce) can great northern beans, rinsed and drained (1½ cups)

This soup is a portal to autumn. Wild rice has an incredible nutty and warm flavor that makes your mouth feel as happy as a child playing in a pile of leaves. This recipe is sort of a vegan answer to a chicken-and-rice soup; a handful of lentils thickens the broth and retains all the flavor goodness of the browned onion. But that's just a little trick; this is certainly not a lentil soup. Since wild rice can be expensive, feel free to use a wild rice blend. That's usually just a mixture of wild and long-grain brown rice. While the soup simmers, you sauté the seitan so that it gets nice and brown. You can definitely serve this soup as dinner on its own or with some bread and a leafy green salad. Also, feel free to add more veggies. Some diced zucchini along with the carrots, or some chopped kale toward the end, would be a good choice.

PREPARE THE SOUP:

Preheat a 4-quart pot over medium heat and add the oil. Sauté the onion in the oil with a pinch of salt for about 5 minutes, until translucent. Add the garlic and sauté until fragrant, about 30 seconds. Toss in the carrots, celery, thyme, tarragon, paprika, and remaining ½ teaspoon salt and give it a stir.

Add the wild rice, lentils, and broth. Cover the pot and bring to a rolling boil. Once boiling, lower the heat a bit so that it's at a rapid simmer, leave the lid slightly ajar, and let cook for about 25 minutes.

PREPARE THE SEITAN:

Meanwhile, about 10 minutes before the soup is ready, sauté the seitan. Preheat a large nonstick pan, preferably cast iron, over medium-high heat. Once the pan is hot, drizzle in the oil to coat the bottom of the pan. Add the seitan and sauté for 5 minutes or so, until nicely browned. Keep covered until ready to use.

When the rice in the soup is tender and the lentils have melted into the broth, add the beans to heat through. Taste for salt and seasonings and add broth or water if necessary, to thicken to your liking.

It tastes best if you let it sit for a few minutes, allowing the flavors to marry. Serve hot, with the seitan slices scattered over the top.

NEW ENGLAND CLAM CHOWDER

serves 6 to 8 · total time: 35 mins
(plus time for soaking the cashews) · active time: 15 mins

This is for all you fish heads out there. A mix of mushrooms stands in for the clams to create a super-satisfying chewiness, while some chopped-up nori gives this chowder a true taste of the sea. It's thick and creamy and loaded with the finer things, like potatoes and carrots. Crumble some saltines over the top and you'll be able to hear the Atlantic Ocean lapping at your feet. For authenticity, make sure to serve this while talking like a character from a Stephen King movie.

How fishy do you like it? Nori is pretty mild as far as seaweeds go, but the potency varies depending on the brand and the freshness of the nori. Start with one sheet, then taste after everything is added at the end. If you think it needs more sea, you can still add another chopped-up sheet. Just mix it in and let the flavor meld, off the heat, for about 10 minutes.

1 tablespoon olive oil

1 large yellow onion, diced

2 medium carrots, peeled and sliced into ¼-inch-thick half-moons

¾ teaspoon salt, plus a pinch

For the cashew cream:

1 cup cashews, soaked for at least 2 hours (see "ABS: Always Be Soaking," page 14)

2 cups vegetable broth

4 teaspoons organic cornstarch

4 ounces shiitake mushrooms, thinly sliced

8 ounces white button mushrooms, sliced ¼ inch thick

3 ribs celery, sliced ¼ inch thick

2 large russet potatoes, peeled and cut into ¾-inch chunks

Freshly ground black pepper

1 or 2 nori sheets, finely chopped (see Notes)

3 cups vegetable broth

2 tablespoons tomato paste

2 tablespoons fresh lemon juice

Chopped fresh flat-leaf parsley or chives, for garnish (optional)

Saltines, for garnish (optional)

Lemon wedges, for serving (optional)

Preheat a 4-quart pot over medium heat and add the oil. Sauté the onion and carrots in the oil with a pinch of salt for about 10 minutes, until the carrots are softened.

Prepare the cashew cream: Drain the cashews and add them to a blender along with the vegetable broth and cornstarch. Blend like crazy, until smooth. This can take anywhere from 1 to 5 minutes depending on your machine. Scrape down the sides with a rubber spatula every now and again to make sure you get everything.

Back to the soup. Add both kinds of mushrooms and the celery. Cook for about 3 minutes, just until the mushrooms are softened. You want them to keep their texture.

Add the potatoes, remaining ¾ teaspoon salt, pepper, nori, and vegetable broth. Cover and bring to a boil. Once boiling, lower the heat to a simmer. Cook for 10 to 15 minutes, or until the potatoes are tender. Be careful to keep a close eye on them so as not to overcook them, or they will turn into mush.

Stir in the cashew cream and gently heat, uncovered, for about 7 minutes, until nicely thickened. Add the tomato paste and lemon juice and taste for seasoning. Add a little extra water if it seems too thick. Serve garnished with parsley and a few saltine crackers, if desired. A wedge of lemon looks pretty, too.

NOTES:

- To efficiently chop nori, chiffonade it. That means roll up and slice! So, tightly roll up your nori sheet like a cigar, and thinly slice. Then run your knife over the curled-up bunches to get them into even smaller pieces.

- If you'd like it even chewier and you have a million dollars to spend on fungi, then go ahead and replace all of the white mushrooms with shiitakes.

ROASTED POTATO
& FENNEL SOUP

serves 6 to 8 · total time: 45 mins · active time: 15 mins

2 pounds Yukon Gold potatoes, cut into 1-inch chunks

Olive oil, for drizzling

1 teaspoon salt

Freshly ground black pepper

2 fennel bulbs (reserve the frilly green fronds)

1 large yellow onion, sliced ½ inch thick

2 cups vegetable broth, warmed

2 cups unsweetened soy milk or almond milk, at room temperature

I tend to go on and on about the delicious benefits of roasting, and here I go again. The scent of potatoes in the oven makes you feel as snuggly as a kitten making muffins on a pillow, and the fennel adds an alluring licorice aroma, making the experience just slightly more intriguing. Because everything is roasted, there's not much else you need to do to make it fabulous. No sautéing, no spices; the oven gives you all the flavor you need. Once it's cooked, all you'll need to do is purée. Life-changing!

Preheat the oven to 425°F. Line two large rimmed baking sheets with parchment paper.

Place the sliced potatoes on one baking sheet. Drizzle with olive oil (1 tablespoon should do, but 2 tablespoons is ideal for browning). Sprinkle with ½ teaspoon of the salt and add several pinches of pepper. Toss with your hands to coat completely. Roast the potatoes for 15 minutes.

In the meantime, prepare the fennel and onion. Slice the fennel bulbs from top to base in ½-inch slices. Place on the other baking sheet with the sliced onion and toss with olive oil, the remaining ½ teaspoon salt, and pepper to coat, just like you did with the potatoes.

After the potatoes have roasted for 15 minutes, remove from the oven and use a spatula to flip them. Return to the oven on the upper rack, and place the fennel and onions on the middle rack.

Roast for 10 minutes, then remove the fennel and onion, flip them, and roast for 5 to 10 more minutes. At this point, the potatoes should be tender and the fennel and onion should be caramelized.

Puréeing in a food processor: Reserve a few pieces of fennel for garnish along with the fronds. Place the potatoes, fennel, and onion in the work bowl along with the broth and milk. Pulse a few times so that it's creamy but still chunky. Don't over-purée or the potatoes will turn gummy. Thin further with water, if needed.

Puréeing with an immersion blender: Reserve a few pieces of fennel for garnish. Add the potatoes, fennel, onion, broth, and milk to a 4-quart pot and blend so that it's creamy but still chunky, thinning with water as needed.

Gently reheat if necessary. Taste for salt and pepper, ladle into bowls, garnish with the reserved roasted fennel slices and the fennel fronds, and serve.

MUSHROOM-BARLEY SOUP
with Garden Herbs

serves 6 to 8 · total time: 40 mins · active time: 15 mins

Mushroom-barley soup doesn't have to be that thick bowlful of murky stuff that your father eats out of a can all winter. In fact, it can be downright right spring-like, with bright flavors from fresh herbs and springtime's bounty of veggies.

I created this soup with fresh herbs from my garden, but I know that not everyone can use fresh herbs from my garden! So if you have to go with just one herb, I recommend the dill. Garnish with extra herbs, if you like.

1 tablespoon olive oil

1 medium yellow onion, thinly sliced

½ teaspoon salt, plus a pinch

8 ounces cremini mushrooms, sliced ¼ inch thick

1 average-size zucchini, sliced into ¼-inch-thick half-moons

4 cloves garlic, minced

1 rib celery, thinly sliced

1 average-size tomato, diced

¾ cup pearled (quick-cooking) barley

6 cups vegetable broth

Several pinches freshly ground black pepper

For the herb mix:

3 tablespoons chopped fresh dill

3 tablespoons chopped fresh cilantro

3 tablespoons chopped fresh basil

2 tablespoons chopped fresh thyme

Preheat a 4-quart pot over medium heat and add the oil. Sauté the onion in the oil with a pinch of salt until translucent, about 5 minutes. Add the mushrooms and zucchini and cook until slightly softened and some of the moisture has been released, about 5 more minutes. Mix in the garlic and sauté for a minute or so.

Add the celery, tomato, barley, broth, remaining ½ teaspoon salt, and pepper. Cover and bring to a boil. Once boiling, lower the heat to a simmer, add the herb mix, cover again, and cook until the barley is tender, about 10 minutes. Taste for seasoning. For the best results, let it sit for at least 10 minutes, uncovered, so that the flavors can marry before serving.

PESTO SOUP

with Gnocchi, Beans & Greens

serves 4 · total time: 35 mins · active time: 20 mins

You've heard me soapboxing about vegan creaminess. Usually creamy texture is brought to us via delicious fatty vehicles like cashews, tahini, and coconut. Here, instead, is an almost fat-free method that might not pack the decadent punch of a cashew-based cream but gets you there all the same. You purée cauliflower with a few other veggies and lots of basil until silky smooth. This is actually a wonderful soup as a starter, but bulked up with pillowy gnocchi, white beans, and wilted greens it becomes a meal unto itself.

2 teaspoons olive oil

3 cloves garlic, minced

1 small head cauliflower (about 1 pound), trimmed and cut into florets

4 cups vegetable broth

½ teaspoon dried thyme

½ teaspoon salt

Several pinches of freshly ground black pepper

1 tablespoon arrowroot or organic cornstarch

1 cup loosely packed fresh basil leaves, plus extra for garnish

8 ounces frozen gnocchi, partially thawed (leave on the counter for 30 minutes or so)

1 small bunch Swiss chard, stems discarded, leaves torn into bite-size pieces

1 (15-ounce) can navy beans, rinsed and drained (1½ cups)

Toasted pine nuts, for garnish (optional)

Preheat a 4-quart stockpot over medium heat and add the oil. Sauté the garlic in the oil for about 1 minute, being careful not to let it burn. Add the cauliflower, 3 cups of the broth (yes, only 3 of the cups! You'll be adding the last cup in a bit), thyme, salt, and pepper. Cover the pot and bring to a boil, stirring every now and again and boiling for about 10 minutes, or until the cauliflower is tender.

In a measuring cup, vigorously mix together the remaining 1 cup broth and the arrowroot until dissolved. Lower the heat a bit so that the soup is at a low boil. Mix in the broth and cook uncovered for 5 more minutes, stirring often, until slightly thickened. Add the basil leaves and remove from the heat. Use an immersion blender to purée until smooth. If you don't have an immersion blender, then use a blender or food processor to purée in batches, being careful to lift the lid once in a while to let steam escape. Taste for seasoning.

Return the soup to the stove over medium heat and add the gnocchi; cover and let cook for 3 minutes or so. Add the greens and beans and cook until the greens are completely wilted and the beans are heated through, about 5 more minutes. Be careful as you stir not to crush the gnocchi or beans. Serve garnished with extra basil and pine nuts, if you like.

BUTTERNUT BISQUE
with a Coconut Swirl

serves 6 to 8 · total time: 1 hour 15 mins · active time: 20 mins

1 large butternut squash (about 4 pounds)

Vegetable oil, for brushing or spraying

1 tablespoon refined coconut oil

1 medium yellow onion, diced

½ teaspoon salt, plus a pinch

3 cloves garlic, minced

1 tablespoon minced fresh ginger

½ teaspoon crushed red pepper flakes

½ cup dry white wine

3 cups vegetable broth

1 cup regular or lite coconut milk, plus extra for garnish (optional)

2 tablespoons pure maple syrup

2 tablespoons fresh lime juice

For serving:
Red pepper flakes

Scallions

MAKE AHEAD:

You can roast the butternut squash a day in advance, and this soup will come together in 20 minutes or so the following day.

Winter evenings are not complete without a gingery bowl of butternut soup. This one is especially easy because the squash is roasted, leaving you plenty of time to build a snowman or do some vegan ice fishing while it roasts away in the oven. Coconut milk, maple syrup, and a dash of lime give the soup an added dimension that will warm you from head to toe. You may need to add extra maple syrup depending on how sweet your butternut is, so let your taste buds guide you once the soup is puréed.

Preheat the oven to 425°F. Line a rimmed baking sheet with parchment paper.

Using a large chef's knife, cut the round part of the butternut squash from the long part. Slice the round part in half and scoop out the seeds. Slice the long part in half as well, lengthwise. Brush or spray the parchment lightly with vegetable oil and place the squash pieces, cut side down, on the baking sheet. Roast for about 45 minutes, or until the squash is very tender. At this point, you can let the squash cool and refrigerate to use the following day, or proceed with the recipe.

Preheat a 4-quart pot over medium heat and add the coconut oil. Sauté the onion in the oil with a pinch of salt for about 7 minutes, until lightly caramelized. Add the garlic and ginger and sauté until fragrant, about 30 seconds.

Mix in the red pepper flakes and the remaining ½ teaspoon salt. Add the white wine and deglaze the pan by scraping the bottom with a wooden spatula. Peel or scoop out the butternut squash and add to the pan along with the broth. If a little of the butternut skin gets in, no big deal. Add the coconut milk, maple syrup, and lime juice and heat everything through.

Use an immersion blender to blend the soup until smooth and creamy. If you don't have an immersion blender and need to use a food processor or blender, remember that steam can build up in there and hurt you. So lift the lid every few seconds to let steam escape. Thin with a little water if necessary, taste for seasoning, and serve. If you like, swirl a little coconut milk into the top of each serving for extra prettiness. Sprinkle with a pinch of red pepper flakes and chopped scallions.

CHEDDARY BROCCOLI SOUP

serves 6 • total time: 30 mins (plus time for soaking the cashews)
active time: 15 mins

No soup chapter could possibly call itself complete without this classic American concoction. Cashews and miso join forces to create a thick, delicious, tangy, and *cheesy* soup. Of course, there's plenty of broccoli, too. And don't worry about chopping everything too perfectly, as it's all going to get puréed in the end anyway. Serve with a big hunk o' bread. It's pure homey bliss!

PREPARE THE SOUP:

Preheat a 4-quart pot over medium heat and add the oil. Sauté the onion in the oil with a pinch of salt just until softened, about 3 minutes. Add the garlic and sauté for 30 seconds or so, just until fragrant.

Add the broccoli, carrots, turmeric, remaining ½ teaspoon salt, and broth. Cover and bring to a boil. Once boiling, lower the heat to a simmer. Cook for about 10 minutes, until the carrots are very tender.

PREPARE THE CASHEW CREAM:

In the meantime, we'll make the cashew cream. Drain the cashews and place in a blender, along with the broth, miso, and nutritional yeast. Blend like crazy, until smooth. This can take anywhere from 1 to 5 minutes depending on your machine. Scrape down the sides with a rubber spatula every now and again to make sure you get everything.

When the carrots are tender, add the cashew mixture to the soup. Use an immersion blender to purée, so that only tiny bits of broccoli and carrot are visible. Keep the soup on low heat, partially covered, for about 10 minutes, until thickened, stirring occasionally.

Once thickened, add the lemon juice and pepper, taste for seasoning, and serve. It thickens even more as it cools, so you'll need to thin out leftovers—if there are any!

For the soup:

1 tablespoon olive oil

1 small yellow onion, diced

½ teaspoon salt, plus a pinch

3 cloves garlic, minced

4 cups chopped broccoli stalks and florets

½ cup peeled and chopped carrots

½ teaspoon ground turmeric

3 cups vegetable broth

Optional garnishes: chopped tomatoes, red onions, and sprouts

For the cashew cream:

1 cup cashews, soaked for at least 2 hours (see "ABS: Always Be Soaking," page 14)

2 cups vegetable broth

3 tablespoons mellow white miso

2 tablespoons nutritional yeast flakes

2 tablespoons fresh lemon juice

Freshly ground black pepper

OLIVE OIL BREAD FOR SOUP

makes one 16-inch loaf · total time: 3 hours · active time: 15 mins

¾ cup warm water

1 tablespoon granulated sugar

1 packet active dry yeast
  (2¼ teaspoons)

¼ cup extra-virgin olive oil, plus extra
  for the bowl and drizzling

2¼ to 2½ cups all-purpose flour

1 teaspoon salt

There's no greater comfort than the aroma of freshly baked bread. I believe this is a scientifically proven fact. This loaf is my absolute favorite soup bread. It's not a recipe passed down through generations or anything fun like that. In fact, it's just something I got off allrecipes.com or some such useful Web site a handful of years ago and tweaked until I got my idea of the perfect bread for soup.

I love a lot of things about it; for one, the ease. I started having pain in my left hand a few years ago and so I don't want anything that I have to knead by hand. This works just perfectly in a standing mixer using a dough hook. Also, the ingredients are super simple, things that anyone who wants freshly baked bread should have around at all times. The olive oil provides a subtle, sweet aroma that just makes it smell and taste even more warm and inviting.

But what I really love is the texture! It's got an almost biscuit-like quality. I love to rip into a chewy crust as much as the next guy, but sometimes with soup I prefer a crispier bite. When lightly toasted, it makes a fabulous crouton. I love to drizzle that with just a tiny bit of olive oil and place it atop my bowl o' soup.

If you don't have a standing mixer, you can knead the dough by hand. Just tack on 10 minutes extra active time.

Add the water and sugar to the work bowl of a standing mixer fitted with a dough hook. Sprinkle in the yeast and let sit for 5 minutes.

Mix in the olive oil. Add 1 cup of the flour along with the salt. Mix on low speed until well incorporated, and then turn the speed to medium and mix for 3 minutes.

Add another ½ cup of flour and mix well, starting on low speed and then switching to medium speed. Then add another ½ cup of flour, again starting on low speed and switching to medium. Knead on medium speed for about 5 minutes. You may occasionally have to get in there with your hands if the dough starts climbing up the hook. It should become smooth and elastic and slightly sticky. At this point, incorporate flour by the tablespoon, kneading on medium speed until the dough is smooth and no longer sticky. When it starts to seem dry, stop adding flour. This could be anywhere between ¼ and ½ cup additional flour.

Meanwhile, drizzle about a tablespoon of olive oil into a large bowl. The dough will double in size, so make sure you have a big enough bowl. Form the dough into a ball and place in the bowl, tossing it around to coat with oil. Cover the bowl with plastic wrap and put in a warm place. Let the dough rise for about an hour, or until doubled in size.

Gently remove the dough from the bowl and place on a clean, dry surface. I don't ever have to flour the surface, but if the dough seems sticky or the surface is very warm, you may need to. Gently form the dough into a long oval. Now roll out and form a loaf that is roughly 14 inches long and 4 inches wide.

Lightly oil a baking sheet and transfer the dough to it. Score it across the top in three diagonal slices, drizzle with a little olive oil, and let rise for about 15 minutes. In the meantime, preheat the oven to 375°F.

Place in the oven and bake for 25 minutes. Lower the heat to 350°F and bake for 10 to 15 more minutes. Use tongs to check the bottom; if it seems to be browning too much, then transfer the bread directly to the oven rack for the remaining baking time.

It's sometimes tough to know whether the bread is baked perfectly, but the outside should be golden brown. Remove from the oven and let sit for 10 minutes before slicing. If the inside is a little undercooked, no worries; just note that for next time. Sometimes there is trial and error involved when baking a new bread. Wrap up any remaining bread (as if!) with plastic wrap to keep fresh.

NOTE:

Even though I'm a self-admitted amateur when it comes to artisan bread baking, I do have a few tips for the home baker!

For one, temperature is important to activate the yeast. Things should be on the warm side, and that includes the equipment. If it's very cold in my kitchen, I make sure to warm my mixer bowl up, either with a brief stint in the oven or by running it under hot water. Same goes for the bowl that the bread rises in. I use a glass bowl, so I can even microwave it for 30 seconds to get it warm. Note: Not hot, just warm!

I also set the bread to rise wherever is warmest. If I'm doing a lot of cooking and baking and my oven is still warm, then often just leaving it on top of the stove will do. But sometimes I place it in my bedroom to rise, because it gets the most sun. An added bonus . . . your bedroom will smell like bread!

For forming the loaf, I don't punch the dough down and knead again after it rises. Instead, I gently lift the dough out onto a clean surface and I form a long oval loaf shape. Then I roll the bread back and forth a bit (as if I were rolling a rolling pin), shaping as I go to keep the ends round, until it reaches the desired shape.

I think this is a great recipe to start off with if you're new to bread baking! If you do it often enough, you can just be making the bread in the background, letting it rise away while you multitask on something else. It just becomes second nature after a while. The most important thing is to get started: Try it once and don't be intimidated. Perhaps before you know it, you'll become the kind of person who bakes his or her own bread!

SALADS

Don't ROLL YOUR EYES at salad!

Hasn't it been through enough already, what with things like Jell-O and marshmallows? Every decade has had its own unique way of destroying a perfectly wonderful concept: fresh ingredients, simply prepared, dressed in something tangy and delicious. This is where you can really let your ingredients shine. Start with veggies that are grown in your area, if you can. Once you're working with the freshest produce possible, everything else will fall into place. All manner of leafy greens (and reds! and purples!), the juiciest tomatoes you can find, fresh herbs, and farmers' market cucumbers will make all the difference. I've included stand-alone recipes for dressings so that you can have a delicious dressing in moments to toss with whatever salad greens you've got on hand. But the modern salad doesn't stop at lettuce (that would make for a pretty boring chapter). Bulked up with beans and grains, simply prepared seitan or tempeh, or pastas and nuts, most of these salads can be served as a dinner unto themselves. The lighter ones need maybe a simple cup of soup and a hunk of bread to complete the meal. Let's make this the salad-for-dinner decade!

SESAME SLAW

with Warm Garlicky Seitan

serves 4 · total time: 20 mins · active time: 20 mins

For the salad:

6 cups shredded red cabbage (about 1 pound)

1 cup shelled edamame (thawed if frozen)

1 batch Miso-Sesame Dressing (recipe follows)

For the seitan:

1 tablespoon toasted sesame oil

1 pound seitan, sliced into thin strips

Pinch of salt

Several pinches of freshly ground black pepper

3 cloves garlic, minced

For the garnish:

½ cup sliced scallions

8 teaspoons toasted sesame seeds (2 teaspoons per serving)

½ cup chopped fresh cilantro (optional)

NOTE:

For a gluten-free option, serve with Sesame Tofu (page 239) instead of seitan.

3 tablespoons rice vinegar

2 tablespoons miso

2 tablespoons water

1 tablespoon toasted sesame oil

2 teaspoons light agave nectar

1 teaspoon sriracha

2 teaspoons minced fresh ginger

Got a big head of red cabbage rolling around in your crisper? Don't we all. This is the easiest, lip-smackingest slaw I know, and it makes quite a substantial lunch. Lots of crunchy cabbage and the occasional plump edamame smothered in a miso-sesame dressing, then topped with garlicky strips of seitan and sprinkled with sesame seeds and scallions. Feel free to customize: Add some shredded carrots and cucumber, top with avocado . . . you know, the usual salad-y things.

PREPARE THE SALAD:

In a large bowl, toss the cabbage, edamame, and salad dressing to coat well. (Reserve a few teaspoons of dressing to drizzle over the seitan.) Let the cabbage marinate while you prepare the seitan.

PREPARE THE SEITAN:

Preheat a large cast-iron pan over medium heat and add 2 teaspoons of the oil. Sauté the seitan in the oil, seasoning with salt and pepper, for about 5 minutes, until lightly browned. Push all the seitan to the side and add the garlic. Drizzle with the remaining 1 teaspoon sesame oil. Briefly mix and cook the garlic in the oil for about 15 seconds, then mix it in with the seitan.

Now divide the salad among serving bowls. Top with the warm seitan, drizzle with the reserved dressing, then garnish with the scallions, sesame seeds, and cilantro, if desired. Serve!

Miso-Sesame Dressing

makes about ¾ cup

This dressing is tangy, salty, and gingery, with a little kick. Not only is it great for slaw, but it's also nice as a side-salad dressing if you're enjoying some noodles, like the Omaha Yakisoba with Red Cabbage and Corn (page 176).

Add all of the ingredients to a small blender and blend until smooth and incorporated. Keep tightly sealed and refrigerated until ready to use. It will keep for up to 5 days.

QUINOA CAESAR SALAD

serves 8 · total time: 45 mins (plus time for soaking the cashews) · active time: 20 mins

"Put some quinoa in it." It has almost become my motto. I mean, why not? Everything needs quinoa! Even Caesar salad. This one really is a meal, and the recipe makes a ton because I love it as leftovers. It tastes great the day after and, honestly, still pretty darn tasty on day three. But feel free to halve it if need be. I am in love with the dressing: It's creamy, garlicky, briny, and tangy—just the kind of stuff you want to drink straight. The little bites of salty smokiness from the tempeh croutons bring everything together. I highly recommend using the simple make-ahead tips for this one; otherwise, it may be too much to pull together on a weeknight.

PREPARE THE TEMPEH:

Mix together the water, tamari, vinegar, liquid smoke, and thyme, and marinate the tempeh in the mixture for at least 30 minutes, giving everything a stir and a flip at least once.

To cook the tempeh, preheat a large, heavy-bottomed pan, preferably cast iron, over medium-high heat and add the oil. Sauté the tempeh in the oil for 10 minutes, until well browned. Add splashes of the marinade a few times as you cook so that it soaks up even more flavor.

TO ASSEMBLE:

Assemble the salad in a very large bowl. Add the greens and quinoa and toss together, and then add the dressing. Serve topped with the tempeh and avocado.

For the marinade and tempeh:

½ cup water

¼ cup tamari or soy sauce

2 tablespoons red wine vinegar

2 teaspoons liquid smoke

½ teaspoon dried thyme, crushed between your fingers

8 ounces tempeh, diced into ½-inch pieces

For everything else:

2 teaspoons olive oil

8 ounces romaine lettuce, chopped

4 ounces baby arugula (or regular arugula, chopped)

6 cups cooked and cooled quinoa

1 batch Briny Caesar Dressing (page 62)

1 avocado, pitted, peeled, and diced into ½-inch pieces

MAKE AHEAD:

- Make the quinoa a day in advance.
- Soak the cashews all day so that you can just come home and whip up the dressing.
- You can also marinate the tempeh all day, but if you do, reduce the amount of soy sauce by 1 tablespoon.

NOTE:

For the roasted garlic, you can either roast a head of it in advance or buy some. Often big fancy places like Whole Foods will have roasted garlic cloves for sale (there are about 15 in a head), or you can even nab some from the salad bar.

VARIATION:

Use the chickpeas from the Ranch Salad with Red Potatoes & Smoky Chickpeas (page 64) instead of the tempeh. If you like, and you're feeling rich and fancy, add some toasted pine nuts as well!

Briny Caesar Dressing

makes 1½ cups

½ cup cashews, soaked for at least 2 hours (see "ABS: Always Be Soaking," page 14)

1 head roasted garlic (about 10 cloves; see Note page 61)

2 cloves garlic

¼ cup capers, with some brine

2 tablespoons nutritional yeast flakes

2 tablespoons grapeseed or olive oil

½ teaspoon salt

Several pinches of freshly ground black pepper

¾ cup water

¼ cup fresh lemon juice

If you don't want to put together the entirety of the Quinoa Caesar Salad, you can use this as a base for the Caesar of your dreams. Mix it up with romaine lettuce and croutons for a more traditional Caesar, then top it with Garlicky Thyme Tempeh (page 236) for a well-rounded meal.

Simply drain the cashews and add all of the ingredients to a small blender or food processor, and purée until smooth. This could take anywhere from 1 to 5 minutes depending on the strength of your machine. Scrape down the sides every now and again to make sure you get everything. Keep tightly sealed and refrigerated until ready to use. It will keep for up to 5 days.

COOL GRAINS ARE COOL!

Grain salads are *the best*. In fact, I probably eat grain salads more often than I eat warm grains. Grains absorb flavor better when cool, and the texture and flavor become more pronounced. But I admit it can be a pain in the asparagus to cook a grain only to have to cool it before eating. It seems like it takes forever! So let me share a couple of tips for fuss-free grain coolness.

1. OF COURSE, YOU COULD MAKE THE GRAIN A DAY IN ADVANCE AND JUST STICK IT IN THE FRIDGE. Then you're looking at negligible prep time and you're not staring at the grain with a growling stomach, anxiously urging it to cook and cool. If you go this route, let the grain come to room temperature in a mesh strainer after cooking, and then just stick it in a sealed container and refrigerate.

2. IF THE URGE FOR A GRAIN SALAD STRIKES WITHOUT NOTICE (AND TRUST ME, IT WILL) AND YOU NEED THAT SPELT BERRY TO HURRY THE HELL UP, HERE IS WHAT YOU DO: Cook the grain as usual, then drain in a mesh strainer or a metal colander with tiny holes (you know, so nothing falls through). Run under a little cold water just to get it cool enough to touch. Then spread it out along the inside of the colander so that it's in the shape of a bowl. Place in the freezer for 10 minutes, tossing once or twice, and voilà—perfectly chilled grains!

GREEK DINER SALAD

serves 6 · total time: 30 mins (plus overnight for the cashew feta) · active time: 15 mins

One bite of this salad and you can practically feel your butt sliding into a red vinyl booth at the diner down the street. So much deliciousness is tossed together in this bowl: crisp romaine lettuce, cukes, tomatoes, and salty kalamata olives. And of course, you can't have a Greek salad without some feta. In this case, cashews that are marinated with lots of acid and seasoning stand in, for delicious, creamy, crumbly bursts of flavor throughout. Make sure to make the cashews a day in advance for maximum flavor!

The cashew idea actually came from my friend Jess, who owns a restaurant here in Omaha called Block 16. The place is far from vegan, but they offer vegan specials every day and take their food very seriously. They understand that vegan salads don't have to mean something from the menu with almost everything that isn't vegan removed, leaving you with a bowl of lettuce and a tomato. Jess boiled some cashews and mixed them up with lemon, oregano, and other Mediterranean goodies, creating a soft feta-like delicacy that is perfect for this salad. I took the idea and went with it, using the cashew mixture as the dressing as well, to minimize the work. The end result is a zippy bowlful that you'll want to serve with some bread to sop up all of the deliciousness. Serve in a big see-through plastic bowl for maximum authenticity.

For the Cashew Feta:

1 cup cashews

2 tablespoons extra-virgin olive oil

¼ cup fresh lemon juice

2 tablespoons red wine vinegar

2 teaspoons dried oregano

1 clove garlic, minced

⅛ teaspoon salt

Freshly ground black pepper

For the salad:

14 ounces romaine lettuce (about 2 heads), chopped

2 cups diced tomatoes (½-inch dice)

2 cups diced cucumbers (½-inch dice)

1 cup kalamata olives, pitted and sliced in half

½ cup diced red onion (½-inch dice)

MAKE IT A MEAL:

A falafel burger right on top makes for a great entrée salad!

PREPARE THE CASHEW FETA:

In a small pot, submerge the cashews in water. Cover and bring to a boil. Remove the lid and let boil for 30 minutes.

Drain the cashews and place them in a bowl. Mash lightly with a fork or a small avocado masher. They should be broken up into chunks, not mashed into a ricotta-like consistency. Mix in the olive oil, lemon juice, vinegar, oregano, garlic, salt, and pepper. Seal tightly and refrigerate overnight.

TO ASSEMBLE:

In a large bowl, toss together the lettuce, tomatoes, cucumbers, olives, and red onion. Pour in the cashew mixture and toss to coat. Taste for seasoning, and serve.

RANCH SALAD
with Red Potatoes & Smoky Chickpeas
serves 6 · total time: 30 mins · active time: 20 mins

1¼ pounds red potatoes, cut into ¾-inch chunks

2 teaspoons olive oil

1 (15-ounce can) chickpeas, rinsed and drained (1½ cups)

2 tablespoons tamari or soy sauce

1 teaspoon liquid smoke

½ cup thinly sliced red onion

½ cup cucumbers sliced into thin half-moons

12 ounces romaine lettuce, chopped

Handful of arugula (optional)

1 batch Avocado Ranch Dressing (recipe follows)

2 tablespoons nutritional yeast flakes

MAKE AHEAD:

To get this done in a snap, steam the potatoes the night before. Perhaps you're steaming some veggies or something else? Simply add the potatoes afterward, and then the salad will come together in a snap on the following day.

NOTE:

For time-management purposes, if you don't have the potatoes prepared in advance, steam those first and then blend the dressing. Everything else will come together quickly.

2 cloves garlic, peeled

1 ripe avocado, pitted and peeled

1 cup vegetable broth

2 tablespoons fresh lemon juice

1 tablespoon olive oil

1 tablespoon onion powder

1 teaspoon sweet paprika

¾ teaspoon salt

¼ cup chopped fresh dill

This salad is dangerous. You could drown in the dressing, for instance. Or just want to eat nothing else for weeks on end. Smoky, salty chickpeas, steamed potatoes tossed with crisp romaine, and a handful of arugula all smothered in a dilly avocado ranch dressing. It's so versatile, making a great lunch on its own. And I can't think of a cuisine in which this salad would be out of place. Italian, Mexican, Indian . . . the flavors are equally at home anywhere. The cool creaminess is especially welcome with a spicy meal.

Prepare your steamer, then add the potatoes and steam for 10 minutes, or until tender. To cool instantly, you can dunk them in an ice bath the moment you remove them from the steamer; otherwise just set aside in a colander and refrigerate when they stop steaming.

Now prepare the chickpeas. Preheat a large pan over medium heat and add the oil. Sauté the chickpeas in the oil for 5 minutes or so, until they're slightly browned. Turn off the heat. Drizzle in the tamari and liquid smoke and roll the chickpeas around to coat completely. Taste the chickpeas for smoke and saltiness and adjust as necessary. Let them cool in the pan.

When the potatoes and chickpeas are cool, mix the onion, cucumbers, and lettuces in a very large bowl with about 1 cup of the dressing and the nutritional yeast. Use tongs (or your hands) to get everything coated completely. Toss in the potatoes. Top with the chickpeas and serve.

Avocado Ranch Dressing
makes 1½ cups

Pulse the garlic in a blender to get it chopped up. Add the avocado, broth, lemon juice, oil, onion powder, paprika, and salt and blend until completely smooth, scraping down the sides with a rubber spatula occasionally to make sure you blend everything. Add the dill and pulse just until the dressing turns a brilliant green with flecks of dill throughout. Taste for seasonings. Remember that the salt flavor will be diluted when you add it to the salad, so make sure it's just a tad saltier than you think it should be. Seal tightly and refrigerate until ready to use.

ROASTED YELLOW BEET SALAD

with Warm Maple-Mustard Dressing

serves 4 · total time: 1 hour 15 mins · active time: 15 mins

It's hard to be inspired to make a salad in the late winter months. Lettuce doesn't exactly warm the soul after said soul has trudged through the slush in single-digit temperatures. But hold off on ordering that pizza, because I've got a remedy! Dress your salad in something warm and inviting. And to sweeten the deal, this dressing has only two ingredients (well, three if you count water, but stop nitpicking!). It comes together easily, too. The beets humbly roast away with minimum prep as you toast the pecans. You'll really only have 15 minutes or so of hands-on time and then earthy, tangy, toasty, sweet flavors will be all yours.

4 small yellow beets, peeled

1 cup whole pecans

6 ounces baby arugula or spinach

1 batch Warm Maple-Mustard Dressing (recipe follows)

1 medium red onion, thinly sliced into half circles

VARIATION:

Replace the pecans with the tempeh croutons from Quinoa Caesar Salad (page 61), as shown.

Preheat the oven to 425°F.

Wrap the beets in aluminum foil and roast for 1 hour. Remove from the oven, unwrap, and slice when they stop steaming. Meanwhile, preheat a pan over medium heat and toast the pecans, tossing until lightly browned, 5 to 7 minutes.

Place the greens in a super-large bowl. Drizzle in the dressing and use tongs to coat. The greens will wilt slightly.

Transfer the salad to plates. Place the sliced beets snugly against the greens. Scatter on the pecans and the onion slices. Serve immediately.

Warm Maple-Mustard Dressing

makes about ⅓ cup

This dressing also does double duty as a dip for french fries or breaded tofu.

¼ cup stone-ground mustard

2 tablespoons pure maple syrup

Mix the mustard and maple syrup together in a bowl. When ready to serve, microwave for 30 seconds (or mix and gently heat in a pan over low heat). Thin with a tablespoon or so of water if it appears too thick.

DRAGON NOODLE SALAD

serves 4 · total time: 30 mins · active time: 20 mins

8 ounces pad thai rice noodles

1 cup thinly sliced radishes

1 cup thinly sliced cucumbers

1 batch Peanut Dragon Dressing (recipe follows)

8 cups crisp salad greens

For the garnish:

4 teaspoons toasted or black sesame seeds

Fresh cilantro sprigs

Summer evenings are incomplete without a noodle salad like this to slurp up. Peanutty, sesame-y, spicy, and loaded with crisp and cooling radishes and cucumbers. To make this even more filling, thinly slice some Sesame Tofu (page 239) over the top while it's still warm. The cool-warm combo is always a fun and delicious one.

Prepare the noodles according to the package directions. It's very important not to overcook them! Set a timer to be safe. Once soft, immediately drain and run cold water over them until cool.

Now assemble the salad: In a very large bowl, toss the noodles, radishes, and cucumbers with most of the dressing, reserving a little bit for drizzling.

Place a bed of greens on each plate and top with the noodle mixture. Sprinkle with the sesame seeds, top with a little cilantro, drizzle with the remaining dressing, and serve.

Peanut Dragon Dressing

makes about 1 cup

½ cup smooth natural peanut butter

2 cloves garlic, peeled

⅓ cup water

3 tablespoons rice vinegar

2 tablespoons soy sauce or tamari

1 tablespoon agave nectar

1 tablespoon sriracha

1 teaspoon toasted sesame oil

½ teaspoon salt, or as needed

This is a very versatile dressing. It's perfect for a salad, of course, but it's also wonderful warm. So if you're looking for something to top some rice and steamed veggies, this dressing is your man.

Place all of the ingredients in a small blender or food processor and blend until very smooth. Keep tightly sealed and refrigerated until ready to use. It will keep for up to 5 days.

FARRO & FENNEL SALAD
with Oranges

serves 6 • total time: 1 hour 30 mins • active time: 20 mins

2 bulbs fennel (reserve fronds for garnish)

1 tablespoon olive oil

Pinch of salt

1 cup dried spelt berries, cooked and cooled (see "Cool Grains Are Cool!" on page 62)

2 cups baby arugula leaves

1 batch Orange Vinaigrette (recipe follows)

1½ cups orange segments

½ cup walnuts, toasted

NOTES:

• For time-management purposes, work in this order: 1.) Preheat the oven. 2.) Prep the fennel. 3.) Toast the walnuts. 4.) Stir together the vinaigrette. 5.) Prep the oranges. 6.) Assemble. 7.) Enjoy!

• How to get pretty orange segments that look like they're from a cooking mag: Slice a thin layer off the top and bottom of the orange, then place the orange on the cutting board. Cut the peel from the orange from the top down, using a chef's knife and following the natural curve of the orange. A little of the white pith left behind is okay; just try to get as close to the orange as you can. If the orange is large (like a navel), then slice it in half through the waist. If it's on the small side, keep it whole. Now slice each segment from top to bottom, avoiding the white membrane where you can. Voilà! Pretty orange segments.

¼ cup fresh orange juice

2 tablespoons red wine vinegar

2 tablespoons extra-virgin olive oil

¼ teaspoon salt

This salad will have you asking the waiter to refill your wine glass, only to realize that you're not seated at a trattoria in Little Italy at all—you're just sitting at your kitchen table eating a salad and your cat is staring at you. No matter!

Roasted fennel, in all its delicious licorice glory, is classically paired with citrus—one bite and you'll see why. Spelt berries (also called farro) are one of my favorite salad grains ever. They've got an awesome firm and springy bite, and if chewing can ever be considered fun, well, this must be the time. A few handfuls of arugula bring a peppery freshness to the dish and roasted walnuts finish it off, creating a feast of texture that will make you reach for the salad tongs again and again.

There are very few ingredients required, and I love that, but each ingredient does take a little work. Not exactly *hard* work, but work all the same. Don't be deterred, though; it really comes together in a cinch and will give you some great skills that will last a lifetime, like how to roast fennel and make orange segments.

Preheat the oven to 425°F. Line a large rimmed baking sheet with parchment paper.

Slice the fennel bulbs from top to base in ½-inch slices. Toss with the olive oil on the baking sheet, add a light sprinkle of salt, and spread out into a single layer. Roast for 15 minutes. Flip the slices over and roast for 5 to 10 more minutes; the fennel should be tender and slightly caramelized. Remove from the oven and let cool. Once cooled, you can slice the fennel into smaller, bite-size strips.

Place the spelt berries, fennel, and arugula in a large bowl. Add the vinaigrette and toss to coat. Fold in the oranges. Scatter the walnuts on top and serve.

Orange Vinaigrette
makes about ½ cup

What a blissfully simple vinaigrette! Try it on a side salad with baby greens, red onion, and olives.

Mix all of the ingredients together in a small cup. Keep tightly sealed and refrigerated until ready to use. It will keep for up to 5 days.

HOW TO COOK LIKE A GRAINIAC

This is my cooking method for spelt berries, or any big and hearty grain for that matter. Instead of steaming in just enough water for the grain to absorb, I boil it more like pasta. Because it's such a hearty grain, it won't fall apart or overcook, and this method is more consistent, since small quantities of water may let the grain burn if the heat isn't just right.

Soak the dry spelt berries in water overnight, or all day, or during whatever 12-hour chunk of time you've got. This will get them to cook faster.

Drain and place in a 2-quart pot. Fill the pot three-quarters full with fresh water and add a big pinch of salt.

Cover and bring to a boil. Once rapidly boiling, keep covered but lower the heat and bring to a slow rolling boil. If the grain has been presoaked, you'll need to cook it for about 20 minutes. If not, then more like 45 minutes. The texture should be firm and springy when fully cooked, but not so firm that it breaks a tooth.

Once cooked, drain into a colander and let cool completely.

FARMER SALAD
with Chive Vinaigrette

serves 4 · total time: 30 mins · active time: 15 mins

This salad is a bit like a Niçoise, only you're not in France, you're at a farmers' market, possibly in the Pacific Northwest, and possibly wearing Birkenstocks and leg warmers. I love the contrast of the rich, creamy baby taters with the fresh crunchy greenness of the snap peas. The Chive Vinaigrette is another burst of fresh onion-ness and also the perfect foil for the peppery arugula. To make it substantial and even more special, some mouthwatering trumpet mushrooms are scattered across the top, still warm. It's such a farmers' market party! If you'd like to add some protein, the Garlicky Thyme Tempeh (page 236) is a great choice, or just a few handfuls of chickpeas.

1 pound baby potatoes

8 ounces trumpet mushrooms, thinly sliced

2 teaspoons olive oil

¼ teaspoon salt

6 cups baby arugula

2 cups trimmed and bias-sliced snap peas

1 batch Chive Vinaigrette (recipe follows)

First, boil the potatoes. Place them in a 2-quart pot, add water to cover, and salt the water. Bring to a boil and then lower the heat and simmer until the potatoes are tender, about 10 minutes. Place them in an ice bath to cool completely, or just run them under cold water.

In the meantime, preheat a large pan (preferably cast iron) over medium-high heat. Sauté the mushrooms in the olive oil with the salt for about 7 minutes, until lightly browned.

In a large bowl, toss together the arugula, snap peas, and potatoes. Add about half of the vinaigrette and toss to coat. Serve in bowls, with the mushrooms scattered on top and additional dressing drizzled all over.

Chive Vinaigrette

makes ⅔ cup

A brilliantly green dressing that is perfect on everything from salad (obviously) to grilled veggies to baked potatoes!

Place all of the ingredients in a small blender or food processor and blend until very smooth. Keep tightly sealed and refrigerated until ready to use. It will keep for up to 5 days.

½ cup chopped fresh chives

1 clove garlic, peeled

2 tablespoons olive oil

3 tablespoons fresh lemon juice

3 tablespoons water

1 tablespoon Dijon mustard

1 teaspoon agave nectar

½ teaspoon salt

Several pinches of freshly ground black pepper

TABBOULEH OF THE SEA

serves 6 · total time: 30 mins · active time: 15 mins

For the couscous:

1 cup whole-wheat couscous

1 tablespoon olive oil

¼ teaspoon salt

1 cup boiling water

For everything else:

1 (15-ounce) can chickpeas, rinsed and drained (1½ cups)

1 cup diced tomato (about ¼-inch dice)

1 cup diced cucumbers (about ¼-inch dice)

1 cup loosely packed fresh flat-leaf parsley, finely chopped

½ cup finely chopped scallions

3 tablespoons capers, drained

2 teaspoons minced garlic

3 tablespoons fresh lemon juice

2 tablespoons olive oil

¼ teaspoon salt

Freshly ground black pepper

I'm not the biggest tabbouleh fan, but I like the idea of it. Grains and herbs and veggies tossed in a simple lemony dressing? Sure, count me in! It's just that I have to do it my way. What I decided to do is play on the fact that mashed chickpeas act a lot like canned tuna. Coupled with briny capers, the result is sort of vegan tuna tabbouleh salad. It makes this a balanced and substantial grain salad that is perfect for lunches on the go, because it even tastes great at room temp.

Oh, and, one more thing: I use couscous instead of bulgur, because it's faster and I always have it on hand. So yeah, this is hardly even tabbouleh anymore. But still.

PREPARE THE COUSCOUS:

Place the couscous in a medium bowl. Drizzle in the oil and sprinkle in the salt. Pour the boiling water over the couscous. Immediately cover the bowl with a plate and steam the couscous for 10 minutes or so. When ready, fluff with a fork and let cool completely (see "Cool Grains are Cool!" on page 62).

PREPARE EVERYTHING ELSE:

In the meantime, using a small masher or fork, lightly mash the chickpeas in a large bowl. They shouldn't be puréed like hummus, or anywhere close to that. Just mash so that there are almost no whole ones left (a few are okay) but they are still recognizable as chickpeas.

Now toss all of the remaining ingredients in with the chickpeas, including the cooled couscous. Mix very well (your hands work well for this) and taste for seasonings. To serve, I usually put everything back in the bowl that the couscous was in because it's a little less messy. Let sit for a few minutes to let the flavors marry, and then serve. This actually tastes even better the next day, and it keeps well in a tightly sealed container in the refrigerator for up to 3 days.

KALE SALAD
with Butternut Squash & Lentils

serves 6 • total time: 1 hour • active time: 20 mins

These are all of my favorite things in the world! This salad just screams *"Isa!"* Sometimes even literally, so don't be freaked out if you hear it. The earthiness of the kale is offset by sweet bits of roasted squash and the zip of the vinaigrette. The lentils really make it a meal.

The trick to preparing kale to eat raw is to work it really hard with your hands, like you're Rolfing it (which is an intense massage-like therapy that looks kind of fun). Work it at every step, including when you rinse and drain it. Use your hands to really scrunch the leaves up to get the water out, almost like wringing out a sponge. Don't worry; kale can take it! In fact, afterward it might feel a little like you after a massage; tender, relaxed, and ready to be smothered in vinaigrette.

1 (1-pound) butternut squash

¼ cup olive oil

½ teaspoon salt

2 tablespoons white wine vinegar

2 teaspoons agave nectar or pure maple syrup

1 teaspoon Dijon mustard

1½ teaspoons finely minced fresh ginger

1 clove garlic, finely minced

8 ounces kale, stems removed, torn into bite-size pieces (about 8 cups)

1½ cups cooked brown lentils (or one 15-ounce can, rinsed and drained)

Preheat the oven to 425°F.

Peel the squash and divide the round part from the long part. Cut the round part in half and scoop out the seeds. Slice everything into ½- to ¾-inch pieces.

Line a large baking sheet with parchment paper. Spread the squash out in a single layer and drizzle with 1 tablespoon of the olive oil. The single layer is important because if the baking sheet is overcrowded the squash won't brown, it'll steam and just get mushy. Sprinkle with ¼ teaspoon of the salt and toss with your hands to coat.

Pop in the oven for about 25 minutes, flipping after 15 minutes or so. It's done when lightly browned on the outside and tender inside. Remove from the oven and let cool.

Stir together the remaining 3 tablespoons olive oil, vinegar, agave nectar, mustard, ginger, garlic, and remaining ¼ teaspoon salt in a large bowl—everything will be going in there, so make sure it's large enough to hold all that kale.

Add the kale and take a minute or so, using your hands, to rub the vinaigrette into the leaves, really swishing them around in there.

Add the cooled squash and the lentils and toss to coat. Give the flavors a few minutes to settle in, then taste for seasoning and serve.

MAKE AHEAD:

Roast a mess of squash an evening or two before as a side dish for dinner and use the leftovers (about 2 cups squash pieces) for this salad.

15-MINUTE OPTION:

Don't feel like butternut squash, or just looking for something a little less labor-intensive? Replace the roasted butternut with uncooked apples. Just peel two tart apples, like Granny Smiths, and dice them into ½-inch pieces.

NOTE:

For the ginger and garlic, you want to get them to be almost a paste. A Microplane grater works perfectly for this, or you can just mince the hell out of them.

SWEET & SOUR BROWN RICE SALAD

with Fresh Herbs

serves 4 to 6 · total time: 15 mins (plus time for cooking the rice)
active time: 15 mins

For the salad:

4 cups cooked and cooled brown rice

⅔ of a 15-ounce can adzuki beans, rinsed and drained (1 cup)

2 cups mung bean sprouts

1 cup thinly sliced scallions

½ cup whole roasted peanuts

¼ cup chopped fresh mint

½ cup chopped fresh cilantro

For the dressing:

2 tablespoons mellow white miso

1 cup sweet chili sauce

¼ cup fresh lime juice

1 teaspoon grated fresh ginger

1 teaspoon agave nectar

Sriracha, for serving

This salad is all about my favorite Vietnamese flavors: lots and lots (and lots!) of fresh herbs and scallions, roasted peanuts, and crunchy sprouts, all tossed together in a spicy, sweet, sour, and salty dressing. It's an out-of-control feast of flavor and texture. I use adzuki beans for protein, but you could also use some sautéed tofu or tempeh.

PREPARE THE SALAD:

In a large bowl, toss together all of the salad ingredients.

PREPARE THE DRESSING:

In a small bowl, use a fork to vigorously mix together all of the dressing ingredients.

Drizzle the dressing onto the salad and toss to coat. Serve with sriracha for some extra heat.

NOTE:

Sweet chili sauce, made from chiles, vinegar, garlic, and sugar, can be found in the Asian aisle of your supermarket. It's great with any Asian-inspired stir-fry and totally worth keeping in your pantry.

HANDHELD

This chapter is all about the  **FUN.**

The fun of eating with your hands, the fun of laying out a bunch of ingredients and putting together your own tacos or forming patties. I don't know, maybe it's not a mid-'90s rave in an abandoned train yard in Brooklyn, but it's a pretty good time. Burger night makes a lot of sense for the busy home cook. And it's easy, too. Mush up a few ingredients, bake or fry them up, top with your favorite ingredients, and you've got yourself dinner. What's more, you can freeze a batch and have them ready for a rainy day. And I always find myself throwing together tacos. If I have no idea what to make, a tortilla as my canvas always provides instant inspiration. But this chapter goes beyond burgers and tacos, revamping a whole lotta classic American sandwiches. Although vegan sloppy joes and tuna sandwiches have been around for decades, I hope that the new spins here will get you excited about them all over again!

BISTRO BEET BURGERS

makes 6 burgers · total time: 1 hour 15 mins · active time: 20 mins

1¼ cups cooked and cooled brown rice

1 cup cooked brown or green lentils, drained well

1 cup shredded beets

½ cup very fine dry bread crumbs

3 tablespoons very finely chopped onion

2 cloves garlic, minced

2 tablespoons smooth almond butter

1 teaspoon dried thyme, rubbed between your fingers

½ teaspoon ground fennel (or finely crushed fennel seeds)

1 teaspoon dry mustard

½ teaspoon salt

Freshly ground black pepper

Olive oil, for the pan

6 burger buns

Shredded lettuce, sliced dill pickles, finely diced onion, and/or ketchup, for topping (I would add a layer of avocado instead of a vegan cheese, but that's just me.)

NOTES:

• One very important part of this recipe is the cooking method. You want to get the burger charred. Not *burned*, but *charred*, which really just means, uh, burned only in some places. The best way to achieve this is with a very hot cast-iron pan. Other pans may react differently to high heat and may not give you that perfect char. So if you're not using a cast-iron pan, the next best thing would be to transfer them to a baking sheet after cooking, brush with oil, and stick them under the broiler for a few minutes.

• If you'd like to bake these instead, do so in a 375°F oven for 8 to 10 minutes per side, then stick them under the broiler to brown.

• I use a food processor to make these happen quickly, so you'll have to do some finagling if you don't have one. You can shred the beets with a hand shredder, then use a potato masher to mash everything together. It will come out a bit chunkier, but still yummy!

Well, everyone loves burgers, and this is a fine, upstanding burger-citizen made with some of my favorite ingredients: brown rice, lentils, and beets! They combine to form the perfect storm of vegan burgerness. It's not that they taste *exactly* like hamburgers or anything, but they *do* taste exactly like awesome veggie burgers: Rice provides hearty texture, to give you a substantial bite. Lentils are my go-to ground meat, so they were a natural addition. And beets give the burgers an intense (and vaguely disturbing) meat-like appearance, but they also add a lot of flavor, earthy and slightly sweet. Just something that takes your VB to the next level. And don't forget the fries! Baked Garlic-Curry Fries (page 87) are the perfect accompaniment. Prepare the mixture the morning of or evening before to have these on the table in no time.

If you have a tree-nut allergy, then sunflower seed butter or tahini will make an excellent substitution for the almond butter.

Put the brown rice, lentils, and shredded beets in the work bowl of a food processor fitted with a metal blade and pulse 15 to 20 times, until the mixture comes together but still has texture. It should look a lot like ground meat.

Now transfer to a large bowl and add the bread crumbs, onion, garlic, almond butter, thyme, fennel, mustard, salt, and pepper. Use your hands to mix very well. Everything should be well incorporated, so get in there and take your time; it could take a minute or two.

Place the mixture in the fridge for 30 minutes to chill.

Preheat a cast-iron pan over medium-high heat. Now form the patties. Use ⅓ cup of the mixture for each patty and form into ¾-inch-thick disks. (See "Perfect Patties Every Time," page 84.)

Pour a very thin layer of oil into the pan and cook the patties for about 12 minutes, flipping occasionally. Drizzle in a little more oil as needed. The burgers should be charred at the edges and heated through.

Serve warm on buns with toppings! They taste pretty great reheated as well, so if you want, cook them in advance, refrigerate, then gently heat in the pan later.

PERFECT PATTIES EVERY TIME!

I'm kind of particular about my veggie burger shape—I really like for it to be neat, with perfectly round, smooth sides. A burger that looks like it's on *America's Next Top Veggie Burger*. To get that shape, just pat your veggie burger mixture into a 3-inch cookie cutter. Don't worry about fingerprints in the burgers; they will flatten out when you flip them. If you don't have a 3-inch cookie cutter, you can get all DIY. Use an empty 15-ounce can and press it into the veggie burger mixture. Then simply pop the patty out of the can!

FREEZE FRAME!

Burgers are ideal candidates for freezing because they reheat so well. I prefer to cook my burgers and *then* freeze them rather than freeze uncooked burger patties. This way, you can just microwave them for a minute or so or let them thaw and then gently reheat in a pan.

To freeze burgers after cooking, let them cool completely on a cooling rack. Stack them up with sheets of wax paper in between each layer, to keep them from sticking together. Place in a storage container or a plastic freezer bag, and freeze away! They will keep for 2 to 3 months.

BURGER FEVER

Why stop at just plain burgers? The Bistro Beet Burger makes a great base for many a variation. Just use the simple fixins below for a different burger every night of the week.

BANH MI BURGER: Vegan mayo with sriracha, fresh cilantro, mint, and the homemade pickles on page 105.

TEX-MEX BURGER: Queso Blanco (page 213), Pico de Gallo (page 233), chopped avocado, pickles, and romaine lettuce.

BURRITO BURGER: Same as the Tex-Mex, but top with a few tablespoons of leftover chili as well. Meaty Beany Chili (page 168) is a great choice.

CHILI BURGER: Simply top with leftover chili and the usual burger fixins: lettuce, pickles, and tomato.

PIZZA BURGER: Marinara sauce, sauce from the Pizza Bowl with Greens, Sausages & Olives (page 204), pickles, and romaine lettuce.

BACON CHEESEBURGER: Smoky Chickpeas (page 64), Queso Blanco (page 213; leave out the jalapeño and cumin), ketchup, sliced red onion, sliced tomato, and romaine lettuce.

CAESAR BURGER: Top the burger with plain Caesar Salad (page 61) and extra dressing for the bottom bun.

FALAFEL BURGERS

makes 8 burgers · total time: 30 mins
(plus time for soaking the chickpeas) · active time: 20 mins

If you want to get your falafel fix but don't feel like forming a bunch of little patties and firing up the deep fryer, then this is the burger for you. Everything you love about falafel, like the spicy aroma, the herbaceous backdrop, the crisp exterior, and the tender interior, is now in burger form!

The secret to perfection here is to simmer dried chickpeas instead of relying on the canned ones. The texture of the canned beans is just too mushy. With this method, you're cooking the chickpeas to firm-tender, just this side of edible, so that they retain their shape and provide lots of toothsome texture. It takes a little advance planning, but it's very easy and hands-off work that is so worth it!

1 cup dried chickpeas

2 cloves garlic

1 cup coarsely chopped yellow onion

½ cup loosely packed fresh flat-leaf parsley

½ cup loosely packed fresh cilantro

¼ cup water

½ cup fine dry bread crumbs

½ teaspoon baking powder

1 tablespoon ground cumin

1 teaspoon sweet paprika

1¼ teaspoons salt

Several pinches of freshly ground black pepper

Olive oil, for the pan

8 sandwich-size pitas

Sliced tomato, cucumber, lettuce, pickles, and/or red onion, for topping

Miso-Tahini Dressing (page 192) or hummus (see page 201), or both (!), for topping

First, partially cook the chickpeas. Place them in a small pot and submerge them in water by about 2 inches. Cover and bring to a boil. Once boiling, lower the heat and simmer for 10 minutes. Then turn the heat off and let the chickpeas soak at room temperature overnight or for 8 hours or so. They should be tender and edible but still very firm, with a similar texture to edamame. Drain before using.

Once the chickpeas are ready, add the garlic (but not the chickpeas!) to a food processor and pulse until finely chopped. Add the onion, parsley, and cilantro, and pulse until the onion is very finely chopped and the herbs are in flecks. Don't purée; you still want coarse texture.

Transfer this mixture to a large bowl. Now place the chickpeas in the food processor and pulse into fine crumbs. Add the water and pulse again until thick and mushy. Again, you still want texture, so don't purée. Transfer the chickpeas to the bowl with the onions.

Now add the bread crumbs, baking powder, cumin, paprika, salt, and pepper to the bowl and mix very well.

Cover tightly with plastic wrap and refrigerate for at least 30 minutes.

Preheat a large heavy-bottomed pan over medium heat. Form the burgers into patties using about ¼ cup of the mixture per patty. Pour a thin layer of olive oil into the pan. It should be enough to cover the bottom of the pan, with some excess. Cook patties four at a time for about 7 minutes on each side, until nicely browned. Drizzle in a little extra olive oil if necessary.

Serve warm in pitas, layered with the toppings of your choice.

NOTES:

- Plan a day ahead. Boil the chickpeas while you're making dinner the night before. Then prepare the burger mixture in the food processor before you do the dishes. This way you can clean up two nights' worth of mess in one day. It's like you're time traveling. Only instead of saving the world from Hitler, you're saving yourself from dirty dishes. Same diff?

- Alternatively, you can start the chickpeas in the morning, let them soak all day, and then prepare the burgers when you get home. The burger mixture requires refrigeration time, so have a snack on hand to hold you over.

BAKED GARLIC-CURRY FRIES

serves 4 · total time: 45 mins · active time: 20 mins

What's a burger without fries? There's a falafel joint down the street from me that makes these amazing curry fries that you can smell from a block away. They are *so* tantalizing, but baked fries are way healthier and totally quench my curry fry craving.

These baked fries *do* take a bit of work. You need to parboil them, plunge them into ice water, and then bake. But I wouldn't include this recipe if it weren't totally worth it! It's everything a fry should be, with a creamy interior and a crispy outside. And it's one of those things that, if you do it once, the next time it won't be such a big deal and the time after that even less so. Looking over the directions, I'm surprised at how much work it looks like when in reality it is so easy!

1½ pounds russet potatoes, sliced
2 tablespoons mild curry powder
½ teaspoon salt
1 tablespoon finely minced garlic
1 tablespoon olive oil, plus more to oil the pan and drizzle onto the fries

NOTES:

- The type of curry powder you use is important. I use the Penzeys sweet curry blend. It's fairly mild with a little kick, and not bitter like some curry powders can be. Oh, and expect yellow garlic-smelling fingers for a few hours because you have to handle the curry powder with your hands. Welcome to my world.

- If you just want plain old baked fries, skip the curry step. Just drizzle on the olive oil and salt and you're good to go! You can also use chili powder or Cajun spice or any spice blend you're totally in love with.

- You want to "steak fry" the potatoes. So slice them about ¼ inch thick and ¾ inch wide.

Bring a large pot of salted water to a boil. In the meantime, you'll prep everything else and preheat the oven to 425°F.

Now prep your work space. Fill a big bowl with ice water. Lay a kitchen towel on the counter and line it with paper towels. You'll be plunging the fries into the ice water after boiling, and then placing them on the towels to blot dry.

Once the water is boiling, add the potatoes and cook for 3 minutes; no longer or they will get mushy, so set a timer if you need to. Drain the potatoes and immediately plunge them into the ice bath to stop them from cooking further.

Once completely cool, place the potatoes in a single layer on the towels to drain. Blot the tops with a paper towel as well so that they're mostly dry. A little moisture is necessary, though, to get the coating to stick. You just don't want a puddle.

Pour the ice water out of the bowl and wipe it dry. Scoop the curry powder into the bowl and mix in the salt. Add the garlic. Add the oil and mix with a fork.

We're in the home stretch now! Spray or lightly brush a large baking sheet with oil. Toss a handful of potato slices into the curry mixture and remove each one, rubbing in the curry powder. Do this in about four batches, being careful not to get huge chunks of curry on any one potato. It should be evenly distributed among the fries.

Place the fries in a single layer on the baking sheet, spray or drizzle with a little oil, and bake for 8 to 12 minutes on each side, until golden brown and tender inside. If you'd like extra browning, place under the broiler for a few minutes, keeping a close eye. Serve hot!

PORCINI-TOFU BURGERS

makes 6 burgers • total time: 30 mins • active time: 30 mins

1 ounce dried porcini mushrooms

14 ounces extra-firm tofu, drained

3 tablespoons smooth almond butter

3 tablespoons tamari or soy sauce

2 tablespoons nutritional yeast flakes

¼ cup very finely chopped yellow onion

2 teaspoons minced garlic

¾ cup panko bread crumbs

Olive oil, for the pan

6 whole-wheat hamburger buns or sandwich-size pitas

Lettuce and sliced tomatoes, for topping

Vegan mayo

NOTE:

- If you can't find dried porcinis, dried portobellos or shiitakes are good alternatives. There are also packages of dried mixed wild mushrooms available, which usually contain porcinis, so grab those if you can.

If mouthwateringly savory is your thing, then this is the burger for you. It's got a lot of umami going on. The preparation involves grinding dried porcini mushrooms to a powder and mashing them up with tofu and panko to form a firm patty with a good, crispy bite. Porcinis have a sultry, woodsy taste that is just out of this world! (No, really, I think porcinis must be from another planet.) You will marvel at how such simple ingredients can create a burger so addictive. It's also a great patty to throw over a salad, and it tastes delish at room temperature, so it's a good candidate for the lunch box as well. It's important to get the onion as finely chopped as possible so that the burgers aren't crumbly. I prefer these with mayo instead of ketchup.

In a blender, pulse the porcinis until they become a powder. This should take 30 seconds to 1 minute, depending on your machine.

In a medium bowl, mash the tofu until it resembles ricotta cheese. Use a potato masher or your hands. Add the almond butter, tamari, nutritional yeast, onion, and garlic and mix it up. Last, add ½ cup of the panko bread crumbs and mix until everything holds together. Definitely use your hands for this part, to really get in there and mush everything up adequately.

Preheat a large heavy-bottomed pan over medium heat. Form patties using about ⅓ cup of the mixture for each. Spread the remaining ¼ cup bread crumbs out on a plate. Press each patty into the bread crumbs on both sides to coat.

Pour a thin layer of olive oil into the pan. It should be enough to cover the bottom of the pan, with some excess. Cook the patties for about 6 minutes on each side, until nicely browned. Drizzle in a little extra olive oil if necessary.

Serve in buns with lettuce, tomato, and vegan mayo.

OLIVE-LENTIL BURGERS

makes 6 burgers · total time: 45 mins · active time: 20 mins

It is unfair to almost any other plant that the olive tree exists. Such an unlevel playing field! Is there another morsel in the world so bursting with flavor? This burger captures their meatiness with every savory bite. With other Mediterranean flavors (like garlic, thyme, and tarragon) contributing, plus mushrooms and lentils, your taste buds will never experience a dull moment when you're chowing down on one of these.

1 tablespoon olive oil

1 small yellow onion, diced

Pinch of salt

8 ounces cremini mushrooms, thinly sliced

3 cloves garlic, minced

½ teaspoon dried thyme

¼ teaspoon dried tarragon

Pinch of freshly ground black pepper

½ cup pitted kalamata olives

1¼ cups cooked brown or green lentils, drained (or one 15-ounce can, rinsed and drained)

2 tablespoons soy sauce

2 teaspoons fresh lemon juice

¼ teaspoon liquid smoke (optional)

1 cup fine dry bread crumbs

Olive oil, for brushing or spraying

6 hamburger buns (focaccia buns are great with these)

Lettuce, tomato, and/or pickles, for topping

Preheat the oven to 350°F.

Preheat a large, heavy-bottomed nonstick pan, preferably cast iron, over medium-high heat and add the oil. Sauté the onion in the oil for about 3 minutes with a pinch of salt. Add the mushrooms, garlic, thyme, tarragon, and black pepper, and sauté for 7 to 10 minutes, until the mushrooms are softened.

Meanwhile, place the olives in a food processor and pulse until they are finely chopped (not puréed). Remove from the food processor. (No need to clean it out for the next step.)

When the mushrooms are cooked, transfer the mushroom mixture to the food processor. Add the lentils, soy sauce, lemon juice, and liquid smoke (if desired), along with ½ cup of the bread crumbs. Pulse until mostly smooth; there should still be a little texture. Transfer to a large bowl. Add the remaining ½ cup bread crumbs to the burger mixture, along with the chopped olives, and thoroughly combine.

Line a baking sheet with parchment paper and spray with oil. Form the mixture into 6 patties that are about ¾ inch thick, spray or brush with a little more oil, and bake for 15 minutes. Flip the burgers and bake for 12 to 15 more minutes, until nicely browned. Serve on buns with toppings.

These taste great served immediately, but they're also excellent at room temperature, so don't be afraid to stuff one into a sandwich and take as a lunch.

ISLAND BLACK BEAN BURGERS

with Nectarine Salsa

makes 8 burgers • total time: 45 mins • active time: 20 mins

Who doesn't love a black bean burger? Here I've gone with a little Caribbean twist—not just *frijoles negros* (that's black beans to you), but black-eyed peas, too. And instead of the usual cumin and friends, I use a healthy dose of Jamaican curry powder. Topped with a sweet nectarine salsa, this tastes like a fabulous island vacay. Unless you already live on a beautiful tropical island, in which case it tastes like home.

I love that these come together in the mixing bowl without any need for sautéing the ingredients first, so they're great for anytime, anywhere. The nectarine salsa is the perfect sweet note here, and you don't even have to peel the fruit since the skin isn't fuzzy like a peach. Or use peaches if you like fuzzy salsa.

For the burgers:

1 (15-ounce) can black beans, rinsed and drained (1 ½ cups)

1 (15-ounce) can black-eyed peas, rinsed and drained (1 ½ cups)

½ cup finely chopped red bell pepper

1 cup finely chopped scallions

3 tablespoons finely chopped fresh cilantro

1 tablespoon plus 2 teaspoons Jamaican curry powder

1 teaspoon salt

¼ cup vegetable broth

2 teaspoons fresh lime juice

1 cup panko bread crumbs

For the Nectarine Salsa:

2 nectarines, diced into ¼-inch pieces

¼ cup finely diced red onion

2 tablespoons chopped fresh cilantro

1 tablespoon fresh lime juice

1 jalapeño, seeded and finely chopped

1 teaspoon agave nectar

Olive oil, for spraying or brushing the pan

8 burger buns

NOTES:

- This recipe halves well! Using only one kind of bean is probably your best bet if you're halving it, and I think regular black beans work better solo.

- If you don't feel like making the salsa (even though it's so easy!), then you can just slice up a couple pieces of mango, nectarine, or pineapple. I love the sweetness here, so I'd say go that route instead of plain old ketchup, but hey, a little ketchup never hurt anyone.

Preheat the oven to 400°F.

PREPARE THE BURGERS:

In a medium bowl, use a small potato masher (or a strong fork) to mash the black beans and black-eyed peas. They should be good and mushy but not totally puréed, with a few beans still identifiable in the mix.

Add the red pepper, scallions, cilantro, curry powder, salt, broth, and lime juice and mix well. Mix in the panko until it all holds together. Refrigerate for 10 minutes or so, or until the salsa is ready.

PREPARE THE SALSA:

Simply mix everything together in a bowl!

COOK THE BURGERS:

Line a baking sheet with parchment paper and spray or brush with oil. Form the burger mixture into 8 patties that are about 1 inch thick (see "Perfect Patties Every Time," page 84). Spray or brush with a little more oil and bake for 15 minutes. Flip the burgers and bake for 12 to 15 more minutes, until nicely browned.

Stuff each burger into a bun and top with salsa. Serve away!

VARIATION:

If you want a more traditional, straight-up black bean burger, no problemo. Use all black beans instead of the black-eyed peas. Instead of the Jamaican curry powder, use 1 tablespoon mild chili powder and 1 teaspoon of cumin. You can top with store-bought salsa if you're feelin' lazy, or a simple *pico de gallo* and chopped avocado.

KOREAN BBQ
PORTOBELLO BURGERS

makes 4 burgers · total time: 45 mins · active time: 20 mins

Portobello mushrooms have become ubiquitous in vegan cuisine for good reason: They're juicy, they char beautifully, and they're the perfect size and shape for stuffing into a bun. These burgers were inspired by—you guessed it—Korean barbecue! Smoky, sweet, and spicy, they're a great way to switch up your portobello burger routine. One bite and maybe you'll be convinced that hamburgers are trying to mimic portobello burgers, and not the other way around. I love these grilled, so that they can get even smokier, but broiling works well, too. I'm supplying directions for both methods.

If you've never had kimchi, you're in for a really pickle-y treat! You can think of it as Korean sauerkraut if you like. It's a spicy, fermented cabbage condiment with a tangy flavor that is at once very fresh tasting but also aged and nuanced. It makes the burger even more fun to eat, with a great variety of texture going on. And yes, things are going to get a little sloppy, but savor it and let those juices run down your hand.

For the marinade:

1 cup water
¼ cup light molasses (not blackstrap)
¼ cup pure maple syrup
¼ cup tomato paste
¼ cup soy sauce
¼ cup red wine vinegar
2 tablespoons liquid smoke
2 teaspoons toasted sesame oil
2 teaspoons sriracha
1 teaspoon onion powder
2 cloves garlic, smashed
4 average-size portobello mushroom caps, stems removed
Olive oil, for spraying or brushing the grill

For serving:

4 large white hamburger buns
Vegan mayo
1 cup kimchi

PREPARE THE MARINADE:

Combine all of the marinade ingredients in a large shallow bowl or pan with enough room to hold the mushroom caps in a single layer. Mix well.

Marinate the mushrooms gill side up for at least 15 minutes and up to 1 hour. Make sure that each mushroom is slathered in marinade.

STOVETOP GRILLING DIRECTIONS:

Preheat a grill pan over high heat. Spray or brush with oil. Place each mushroom gill side up in the pan and partially cover with a large lid. Cook for about 5 minutes; spoon a little more marinade on about halfway through. Flip each mushroom and cook for another 5 minutes, or until the center where the stem was seems tender and juicy and the mushroom is nicely charred.

BROILING DIRECTIONS:

Preheat the broiler to high. Spray a rimmed baking sheet with oil and arrange the oven rack about 6 inches from the heat. Place each mushroom gill side up on the baking sheet and broil for about 5 minutes per side. Spoon some marinade over the mushrooms while they are cooking.

TO ASSEMBLE:

Spread each bun with a little mayo. Place burger on bun and top with kimchi. I like to cut my burger in half with a steak knife and dig in!

NOTES:

- Don't remove the gills from the porto-bellos, even if you've seen them do that on cooking shows. They are loaded with flavor and texture, not to mention the fact that the gills soak up marinade beautifully. Gently wash your caps before marinating and you are A-OK.

- Portobellos vary in size pretty drastically. They can be anywhere from the size of a hockey puck to the size of a small Frisbee. For burgers, I like mushrooms that are somewhere in between: about 5 inches in circumference. Try to grab nice firm ones that are uniform in size and not limp or wrinkled. If you're going to keep them stored in the fridge for a few days, wrap them in a clean kitchen towel instead of in plastic. They need a little air to stay fresh.

JERK SLOPPY JOES

with Coconut Creamed Spinach

makes 6 sandwiches · total time: 40 mins · active time: 40 mins

For the sloppy joe filling:

1 tablespoon plus 1 teaspoon refined coconut oil

1 medium yellow onion, diced

½ teaspoon salt, plus a pinch

1 pound seitan, chopped into bite-size pieces

3 cloves garlic, minced

1 tablespoon minced fresh ginger

2 tablespoons chopped fresh thyme

1 tablespoon sweet paprika

½ teaspoon ground allspice

½ teaspoon crushed red pepper flakes

⅛ teaspoon ground cinnamon

Several pinches of freshly ground black pepper

1 (14-ounce) can crushed tomatoes

2 tablespoons pure maple syrup

1 tablespoon fresh lime juice

2 teaspoons yellow mustard

For the spinach:

2 cloves garlic, minced

2 teaspoons refined coconut oil

1 pound spinach, stems removed

1 cup regular or lite coconut milk

2 star anise pods

¼ teaspoon salt

For serving:

6 big burger buns (kaiser rolls would be great)

This sandwich is definitely the result of a Brooklyn girl moving to the Midwest. It combines my love for the sautéed callaloo and West Indian jerk sauces that I enjoyed in my old neighborhood with my love for sloppy, saucy Midwestern sandwiches. Callaloo comes from the leaves of the taro plant, which is virtually impossible to find where I live now, but spinach makes a great stand-in. This sloppy joe, made with seitan, is stick-to-your-ribs spicy and tangy, and the spinach is cooling and creamy with coconut and the ethereal sweet licorice flavor of star anise, which is a component in lots of Jamaican curry powders.

Of course, you can enjoy the sloppy joes on their own sans spinach (but don't you love your veggies?) or enjoy the spinach alongside any other jerk sorta' recipe. And if you don't feel like having sandwiches, this would be pretty awesome over rice, too.

PREPARE THE SLOPPY JOE FILLING:

Preheat a large, heavy-bottomed pan over medium-high heat and add 1 tablespoon of the oil. Sauté the onion in the oil with a pinch of salt until translucent, 3 to 5 minutes.

Add the seitan and cook for about 5 minutes, until nicely browned, stirring often. Push the seitan and onions to one side of the pan so that you have space to quickly sauté the garlic and ginger. Put the remaining 1 teaspoon coconut oil in the pan and toss in the garlic and ginger to cook, stirring as they sizzle, for about 15 seconds. Then mix it all up with the seitan and onions.

Add the thyme, paprika, remaining ½ teaspoon salt, allspice, red pepper flakes, cinnamon, and black pepper and toss to coat everything and toast the spices a bit.

Add the tomatoes and cook for about 10 more minutes, tossing often. Last, mix in the maple syrup, lime juice, and mustard. Let cook for a minute or so, then taste for seasonings. Keep warm until ready to serve.

PREPARE THE SPINACH:

Preheat a large, heavy-bottomed pan over medium heat. Quickly sauté the garlic in the coconut oil, just so it sizzles for a few seconds, being careful not to let it burn. Add the spinach in batches, tossing with tongs, until it is all wilted and fits in the pan. Cook for about 3 minutes, until a lot of moisture is released.

Now we're going to get rid of the excess moisture, but we'll try not to lose any garlic or spinach in the process. Shove the spinach off to one side, and carefully (don't burn yourself!) lift the pan and drain the excess water into the sink. The spinach might all just behave itself and stay on one side of the pan, but use the tongs to keep it from falling into the sink just in case.

Return to the heat and add the coconut milk, star anise, and salt. Bring the coconut milk to a boil and stir often, cooking for about 5 minutes so that the star anise releases its flavor. Turn off the heat and let it rest for about 10 minutes, so that it can be soaking up the coconut milk yumminess. Discard the star anise before serving.

Spoon the sloppy joe mixture over each bun and top with the spinach. Close bun, get sloppy, and enjoy!

NOTES:

- Spinach is one of those greens that tends to collect a lot of dirt. For that reason alone, a prewashed bag of spinach is ideal for a weeknight meal. If you don't have access to bags of spinach, then the best way to wash it is to remove rough stems and place the spinach in a very large bowl of very cold water for a few minutes. The dirt should sink to the bottom. Remove from the water (don't spill it into a colander or the dirt will just collect on the spinach again) and place in a colander for another quick rinse. Your spinach is now ready to use!

- To time everything right, start the spinach in a separate pan when you add the tomatoes to the seitan pan.

- Gluten-free option: You may substitute 2 cups cooked lentils for the seitan, or 1 (14-ounce) package extra-firm tofu, crumbled into bite-size pieces.

RED-HOT BLTs

makes 4 sandwiches · total time: 20 mins (plus time for marinating the tempeh) · active time: 20 mins

For the marinated tempeh:

½ cup Louisiana-style hot sauce (like Frank's RedHot)

¼ cup water

1 tablespoon tamari or soy sauce

2 teaspoons liquid smoke

8 ounces tempeh, cut into ¼-inch slices (see Notes)

For serving:

8 slices sourdough bread

Vegan mayo

8 slices beefsteak tomato

1 romaine lettuce heart, sliced into large pieces

NOTES:

- I usually purchase the rectangular tempeh and I slice it widthwise. I'd say the slices end up being 3 inches long and ¾ inch wide. If you have a different-size block of tempeh, just do your best to make them into ¼-inch-thick strips that will fit into a sandwich.

- Big, juicy beefsteak tomatoes are perfect here, but this is also a wonderful place to use gorgeous heirloom varieties with brilliant Technicolor stripes, or any tomato that is just too joyfully plump to cook with. In any case, save the plum tomatoes for sauce, and pick something you can really sink your teeth into for this sandwich.

- For extra oomph, try mixing some of the remaining marinade with ¼ cup of mayo and using that as the spread instead of plain ol' mayo.

When I moved to Omaha, I got my boyfriend hooked on Frank's RedHot sauce, so I have only myself to blame. But I start to feel a little worried about him when he puts it on everything (uh, cookies?). This sandwich is an attempt to quell his appetite for gallons and gallons of Frank's in a civilized manner. The "bacon" is made from tempeh that's been soaked in Frank's and a little liquid smoke. It's the perfect afternoon pick-me-up! Despite the copious amount of hot sauce used, it doesn't end up being too hot, especially with the cooling mayo and lettuce. I love it made with sourdough, but multigrain bread is fine too. I use only the romaine lettuce heart, because you really want those inner leaves for maximum crunch.

PREPARE THE TEMPEH:

In a large bowl or a plastic bag, mix together the hot sauce, water, tamari, and liquid smoke. Marinate the tempeh slices in the mixture for at least 1 hour and up to overnight. Flip once or twice to make sure all the slices are coated.

Preheat a large nonstick pan over medium heat. Coat the bottom of the pan with oil and add the tempeh strips in a single layer, shaking off any excess marinade.

Cook for about 7 minutes, flipping a few times to get each side cooked. In the last minute, add splashes of marinade to coat the slices in extra flavor.

While the tempeh is cooking, get ready to assemble your sandwiches. Spread all of the bread slices with mayo (I like more on the top slice, but a little on the bottom, too). To assemble, lay strips of tempeh onto the bottom slice of bread. Top with tomato slices and romaine. Close sandwich (duh) and eat!

CHICKY TUNA SALAD SANDWICHES

makes 6 sandwiches · total time: 15 mins · active time: 15 mins

I said it in my first cookbook, *Vegan with a Vengeance,* and I'll say it again: It's still no secret that chickpeas taste a little like tuna fish! And they are both born in a can, right? This filling is invaluable to me. I make it weekly for sandwiches on the go, or for plopping on top of a salad. It's another one of my boyfriend's favorites, and he simply asks for it by saying, "Can you make chickpea?" (Yes, that sounds like something a five-year-old would say.)

Sometimes in the summertime, instead of bread, I roll it up into a raw chard leaf for a light and yummy way to get a little green in. Oh, but if you're eating on bread, toasted whole wheat is a must!

In recent years people have started using sunflower seeds instead of chickpeas to create a vegan tuna sandwich, and I decided to combine the two to see what happened. Result: I loved it, obviously! Chickpeas have a soft meatiness, and then the little pieces of sunflower seed provide some bite. Carrots and celery stud the salad with lots of fresh crunch. Since I make this so often, I use a large food processor to get it done in just about 5 minutes, but I'll also give instructions for making it with nothing but a knife, a cutting board, and the hands your mama gave you. *However,* if you have the food processor that your mama gave you, that's even better. And if you've got some seaweed ingredients lying about, now would be the time to use them! They add a tasty fishiness to the salad, but if you don't have anything like that, no problem. I don't use them every time; it just depends on whether I'm in a really fishy mood.

1 large carrot, peeled

1 rib celery, leaves removed

¼ medium white onion

1 (15-ounce) can chickpeas, rinsed and drained (1½ cups)

½ cup sunflower seeds

⅓ cup vegan mayo, plus more for serving

1 teaspoon apple cider vinegar or fresh lemon juice

1 tablespoon kelp or dulse flakes (optional)

¼ teaspoon salt

Freshly ground black pepper

12 slices whole-wheat bread, toasted

Lettuce, sliced tomato, and/or sprouts, for topping

FOOD PROCESSOR DIRECTIONS:

Cut the carrot and celery into a few large chunks (5 or so). Add them to the food processor, along with the onion. Pulse until everything is chopped, but be careful not to purée. The veggies should range from pea-size to chickpea-size, more or less. Transfer to a large bowl, scraping the work bowl with a rubber spatula to get as much out as you can, but it doesn't have to get totally clean.

Pulse the chickpeas and sunflower seeds in the food processor to mash them. They should remain somewhat chunky, with bits of whole chickpea left, not puréed like hummus. Transfer to the bowl and combine with the veggies.

Add the mayo, vinegar, seaweed flakes (if desired), salt, and pepper, and mix well.

(recipe continues)

NOTE:

If you'd like to make this even more quickly, use a handful of baby carrots instead of whole carrots.

VARIATIONS:

- **Curried Chicky Sandwiches:** Start with about 1 tablespoon of curry powder and taste from there. I also like to add something sweet to the curry sandwich, so try a handful of raisins or ½ cup of halved seedless grapes.

- **Chicky Avocado Wrap:** Fold diced avocado into the chickpea mixture. Roll up in a wrap with lettuce, tomato, sprouts, and extra mayo.

DIRECTIONS FOR CHOPPING BY HAND:

Use a mini potato masher or a strong fork to mash the chickpeas in a large bowl. They should retain some of their texture and not appear puréed. Now prep the veggies. Finely chop the carrot, celery, and onion into just about pea-size pieces. Combine the veggies with the mashed chickpeas.

Spread the sunflower seeds out in a single layer on the cutting board. Use your chef's knife to chop them up a bit, but don't worry—some can be left whole. Just rock your knife back and forth over them for 30 seconds or so and whatever happens, happens. Add them to the bowl.

Add the mayo, vinegar, seaweed flakes (if desired), salt, and pepper, and mix well.

No matter which method you use, taste for seasoning, and serve in sandwiches with toppings!

BLACK-EYED PEA & COLLARD TACOS

with Apple-Avocado Salsa

makes 6 tacos · total time: 30 mins · active time: 30 mins

I guess you could call these soul tacos! Refried black-eyed peas laced with Louisiana hot sauce, stewed collards, and your new favorite flavor combo—a simple salsa of Granny Smith apples and avocado. This taco is fun and comforting, with lots of texture and hints of fall flavor. I love a big flour tortilla here.

PREPARE THE BLACK-EYED PEAS:

Preheat a 2-quart pot over medium heat and add the oil. Sauté the onion in the oil for 3 to 5 minutes, until translucent. Add the garlic, coriander, cumin, and salt. Sauté for another minute or so. Add splashes of water if it appears dry.

Add the black-eyed peas and mash with a fork or a mini potato masher (or avocado masher). You want a little texture, so don't mash it to a purée. Add the broth and hot sauce and mix well. Cook for 5 more minutes or so—the beans should be thick and velvety. Taste for salt and hot sauce. Keep covered until ready to use.

PREPARE THE COLLARDS:

Preheat a large pan over medium heat and add the oil. Sauté the garlic in the oil for only about 15 seconds. Have the other ingredients at the ready so that the garlic doesn't burn. Add the collards, broth, and salt, and toss to incorporate the garlic. Cover the pan and let cook for about 10 minutes, stirring occasionally.

Remove the lid and continue to cook until the collards are tender and most of the liquid has cooked away. It shouldn't take more than 5 minutes. Cover to keep warm until ready to serve.

PREPARE THE SALSA:

Simply mix all of the ingredients together in a bowl, drizzling the lemon juice on at the end. Keep covered and chilled until ready to serve.

TO ASSEMBLE:

Lightly toast the tortillas in a dry pan if desired, or microwave briefly (15 seconds or so) just to warm through. Layer the tortillas with the black-eyed peas, greens, and apple salsa. Sprinkle with the pumpkin seeds and serve.

For the black-eyed peas:
2 teaspoons olive oil
1 small yellow onion, finely chopped
2 cloves garlic, minced
1 teaspoon coriander seeds, crushed
1 teaspoon ground cumin
½ teaspoon salt
2 (15-ounce) cans black-eyed peas, rinsed and drained (3 cups)
1 cup vegetable broth
3 tablespoons Louisiana-style hot sauce (like Frank's RedHot)

For the collards:
1 teaspoon olive oil
2 cloves garlic, minced
1 pound collard greens, stems discarded, leaves coarsely chopped
1 cup vegetable broth
¼ teaspoon salt

For the Apple-Avocado Salsa:
1 Granny Smith apple, peeled and diced
1 avocado, pitted, peeled, and diced
½ cup chopped scallions
2 tablespoons fresh lemon juice

For serving:
6 (10-inch) flour tortillas
Shelled pumpkin seeds (optional)

NOTE:

Louisiana-style hot sauce has a particular flavor and a low to moderate heat level that I think is perfect for this recipe. If you want to play around with other hot sauces, you can, of course, but start slowly and work up. For instance, sriracha is much hotter than Frank's.

CUCUMBER-AVOCADO TEA SANDWICHES

with Dill & Mint

makes 6 sandwiches • total time: 20 mins • active time: 20 mins

For the Avocado Spread:

2 ripe avocados

2 tablespoons fresh lemon juice

½ teaspoon salt

½ cup chopped cucumber

2 tablespoons chopped fresh mint, plus extra for garnish

2 tablespoons chopped fresh dill, plus extra for garnish

For serving:

12 slices white bread (or 6 slices white and 6 slices whole wheat)

1 small cucumber, very thinly sliced

NOTE:

Avocado browns very quickly, so prepare the filling as close to serving time as you can. If you do need to let it sit around for a while, place in a container along with the pits from the avocados and squirt on a little extra lemon juice. Then place a layer of plastic wrap directly on the surface of the mixture. Keep refrigerated until ready to use. But even with this method, I don't recommend letting it sit around for more than a few hours.

I created these tea sandwiches on a particularly sweltering summer's eve, when I was having friends over but just didn't feel like cooking. My laziness paid off and made me appear incredibly fancy, because only fancy people serve tea sandwiches, I do declare.

These are essentially my take on tradition: cream cheese and cucumber tea sandwiches. Avocado breaks free from its guacamole shackles and instead is infused with lemon, fresh dill, and mint. The end result is a nod to the old foil-wrapped cream cheese brick, but a creamy, tangy, silky experience that is all its own. Use a slice of white and a slice of wheat bread in each sandwich for maximum impressiveness. Oh, and you can't have tea sandwiches without tea! I recommend Lady Grey. The hints of citrus are the perfect complement to the fresh herbs. Load up your prettiest vintage plates and you'll feel to the manor born.

PREPARE THE SPREAD:

Remove the pit from the avocados and scoop the green goodness into a food processor along with the lemon juice and salt. Purée until completely smooth, scraping down the sides with a rubber spatula as necessary. Add the cucumber and pulse until finely chopped. Add the mint and dill and pulse again just to combine. You just want the herbs well incorporated into the mix, but not puréed. Taste for seasonings.

Arrange the slices of bread on the counter (you may alternate so that half of the bottom slices are whole wheat and half are white). Spread the avocado mixture onto all 12 slices. Add a single layer of cucumber on 6 of the slices. Now close each sandwich. Use a sharp knife to cut off the crusts. With a gentle touch (so as not to squish the filling out too much), slice each sandwich into quarters, either squares or triangles. Serve garnished with extra herbs. (Or top with anything pretty and green, like shredded lettuce or pea shoots.) Serve immediately.

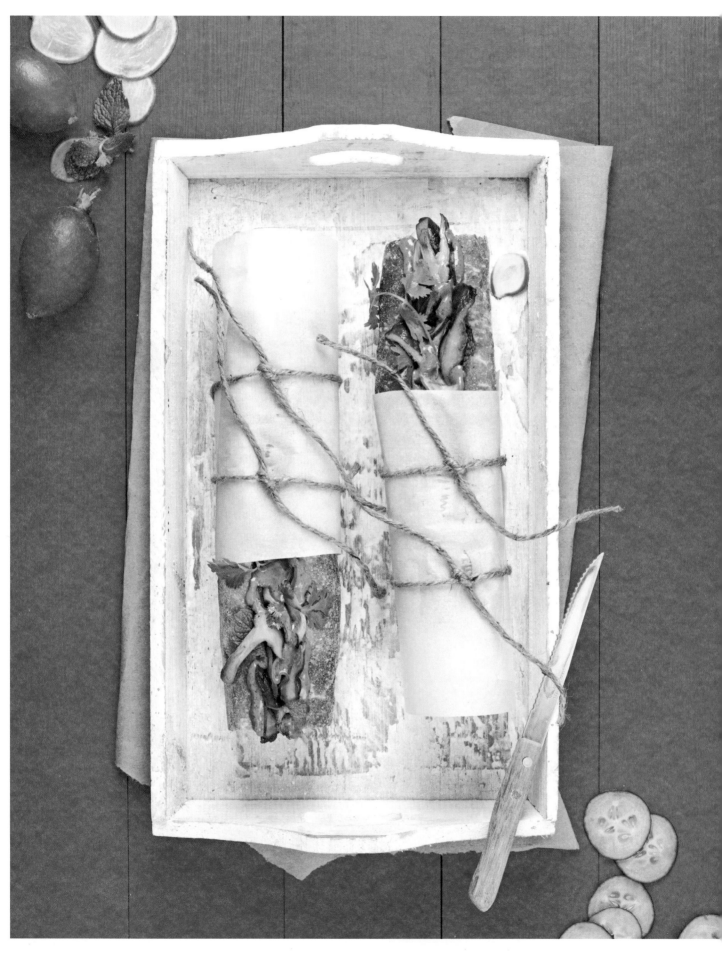

SHIITAKE BANH MI

makes 2 large sandwiches · total time: 20 mins · active time: 20 mins

I came to the *banh mi* late in life (as I imagine most Brooklyn Jews did), but when I fell for it, I fell hard. The general idea is crusty bread, charred meat (seitan and tofu most often in the vegan versions I've tried), super-spicy creamy spread, pickled veggies to help cool you down, and fresh cilantro and mint to make the whole thing. I decided to use shiitakes as my meat, first of all because I'd never seen anyone else do it but also because I wanted something relatively light but still entirely meaty. I love a hot-cold contrast in sandwiches, and this one doesn't disappoint.

The spread is made from almond butter, but don't worry; it doesn't taste anything like an almond butter sandwich. It is transformed with a few other ingredients into a spicy, creamy, almond-chili spread that causes the whole shebang to melt in your mouth. Instead of making pickles, I decided to just toss some cucumbers and red radishes with rice vinegar and agave and let them sit for as long as it took to prep everything else. It gets the job done quickly and pickley!

For the pickles:
½ cup thinly sliced red radishes
½ cup thinly sliced cucumbers
2 tablespoons rice vinegar
2 teaspoons agave nectar
Pinch of salt

For the shiitakes:
1 tablespoon peanut oil
8 ounces whole shiitake mushrooms, stems trimmed
2 cloves garlic, minced
1 tablespoon tamari or soy sauce

For the Almond-Chili Spread:
¼ cup almond butter, at room temperature
1 tablespoon rice vinegar
1 teaspoon agave nectar
1 tablespoon sriracha
¼ teaspoon salt

For serving:
2 (6- to 8-inch) baguettes, split in half
A large handful of fresh cilantro sprigs
½ cup fresh mint leaves

PREPARE THE PICKLES:

Toss all of the ingredients together in a bowl and let sit until ready to serve. Give the ingredients a stir every now and again when you remember.

PREPARE THE SHIITAKES:

Preheat a large cast-iron pan (or any heavy-bottomed pan) over medium-high heat. Drizzle in the oil, then add the shiitakes. Cover and let the shiitakes cook for about 5 minutes, stirring occasionally. They should soften up a bit and release moisture. Uncover and cook for 3 more minutes or so, until they are slightly browned in spots. Add the garlic and sauté for 1 more minute. Last, add the tamari and stir until it's well incorporated. Remove the mushrooms from the pan as soon as they're done to prevent overcooking.

PREPARE THE ALMOND-CHILI SPREAD:

Combine all of the ingredients in a small blender or food processor and purée until completely smooth. I've attempted to do this with just a fork and a small bowl, but it doesn't get as creamy as I like, and so I strongly suggest using a machine. Add a little bit of warm water if it doesn't seem to be getting creamy enough.

TO ASSEMBLE:

Spread the insides of the baguettes with the almond-chili spread. Layer on the mushrooms, followed by the pickles, and finally the cilantro and mint. Close the sandwiches and chow down.

NOTES:

- For the almond butter, any smooth, unsweetened variety will do, salted or not. But if it's not salted you'll need to add a bit of extra salt. Also, since the amount of oil varies from brand to brand, you may need to add a little water to get the almond-chili spread to be a smooth, creamy consistency.

- To get this done in 20 minutes, make the almond-chili spread while the shiitakes are cooking.

ROASTED VEGETABLE
ROMESCO SANDWICHES

makes 4 sandwiches · total time: 45 mins · active time: 25 mins

For the roasted vegetables:

1 small head cauliflower, trimmed and sliced into ½-inch slices (see Notes)

2 medium zucchini (about 12 ounces), sliced on a long bias ½ inch thick

2 tablespoons olive oil, plus more as needed

½ teaspoon salt

Freshly ground black pepper

For the Romesco Spread:

¾ cup sliced almonds

2 cloves garlic, minced

2 roasted red peppers (see Notes), chopped

1 tablespoon olive oil

1 tablespoon red wine vinegar

2 teaspoons sweet paprika

¼ teaspoon salt

For serving:

4 sturdy white buns (like focaccia or ciabatta)

2 roasted red peppers (see Notes)

Handful of fresh basil leaves

NOTES:

• The cauliflower in this recipe is sliced to sandwich size. Just place the cauliflower on the cutting board, stem side down, and use your chef's knife to get ¾-inch-thick slices. Now, you'll probably get a few smaller pieces that fall away, and that is totally fine! Roast those up as well, and if they don't make their way into the sandwich, you'll have a nice little snack.

• You can roast the red peppers (see page 118) for the sauce, but they need a lot of time to cool before you can peel the skins off, so for simplicity's sake, I suggest using jarred roasted reds here.

Sometimes, when the weather is gray but it's not raining and not too cold, I love to pull on a hoodie and sit outside at my brick red picnic table to eat a warm meal. There's something so soothing about the birds chirping away, the traffic whizzing by, and the stillness of the slate sky. And nothing hits the spot like this roasted veggie sandwich. As a bonus, your place will still smell amazing when you step in from the cool air. If you don't have a picnic table, sit on your fire escape, or just, I don't know, stick your head out the window.

PREPARE THE VEGETABLES:

Preheat the oven to 425°F and line a large rimmed baking sheet with parchment paper. Brush or spray the parchment with oil.

Place the cauliflower and zucchini on the sheet, drizzle with the oil, and sprinkle with salt and black pepper. Toss to coat, and arrange in a single layer.

Roast the veggies for about 20 minutes. Remove from the oven and flip the cauliflower and zucchini. Spray or brush with a little extra oil if they appear dry. Continue to roast for 10 to 15 more minutes, until the veggies are nicely brown and soft.

PREPARE THE SPREAD:

First, toast the almonds. You can skip this step if you're feeling lazy, but it does add a lot of flavor! Preheat a large, heavy-bottomed pan over medium-low heat. Spread the almonds out in a single layer and toss frequently until fragrant and honey brown, 5 to 7 minutes.

Transfer the almonds to a blender or food processor and pulse into fine crumbs. Add the garlic and pulse to chop. Add the roasted red peppers, olive oil, vinegar, paprika, and salt, and purée until relatively smooth, scraping down the sides every now and again to make sure you get everything. Depending on the machine you're using, you may be able to purée without adding any water, but if it doesn't seem to be blending, add water by the tablespoon until it decides to cooperate. Taste for seasoning. Keep tightly sealed and refrigerated until ready to use.

Spread the inside of the buns with a thick amount of spread. Add layers of zucchini, roasted red pepper, and cauliflower, and top with the basil. Close the sandwich (obviously), go outside, and enjoy!

EDAMAME HUMMUS & TOFU WRAPS

makes 4 wraps · total time: 20 mins · active time: 20 mins

This isn't your average hummus wrap! Not that there is anything *wrong* with your average hummus wrap, but this one is turned up a notch. It's spicy and green, made with edamame and a bit of wasabi powder. The tofu here is really simple and delicious, too. Sautéed in sesame oil until golden, it makes for a wonderful Japanese-inspired wrap with big flavors and not too many ingredients. I love to use a long and strong sprout in these. Try to find big broccoli sprouts, or even pea shoots.

Since wasabi powder can vary in strength from brand to brand, maybe start with a teaspoon and go from there. I use just enough so that I can feel it in my nose! Also, since the amount of moisture in tahini varies, as well as the amount of moisture in edamame and the strength of your blender versus my blender, you may need to add up to ½ cup extra water.

For the tofu:
1 tablespoon toasted sesame oil

14 ounces extra-firm tofu, cut into ¾-inch cubes

¼ teaspoon salt

For the Edamame Hummus:
2 cloves garlic

1 ½ cups shelled frozen edamame, thawed completely

⅓ cup water, plus more as needed

¼ cup fresh lemon juice

¼ cup tahini

¼ cup olive oil

1 ½ teaspoons wasabi powder (see headnote)

½ teaspoon salt

For serving:
4 (8-inch) whole-wheat wraps

2 cups hearty sprouts, like broccoli or sunflower sprouts

PREPARE THE TOFU:
You'll need a cast-iron pan, or something nonstick that can take very high heat. Preheat the pan over high heat. Once the pan is good and hot, add the sesame oil. Add the cubed tofu and sprinkle with salt. The tofu should immediately sizzle when it hits the hot oil; otherwise, turn the heat up. Cook for about 10 minutes, tossing often, until it's nicely browned. While the tofu is browning, start the hummus.

PREPARE THE HUMMUS:
Pulse the garlic in a blender or food processor to chop it up a bit. Add the remaining hummus ingredients and purée until smooth, adding a little extra water as needed to thin. Taste for seasonings. Refrigerate in a tightly sealed container if not using immediately.

TO ASSEMBLE:
Spread a very thick layer of hummus in the center of each wrap. Add a handful of tofu cubes and a good bunch of sprouts. Wrap them up, slice in half, and go for it!

ANCHO-LENTIL TACOS

serves 6 · total time: 20 mins · active time: 20 mins

For the Ancho Spice Mix:

2 teaspoons ground ancho chile

1 teaspoon ground cumin

½ teaspoon ground coriander

½ teaspoon dried oregano

½ teaspoon salt

For the lentils:

2 teaspoons olive oil

1 small yellow onion, minced

2 cloves garlic, minced

Pinch of salt

2 ½ cups cooked brown lentils

3 tablespoons tomato paste

2 tablespoons hot sauce (preferably Cholula)

For serving:

6 corn tortillas

Shredded lettuce

Salsa

Sliced avocado or guacamole

Lentils are my all-time favorite vegan ground meat. Sautéing the lentils and lightly mashing them gives them a traditional taco-filling texture that is good, hearty, sloppy fun. Ancho chiles are dried poblanos, and I love to use them straight up (as opposed to in a mixed chili powder) for their deep, fruity, naturally smoky flavor. But you can use regular old blended chili powder here if you don't have ancho chile; just promise me to pick up ground ancho chile powder sometime and see if you don't love it.

The filling is not too spicy, but it does have a little kick from the hot sauce (Cholula is my choice for Mexican-inspired foods). A few squirts of tomato paste provide moisture and binding and really help to lend a convincingly meaty texture. The idea here is to mash the lentils until they hold together, adding splashes of water along the way to keep the mixture juicy.

I like to serve this taco with cooling ingredients: cilantro for bright freshness, lime for tanginess, avocado (or guacamole) for creaminess, and, of course, some fresh salsa. If you'd like, try the *queso* from the Nacho Night (page 232) squirted on top.

PREPARE THE SPICE MIX:

First, combine all of the ingredients for the spice mix.

PREPARE THE LENTILS:

Preheat a large skillet over medium-high heat and add the oil. Keep a cup of water within reach; you'll need to add splashes as you cook. Sauté the onion and garlic in the oil with a pinch of salt for about 3 minutes, until lightly browned. Add the spice mix and toss for 30 seconds or so to toast.

Lower the heat to medium, and add the lentils, a few splashes of water, the tomato paste, and hot sauce; use a spatula to mash the lentils a bit as they cook, until they hold together. If your spatula isn't working to accomplish this, just use a fork. Do this for about 5 minutes, adding splashes of water as necessary if it appears dry. Taste for seasoning; you may want to add more spices or hot sauce. And that's it!

TO ASSEMBLE:

Lightly toast the tortillas in a dry pan if desired, or microwave briefly (15 seconds or so) just to warm through. Stuff with filling and fixings and serve!

CHIPOTLE-OYSTER MUSHROOM TACOS

makes 6 tacos • total time: 30 mins • active time: 30 mins

With their chewy and meaty texture, oyster mushrooms make a fabulous taco ingredient. These are spicy and smoky and here they are rounded out with pinto beans for a complete meal. The slaw is really easy to pull together and is a welcome fresh and crunchy cooling element to counterbalance the spicy filling. And of course you can't forget the avocado! Throw together the slaw while the mushrooms are cooking and it's taco time in no time.

PREPARE THE FILLING:

Preheat a large pan over medium heat and add the oil. Sauté the onion in the oil with a pinch of salt for about 3 minutes, just until slightly softened. Add the garlic and sauté for 30 more seconds.

Add the mushrooms and sprinkle with the remaining ¼ teaspoon salt. Sauté until lightly browned and releasing moisture, about 5 minutes. Add the tomatoes, chipotles, cilantro, and cumin and turn the heat up, cooking for 5 more minutes. The tomatoes should break down a bit and everything should appear juicy.

Lower the heat, add the pinto beans and lime juice, and heat through for about 2 minutes. Taste for salt and keep warm until ready to serve.

PREPARE THE SLAW:

Simply toss all of the ingredients together in a small bowl, making sure to coat the cabbage.

TO ASSEMBLE:

Lightly toast the tortillas in a dry pan if desired, or microwave briefly (15 seconds or so) just to warm through. Stuff with filling and fixings and serve!

For the filling:

1 tablespoon olive oil

1 medium red onion, thinly sliced

¼ teaspoon salt, plus a pinch

3 cloves garlic, minced

10 ounces oyster mushrooms, cut into 1- to 2-inch pieces (see Notes)

1 medium tomato, chopped

3 tablespoons chipotles in adobo sauce, seeded

¼ cup chopped fresh cilantro

1 teaspoon ground cumin

1 (15-ounce) can pinto beans, rinsed and drained (1½ cups)

2 tablespoons fresh lime juice

For the slaw:

6 ounces cabbage, shredded (about 3 cups)

1 tablespoon olive oil

2 tablespoons fresh lime juice

⅛ teaspoon salt

For serving:

6 (8-inch) soft tortillas of your choice

Diced avocado

NOTES:

• Oyster mushrooms can be hard to find year-round, so sub shiitakes if necessary. Just note that they'll cook a bit faster. Oysters often come bunched up and I don't like to slice them too small, so I just try to separate them at the stem. If any are very large, I slice into 1-inch pieces. But try to keep the mushrooms as intact as possible to retain their flavor and texture.

• For the slaw, you can use red or green cabbage, or even a bag of cabbage slaw mix.

PASTA & RISOTTO

PASTA is easily the most EFFICIENT

way to get a healthy, hearty, and delicious meal on the table in a matter of minutes. It's all too common to fall into a pasta rut, though. This chapter offers a nod to the classics, as well as a few fresh ideas to help liven up your pasta pot. With pasta, I always make the most of sauces. Obviously everyone loves a classic tomato sauce, and I've got you covered there, but there are so many different sauce methods to learn. Garlic and wine, lentils, cashew cream, pesto—having pasta a few nights a week really doesn't have to be repetitive or involve lots of empty carbohydrates. Fill your bowls with plenty of veggies and yummy whole foods like nuts and beans. Try some tempeh and tofu prepared in simple but tasty ways. Take advantage of all of the new pastas out in the market these days; whole wheat, brown rice noodles, and quinoa pasta are just a few of my favorites. A classic semolina pasta is great too, but it's nice to have variety, isn't it? My number-one time-management tip for pasta is this: Before you do anything, and I mean the instant you walk through the door, put on a big pot of salted water. That way the water is waiting for you, not the other way around.

SUNFLOWER MAC

serves 4 · total time: 30 mins (plus time for soaking the
sunflower seeds) · active time: 20 mins

1 cup unroasted sunflower seed
  kernels, soaked for at least 2 hours
8 ounces elbow macaroni or other
  small pasta
1 tablespoon olive oil
½ cup thinly sliced carrots
1 small yellow onion, diced
½ teaspoon salt, plus a pinch
3 cloves garlic, minced
3 cups vegetable broth
2 tablespoons organic cornstarch
¼ cup nutritional yeast flakes
2 tablespoons tomato paste
1 tablespoon fresh lemon juice
Sweet paprika, for garnish

The most important people in my life are my recipe testers. One of
my most favoritest testers, who has been there with me from the
very beginning, is Jess Sconed. This recipe, created in her honor, is
totally fitting because she's a lot like a sunflower. One with dyed-
black pigtails and purple nail polish, but a sunflower all the same!

I know how she feels about raw onions and cilantro (not too
good), and so I often come up with recipes keeping that in mind.
She also has a tree-nut allergy, so my cashew lust does not
fare well. Knowing how much Jess loves vegan macs, I created
this recipe for a cheezy sauce that I knew she would love, using
ingredients that would be good for her, too. And so I pulled out the
sunflower seeds.

Sunflower seeds have a mellow, nutty quality that fits right
into a cheezy sauce. The backdrop of garlic and onion, with a hint
of vegetable sweetness from carrots and the rich toastiness from
the sunflowers, had me at the first creamy forkful.

This recipe makes more sauce than you'll need for the pasta,
so if you're like me and serve tons of steamed kale over your mac,
then don't worry: There is plenty of sauce to go around!

Place the sunflower seeds in a bowl and submerge in water. Let soak for about
2 hours or up to overnight. Drain well.

Bring a large pot of salted water to a boil for your pasta. Once boiling, cook the
pasta according to the package directions. Drain, return to the pot, and set aside.

Meanwhile, preheat a saucepan over medium heat and add the oil. Sauté the
carrots and onions in the oil with a pinch of salt for about 10 minutes, until
the onions are translucent and the carrots are slightly softened. Add the garlic
and sauté for 30 seconds or so, then remove from the heat.

Place the mixture in a blender or food processor. Add the broth, cornstarch,
nutritional yeast, tomato paste, remaining ½ teaspoon salt, and sunflower
seeds. Blend until very smooth. This could take up to 5 minutes depending on
the power of your machine, so give your blender motor a break every minute
or so and test the sauce for smoothness. It should be very smooth, with only a
slight graininess.

Transfer the sauce back to the saucepan. Turn the heat to medium and let
cook, stirring very often, until thickened. This should take about 15 minutes.
Add the lemon juice and taste for seasoning.

Pour most of the sauce over the pasta, reserving some to pour over individual
servings. Mix it up, and serve with extra sauce and a sprinkling of paprika.

ROASTED RED PEPPER
MAC & CHEESE

serves 4 • total time: 30 mins (plus time for soaking the cashews) • active time: 20 mins

---

2 teaspoons olive oil

1 small yellow onion, diced

½ teaspoon salt, plus a pinch

2 cloves garlic, minced

8 ounces elbow macaroni or other small pasta

¾ cup cashews, soaked for at least 2 hours (see "ABS: Always Be Soaking," page xx)

2 cups vegetable broth

1½ tablespoons organic cornstarch

1 tablespoon nutritional yeast flakes (optional)

1 roasted red pepper (store-bought or homemade; see page xx)

1 tablespoon tomato paste

1½ teaspoons pizza seasoning (see Notes)

1 teaspoon dry mustard

½ teaspoon ground turmeric

NOTES:

- If you don't have any pizza seasoning around, simply use these spices: ¼ teaspoon fennel seeds or ground fennel, ¼ teaspoon dried oregano, ½ teaspoon dried thyme, and ½ teaspoon granulated garlic.

- I always have a jar of roasted red peppers on hand, but making your own doesn't take much time or effort. If you've got the oven on to cook something else, anywhere between 350° and 425°F, simply sneak in a pepper or three on a small baking pan. Roast whole for 20 to 30 minutes, or until the pepper appears collapsed, then transfer to a paper bag immediately and close the bag up securely. This will steam it, so that when cool the skin comes off easily. Once you get the skin off, open the pepper up (if it hasn't already broken open) and discard the seeds. Voilà!

This is a beautiful, bright orange mac, flavored with pepperoni-type pizza seasonings—fennel, thyme, and oregano. There's plenty of sauce, so load it up with your favorite veggies.

You can make this a baked mac, if you prefer. Transfer the whole shebang to an 8-inch square casserole dish and bake at 350°F for 20 minutes.

Preheat a 2-quart sauce pot over medium heat and add the oil. Sauté the onions in the oil with a pinch of salt for 5 to 7 minutes, until the onions are translucent. Add the garlic and sauté for 30 seconds or so, and then transfer to a blender or food processor.

Bring a large pot of salted water to a boil for cooking the pasta. Once boiling, cook the pasta according to the package directions. Drain, return to the pot, and set aside.

Drain the cashews and add them to the blender along with the broth, cornstarch, nutritional yeast (if using), red pepper, tomato paste, pizza seasoning, remaining ½ teaspoon salt, dry mustard, and turmeric. Blend until very smooth. This could take anywhere from 1 to 5 minutes depending on the strength of your blender. Scrape down the sides every 30 seconds or so and test for smoothness.

Transfer the sauce in the blender back to the sauce pot in which you cooked the onions. Turn the heat to medium and let cook, stirring very often, until thickened. This should take 10 to 15 minutes. Taste for salt.

Add the sauce to the pasta in the pot and use a large slotted spoon to mix well, taking care not to break the pasta. Serve.

TEMPEH MEATBALLS & SPAGHETTI

serves 4 · total time: 1 hour · active time: 30 mins

If ever there was a dish that screams "family," this is it. Whether it be the family that you were born into, or your six roommates in a Brooklyn loft with no heat, spaghetti and meatballs is what brings everyone together. So many of my best memories revolve around a big juicy meatball and lots of slurpy, garlicky marinara. I picture my grandma's dinner table with a big platter of her meatballs right in the center of it. There were always a few burned ones that everyone tried to grab first. I also picture my best friend's mom, a beautiful Italian woman with jet black hair and catlike blue eyes, feeding me almost every night of the week. And later, when I went vegetarian, I remember cooking tofu balls and spaghetti with my mom and sis. Even decades later, when I lived in the aforementioned heatless loft, every Sunday night we'd watch *The Sopranos* and eat spaghetti and meatballs made from some store-bought soy sausage stuff.

Well, this recipe is none of those exactly, but it draws on all of my spaghetti-and-meatballs memories. I love the texture of tempeh in meatballs. It's succulent and satisfying. A few condiments and pantry spices give me the childhood flavors that I crave. Definitely double this recipe for family occasions, and don't forget to burn a few—those are always the best loved.

For the meatballs:

1 pound tempeh
1 cup water
1 tablespoon tamari or soy sauce
1 tablespoon olive oil
2 cloves garlic, minced
3 tablespoons ketchup
1 tablespoon Dijon mustard
½ teaspoon dried oregano
½ teaspoon dried thyme
½ teaspoon salt
Several pinches of freshly ground black pepper
½ cup very finely chopped yellow onion
1 cup panko bread crumbs
Olive oil, for panfrying

For everything else:

8 ounces spaghetti
4 cups marinara sauce (store-bought or homemade; page 121)
Crushed red pepper flakes
Freshly ground black pepper

Bring a pot of salted water to a boil for the spaghetti.

PREPARE THE MEATBALLS:

Meanwhile, crumble the tempeh into small pieces in a 2-quart pot. Add the water, tamari, and olive oil. Cover and bring to a boil. Once boiling, lower the heat and simmer, with the lid slightly ajar so that steam can escape, for 15 minutes. Most of the water should be absorbed. If there is excess water left, drain it; place the tempeh in a bowl and place in the freezer to cool. It should take 10 minutes or so. Give it a stir after 5 minutes to help it cool evenly.

Once the tempeh is cool, add the garlic, ketchup, mustard, oregano, thyme, salt, and pepper. Mix well. Mix in the onion. Now add the panko bread crumbs and use your hands to mix until it holds together very well. If it seems loose, add extra bread crumbs by the tablespoon until you can form very tight, compact balls. Scoop up roughly golf ball–size amounts and roll between your hands to form the balls.

(recipe continues)

MAKE AHEAD:

I admit this recipe might be ambitious for a weeknight, especially if you're already very hungry. Boiling and cooling the tempeh before proceeding takes time. You can do that step an evening in advance if you like, and then all you have to do the following day is put together the mixture and panfry.

NOTE:

The onion has to be very finely chopped here, to ensure that the meatballs don't fall apart. Aim for pea-size pieces.

Preheat a large nonstick pan (preferably cast iron) over medium heat. Coat the pan with a thin layer of olive oil. Add the meatballs one by one, rolling them in the pan to coat in oil. If your pan is not big enough to fit all of the balls comfortably, then do them in two batches. Panfry for about 10 minutes, rolling them frequently to cook evenly.

PREPARE THE SPAGHETTI:

Cook the spaghetti in the boiling water. Drain and toss with the marinara in the pot you boiled it in. Serve the spaghetti in big bowls, with 3 or 4 meatballs each. Top with red pepper flakes and black pepper and slurp it up!

Spicy Slurpy Spaghetti Sauce

makes 4 cups · total time: 30 mins · active time: 5 mins

This sauce is made slightly sweet thanks to a caramelized onion base. It beats the jarred stuff by a long shot! If you're not feeling the spicy, you can reduce the amount of red pepper flakes or omit them altogether.

1 tablespoon olive oil

1 small yellow onion, finely chopped

3 cloves garlic, minced

1 tablespoon light brown sugar

1 teaspoon dried thyme

1 teaspoon dried oregano

1 teaspoon crushed red pepper flakes

Freshly ground black pepper

1 (24-ounce) can crushed tomatoes with basil

1 teaspoon salt

Preheat a 2-quart pot over medium-low heat and add the oil. Sauté the onion in the oil for about 5 minutes, until slightly browned. Add the garlic and sauté until fragrant, about 30 seconds. Add the brown sugar and cook for about 1 minute, until the sugar is dissolved and coats all the onions. Mix in the thyme, oregano, red pepper flakes, and black pepper. Add the tomatoes and salt and stir everything together. Cover the pot, leaving a little gap for steam to escape, and cook for 15 minutes. Taste for seasoning and serve.

GARDENY SHIITAKE & CHARD FUSILLI

serves 4 • total time: 30 mins • active time: 30 mins

8 ounces fusilli

1 tablespoon olive oil

5 cloves garlic, minced

8 ounces shiitake mushrooms, thinly sliced

1 teaspoon salt, plus a pinch

1 cup chopped fresh tomatoes

Several pinches of freshly ground black pepper

8 ounces Swiss chard, stems thinly sliced, leaves torn into bite-size pieces

¼ cup chopped fresh basil leaves

2 tablespoons fresh cilantro

2 tablespoons lemon juice

2 tablespoons nutritional yeast flakes

I've always felt that chard and shiitakes are a natural match, and I hope that the rest of the world catches on. I love the, for lack of a better word, "gardeniness" of this combo. It automatically makes me think of digging in the rich soil on a perfect day. Which isn't too far off base, since every summer I have an army of chard constantly waving at me from the garden like a bunch of cheerleaders with green and red pom-pom leaves.

Anyway, this recipe demonstrates a very basic type of dish that I love to prepare with pasta. Something green and succulent that melds with the sauce that comes simply from fresh tomatoes. Oh, and garlic. Lots and lots of it! Throw in some fresh herbs and you've got a pasta garden party. If you don't love cilantro, then dill would be a good replacement.

If you'd like to bulk it up, Garlicky Thyme Tempeh (page 236) goes just perfectly, or you can toss in 1½ cups white beans at the end of the cooking time.

Bring a pot of salted water to a boil for the pasta and cook according to the package directions and drain. Keep warm until ready to serve.

Preheat a large pan over medium heat and add the oil. Sauté the garlic in the oil just until fragrant, about 30 seconds. Add the mushrooms with a pinch of salt and sauté until softened, about 3 minutes.

Add the tomatoes, the remaining 1 teaspoon salt, and pepper, cover the pan, and turn the heat up to get the tomatoes to break down faster, cooking them for about 3 minutes. Add the Swiss chard stems and leaves and cook, uncovered, until the stems are softened and the leaves are wilted, about 5 minutes.

Add the basil, cilantro, lemon juice, and nutritional yeast and mix.

Add the pasta to the pan, turn off the heat, and toss to coat. Serve!

ROASTED
BUTTERNUT ALFREDO

serves 4 · total time: 1 hour (plus time for soaking the cashews; · 30 mins if using canned squash) · active time: 20 mins

In mid-November, when you've already done just about everything you think you can do with butternut squash, this recipe provides a welcome break. The squash is roasted first and then puréed with cashew cream to make a thick, autumnal sauce that is lush, creamy, and, most important, savory. White wine, some sautéed onions and garlic . . . oh yes, keep it coming! For extra squash yumminess, reserve some extra roasted squash to scoop on top of the pasta before serving.

Bring a pot of salted water to a boil for the pasta. Cook the pasta according to the package directions and drain. Set aside, keeping warm until ready to serve.

PREPARE THE SAUCE:
Drain the cashews and place them in a blender with the broth. Blend until very smooth; this could take anywhere from 1 to 5 minutes depending on the strength of your blender. Rub a bit of the sauce between your fingers to test, and when hardly any grittiness remains, add the roasted butternut, miso, nutritional yeast (if using), and lemon juice. Purée until smooth, scraping down the sides with a rubber spatula to make sure you get everything.

PREPARE EVERYTHING ELSE:
While the sauce is blending, start the onions. Preheat a large cast-iron pan over medium heat and add the oil. Sauté the onion in the oil with a pinch of salt for about 7 minutes, until lightly browned. Add the garlic and sauté for 30 seconds or so, just until fragrant. Mix in the sage and pepper. Then add the wine and remaining ½ teaspoon salt and turn the heat up to bring the wine to a boil. Let boil for about 2 minutes to reduce a little.

Turn the heat down to medium-low. Add the butternut cream to the pan and stir to incorporate the onions and everything. Heat through, stirring occasionally, for about 5 minutes. The sauce should thicken a bit. Taste for seasonings.

Set aside about half of the sauce for later use (you can reserve a cup or so for veggies if you'd like to throw some on top). Add the pasta to the pan, and toss to coat. Serve topped with additional roasted squash and a sprinkle of nuts.

8 ounces gemelli pasta (really, any pasta works here)

For the sauce:
½ cup cashews, soaked for at least 2 hours (see "ABS: Always Be Soaking," page 14)

1½ cups vegetable broth

1½ cups mashed roasted butternut squash from 1 squash (see page 50) or from 1 (15-ounce) can puréed squash

2 tablespoons mellow white miso

2 tablespoons nutritional yeast flakes (optional)

1 tablespoon fresh lemon juice

For everything else:
1 tablespoon olive oil

1 medium yellow onion, quartered and thinly sliced

½ teaspoon salt, plus a pinch

3 cloves garlic, minced

1 teaspoon dried rubbed sage

Several pinches of freshly ground black pepper

¾ cup dry white wine

For the garnish:
Extra mashed roasted squash

Pepitas or chopped pecans, walnuts, or hazelnuts

CREAMY SUN-DRIED TOMATO PENNE

with Broccoli

serves 4 · total time: 30 mins (plus time for soaking the cashews) ·
active time: 30 mins

8 ounces penne

For the Sun-Dried Tomato Cream:

¼ cup sun-dried tomatoes (not the oil-packed kind)

¾ cup cashews, soaked for at least 2 hours (see "ABS: Always Be Soaking," page 14)

1½ cups vegetable or mushroom broth

For everything else:

1 tablespoon olive oil

1 medium red onion, quartered and thinly sliced

½ teaspoon salt, plus a pinch

4 cloves garlic, minced

¼ cup sun-dried tomatoes (not the oil-packed kind), thinly sliced

½ cup vegetable broth

⅓ cup dry red wine

Several pinches of freshly ground black pepper

4 cups broccoli florets and julienned stems

½ cup loosely packed fresh basil (about 15 leaves)

NOTE:

This recipe calls for the dry kind of sun-dried tomatoes, not the kind packed in oil. It's a much more economical choice, and the dried kind keep forever. Plus, less oil is always nice! But make sure you're not digging overly dry sun-dried tomatoes out of a bulk bin. They shouldn't feel like wood chips (yuck); they should be dried but still pliable, with some moisture to them. If you can, try to find some in an airtight package.

This dish is so easy, but it still reminds me of a great restaurant dish. Maybe a great restaurant dish from the '90s, what with the sun-dried tomatoes, but hey, they're delish! And there's just something about sun-dried tomatoes and cream. The tanginess of the tomatoes is represented twice: once blended up in the cream, and then again in little strips, which give you surprise bursts of flavor throughout. It's really a good time and might give you an updated appreciation for the sun-dried tomato.

Bring a pot of salted water to a boil for the pasta. When it comes to a full boil, cook the pasta according to the package directions and drain. Set aside, keeping warm.

PREPARE THE TOMATO CREAM:

Pulse the sun-dried tomatoes in a blender just to get them chopped up. Then drain the cashews and add them to the blender, along with the broth. Blend until very smooth. This could take anywhere from 1 to 5 minutes depending on the strength of your machine. Scrape down the sides with a rubber spatula now and again to make sure you get everything. Set aside.

PREPARE EVERYTHING ELSE:

Preheat a 4-quart pot over medium heat and add the oil. Sauté the onion in the oil with a pinch of salt for about 3 minutes, until translucent. Add the minced garlic and sauté for 30 seconds or so.

Add the sun-dried tomatoes, broth, wine, remaining ½ teaspoon salt, and pepper, cover the pot, and turn the heat up to bring to a boil. As soon as it starts to boil, add the broccoli and cover the pot. Cook for about 5 minutes. No need to stir; you're just braising the broccoli so that it cooks through but is still bright and crisp.

Once the broccoli is cooked, pour in the cashew mixture and stir in the basil. Let thicken for about 3 minutes, stirring occasionally. You may want to thin the sauce a little bit depending on how much of it reduced, so you can add up to 1 cup of water depending on how thick you like it. Taste for seasoning. Add the penne and toss to coat, making sure that plenty of sauce fills the pasta tubes. Serve right away!

EGGPLANT &
BREAD CRUMB FETTUCCINE

serves 4 · total time: 30 mins · active time: 30 mins

Are you ever in the middle of cooking a fancy dinner when a case of the lazies strikes and you say "Fork it!" and throw everything into a big pan, come what may? That's how this pasta came into my regular rotation. I really wanted eggplant Parmesan, but really *did not want* a million dishes, along with the breading, the frying, the baking, and all of the special hell that comes along with eggplant Parmesan. I swear that this version gets you what you want without all the work. Toasty bread crumbs, creamy eggplant, and yummy spaghetti sauce. And it all happens in less than 30 minutes. It's not the fanciest dish in the world, but it is one of the tastiest.

2 tablespoons olive oil, plus extra for drizzling

1 pound eggplant, sliced into ¼-inch-thick half-moons

½ teaspoon salt

½ cup fine dry bread crumbs

½ teaspoon dried thyme

8 ounces fettuccine

1 batch Spicy Slurpy Spaghetti Sauce (page 121) or 4 cups store-bought spaghetti sauce, warmed

Preheat a large nonstick or cast-iron pan over medium heat. Add the olive oil to coat the bottom, then add the eggplant in a single layer (as best you can and still fit them all), and sprinkle with the salt. Cook, flipping the pieces occasionally until the eggplant is softened and lightly browned, about 15 minutes. As it's cooking, keep spraying with or drizzling a little oil in to make sure the eggplant stays moist.

Meanwhile, bring a large pot of salted water to a boil for the pasta.

When the eggplant is done cooking, add the bread crumbs and thyme and stir to coat. The crumbs should toast and become a few shades darker in about 2 minutes. Once toasty, turn off the heat off.

Cook the pasta according to the package directions, drain, and then place it back in the pot. Add the eggplant to the pasta and stir it in with a pasta spoon, trying not to break the eggplant up too much. Make sure to add any leftover bread crumbs from the pan as well. Stir in the sauce and toss to coat and heat. Serve!

PESTO-CAULIFLOWER PASTA
with Breaded Tofu

serves 4 · total time: 40 mins · active time: 40 mins

For the tofu:

¾ cup fine dry bread crumbs (I use whole wheat)

½ teaspoon dried thyme, crushed between your fingers

½ teaspoon dried rosemary, crushed between your fingers

½ teaspoon dried basil

1 teaspoon garlic powder

3 tablespoons tamari or soy sauce

14 ounces extra-firm tofu, cut into ½-inch cubes

Olive oil, for brushing

For everything else:

8 ounces linguine (I love to use quinoa pasta here)

1 medium head cauliflower (1½ to 2 pounds) chopped into ½-inch pieces

1 batch Bestest Oil-Free Pesto (page 128)

NOTES:

• If you have a little extra time and want to add even more flavor to this dish, instead of boiling, you can roast the cauliflower. Drizzle with olive oil, sprinkle with salt, and roast on a baking sheet at 375°F for about 20 minutes, flipping once.

• I use my Bestest Oil-Free Pesto here, because I really do eat it often enough that I don't want all the extra decadence of the Bestest Pesto (page 140). I do like to drown it in sauce. But use whichever you prefer!

This is in regular rotation here in my Omaha estates, where it is affectionately called "Cauli Pesti." Mostly by me. It combines two of my deepest cravings—cauliflower and pesto—with what my boyfriend always, always, *always* wants to eat: breaded tofu.

Once upon a time I'd go above and beyond for breaded tofu. Dipping it in this and dredging it in that, marinating, frying, and doing a little ritualistic dance that ensured the breading would remain in a perfectly crisp and even coat from beginning to end. And it got so that when I asked John what he wanted to eat that night I would dread the inevitable reply: "Breaded tofu."

Times have changed, and I've gotten a lot less picky about exactly how I bread my tofu. And I've stumbled upon something pretty effortless. This method produces a down-and-dirty breaded tofu that may not look like a $30 entrée but tastes pretty fabulous. And it is simple. You give each tofu cube a quick dip in some soy sauce, then toss them in a simple mixture of bread crumbs and spices, then into the pan it all goes! A thin layer of olive oil is all it takes.

The cauliflower florets are boiled in the pasta water, so everything comes together easily. The end result is a creamy, seductive sauce smothering succulent cauliflower and slurpy linguine, topped with homey, herby cubes of yumminess with a crisply beautiful exterior. It's perfect any day of the week and any time of the year!

Bring a 4-quart pot of salted water to a boil for the pasta and cauliflower.

PREPARE THE TOFU:

Preheat a large nonstick pan, preferably cast iron, over medium-high heat. On a dinner plate, use your fingertips to mix together the bread crumbs, thyme, rosemary, basil, and garlic. Pour the tamari onto a separate plate.

Place a handful of tofu cubes in the soy sauce and toss to coat. Then dredge them in the bread crumbs, tossing to coat. (Use your dry hand to handle the tofu in the bread crumbs; otherwise you'll get a crumb mitten on your hand.) Put the coated tofu off to the side of the plate and continue until all the tofu is coated.

(recipe continues)

NOTES:

- The tofu breading stays put as long as you follow a few simple rules. Make sure that the pan is preheated and ready to roll; the tofu should sizzle as it touches down, or else the breading might just get mushy and fall off. Also, make sure you're using a thin metal spatula that glides easily between the pan and the breading. Rubber or wood will just knock the breading right off. And last, the pan has to be nonstick. My preference, as always, is for well-seasoned cast iron. If you don't get it perfect the first time, no sweat; it will still be yummy. It'll be even better the second time you make it and maybe perfect the third!

- This really is the lazy man's preparation. I don't even press the tofu, and I think if you did, it would soak up too much soy sauce and get too salty. Instead, use the moisture in the tofu to your advantage. Just give the block a quick squeeze over the sink and you're good to go.

- If you'd like even more flavor and a bit of toastiness, you can roast the cauliflower instead of boiling it. Here's how: Line a large rimmed baking sheet with parchment paper. Spread the cauliflower onto the sheet and drizzle olive oil over it. Sprinkle with ¼ teaspoon salt. Toss with your hands to make sure everything is coated. Spread the cauliflower in a single layer and bake at 375°F for 10 minutes; then use a spatula to flip. You don't have to flip each and every one, so don't get OCD about it. Bake for another 15 to 20 minutes, until lightly browned, tender, and toasty.

Spray a pan with olive oil or put a thin layer of oil in the pan, and then transfer the tofu cubes to the pan. Be careful not to crowd the pan. If it isn't big enough, cook them in two batches. Spray or drizzle the tofu with a little oil, let cook for a few minutes, then flip, using a thin metal spatula so that you don't scrape off the breading. Cook for about 7 minutes total, spraying more oil or adding a little extra to the pan as needed and flipping occasionally until browned on most sides.

PREPARE EVERYTHING ELSE:

When the water is boiling, add the pasta. After about 4 minutes, add the cauliflower, too. Cook for about 8 more minutes; the pasta should be done and the cauliflower tender. Drain into a large colander. Immediately add them back to the pot in which you cooked them and mix in the pesto. Divide into bowls, top with the breaded tofu, and serve.

Bestest Oil-Free Pesto

makes 1½ cups

> This is a version of Bestest Pesto (page 140) without oil. Instead I use extra broth and nutritional yeast for a super-creamy sauce. I also use all pine nuts so that it's as smooth as possible. If pine nuts are prohibitively expensive, cashews will work, too!

2 cloves garlic
⅓ cup pine nuts or cashews
3 cups loosely packed fresh basil leaves
½ cup fresh cilantro sprigs

¾ teaspoon salt, plus more as needed
½ cup vegetable broth
¼ cup nutritional yeast flakes
1 tablespoon fresh lemon juice
Freshly ground black pepper

Pulse the garlic and pine nuts into coarse crumbs in a food processor. Add the basil, cilantro, salt, broth, nutritional yeast, and lemon juice and purée as smooth as possible, scraping down the sides with a rubber spatula to make sure you get everything. Add water to thin as needed. Taste for salt and finish with black pepper. Keep sealed and refrigerated until ready to use.

PUTTANESCA POMODORO

serves 4 • total time: 30 mins • active time: 15 mins

Olives and more olives tossed with garlicky fresh tomato sauce. Puttanesca is said to have been invented in Italy by ladies of the evening, who prepared this fast and tasty pasta when they had a few minutes to spare between clients. But you can make it when you get home from your vanilla job as well. It really hits the spot when you're looking for something complex in no time at all.

First bring a large pot of salted water to a boil for the pasta. Prep everything while it's boiling. Once boiling, cook the pasta according to the package directions and drain.

Meanwhile, preheat a 4-quart pot over medium-low heat and add the oil. Sauté the garlic in the oil for about 1 minute, being careful not to burn.

Add the tomatoes, black and green olives, capers, oregano, crushed red pepper flakes, salt, black pepper, and basil leaves, and stir. Cover the pot and turn the heat up to medium-high. Let cook for about 15 minutes, stirring often.

At this point, the tomatoes should be broken down and saucy. Toss in the spaghetti and toss to coat. Serve topped with extra basil.

8 ounces linguine

2 tablespoons olive oil

4 cloves garlic, minced

2½ pounds tomatoes, coarsely chopped

¼ cup pitted kalamata olives, coarsely chopped

¼ cup pitted green olives, coarsely chopped

¼ cup capers

1 teaspoon dried oregano

½ teaspoon crushed red pepper flakes

½ teaspoon salt

Several pinches of freshly ground black pepper

8 large fresh basil leaves, torn into pieces, plus extra for garnish

TOFU-MUSHROOM STROGANOFF

serves 4 · total time: 30 mins (plus time for soaking the cashews) · active time: 20 mins

8 ounces fusilli

¾ cup cashews, soaked for at least 2 hours (see "ABS: Always Be Soaking," page 14)

1½ cups vegetable or mushroom broth

For the tofu:

14 ounces extra-firm tofu, sliced into thin strips

1 tablespoon olive oil

Pinch of salt

For the sauce:

1 tablespoon olive oil

1 medium yellow onion, quartered and thinly sliced

½ teaspoon salt, plus a pinch

4 cloves garlic, minced

8 ounces cremini mushrooms, thinly sliced

1 teaspoon dried thyme

½ cup dry white wine

2 tablespoons tomato paste

Several pinches of freshly ground black pepper

Chopped fresh flat-leaf parsley, for garnish (optional)

Stroganoff—just the mere mention of it makes you feel warm and cozy. I had been using the same vegan stroganoff recipe for about twenty years and felt it was time for an update! This version is full of creamy and heavenly mushroom flavor, with hints of white wine and thyme. Lightly sautéed strips of tofu make it even more filling and delicious. I love how fusilli catches the sauce in its curves, but wide noodles like fettuccine or rombi are good choices, too.

To get the strips of tofu for this recipe, slice tofu in half through the equator, like a clam. Then slice each half into ¼-inch-thick strips. You should end up with slices that are about 3 inches long by 1 inch wide.

Bring a large pot of salted water to a boil for the pasta. When it's boiling, cook the pasta according to the package directions. Drain and set aside.

Drain the cashews and add them to a blender along with the vegetable broth. Blend until very smooth, with only a slight graininess. This could take anywhere from 1 to 5 minutes depending on the strength of your machine. Scrape down the sides with a rubber spatula now and again to make sure you get everything.

PREPARE THE TOFU:

Preheat a large, heavy-bottomed pan over medium heat and add the oil. Sauté the tofu along with the salt for 5 minutes or so, until it's just slightly browned. Set the tofu on a plate covered with aluminum foil as you prepare the sauce.

PREPARE THE SAUCE:

In the same pan in which you cooked the tofu, still on medium heat, add the oil and sauté the onion in the oil along with a pinch of salt for about 5 minutes, until translucent. Add the minced garlic and sauté for 30 seconds or so.

Now add the mushrooms and thyme and cook until the mushrooms are lightly browned, about 5 more minutes. Add the wine, tomato paste, remaining ½ teaspoon salt, and pepper, stir, and turn the heat up to high. Let the wine reduce by about half. This should take 5 minutes or so. Turn the heat back down to medium.

Pour in the cashew mixture. Stir until well combined and let thicken for about 5 minutes. Taste for seasoning. Add the tofu and toss to coat, carefully, so as not to break the tofu. Serve over the pasta, and garnish with fresh parsley, if you like.

OLIVE ANGEL HAIR

with Seared Brussels Sprouts

serves 4 · total time: 30 mins · active time: 30 mins

I know it's easy to run out of pasta ideas or fall into a pasta rut. But just a little produce and a few pantry items can pull you out! Salty olives and perfectly cooked Brussels sprouts, with their delicate layers and caramelized outer leaves, make this a totally satisfying dish that isn't exactly run-of-the-mill. Chopped-up walnuts add some texture and help get the flavors to cling to the pasta.

I feel fulfilled when my pasta is a complete meal that can come together with just the pot of pasta and one other pan full of lots of awesome stuff. This dish utilizes a few time-management (and dish-management) techniques that will always come in handy. Use one pan to toast up some walnuts, and then use that same pan to prepare all of the other ingredients. While you're doing that, use the pasta water to steam some veggies to be used in the dish. In this case, we're steaming quartered Brussels sprouts so that they're cooked through, and then all you have to do is sear them in the pan.

8 ounces Brussels sprouts, quartered

8 ounces angel hair pasta

½ cup shelled walnuts

1 medium yellow onion, quartered and thinly sliced

2 tablespoons olive oil

½ teaspoon salt, plus a pinch

4 cloves garlic, minced

1 teaspoon dried thyme

½ teaspoon crushed red pepper flakes

Freshly ground black pepper

½ cup kalamata olives, coarsely chopped

½ cup to 1 cup vegetable broth

2 tablespoons white balsamic vinegar or fresh lemon juice

First put on a large pot of salted water to boil. When it's boiling, steam the Brussels sprouts for 3 minutes (see Note) and set aside. Then cook the pasta according to the package directions. Drain and set aside.

In the meantime, preheat a large, heavy-bottomed pan over medium heat. Toast the walnuts for about 5 minutes, tossing occasionally, until fragrant and toasty. Remove from the pan and place on a cutting board. When cool enough to handle, chop the walnuts into pea-size pieces.

Using the same pan, turn the heat up to medium-high and sauté the onion in 1 tablespoon of the olive oil and a pinch of salt just until translucent, about 3 minutes. Add the steamed Brussels sprouts to the pan, along with the remaining 1 tablespoon olive oil. Try to make sure that the sprouts are touching the bottom of the pan, not resting too much on the onions, so that they sear. Cook for about 5 minutes, stirring occasionally, until seared on at least one side.

Add the garlic, thyme, red pepper flakes, and black pepper, and cook until fragrant, about 30 seconds.

Add the olives, remaining ½ teaspoon salt, ½ cup of the vegetable broth, and vinegar and mix well. Add the pasta and toss to coat. Add the walnuts and toss again. Make sure to get any crumbs from the walnuts, too. If the dish seems dry, add up to ½ cup additional vegetable broth. Taste for seasoning, and serve.

NOTES:

- Once the water for your pasta is boiling, you're going to use that water to steam the Brussels sprouts before cooking the pasta. You can use this trick if you just need some steamed veggies to throw into your dish, or if your veggies need to be steamed before searing, roasting, or sautéing. Place the vegetables in a colander that can easily rest on the pot edge, above the water. Ideally, it should be small enough to fit into the pot and still have a lid sit comfortably on top. It should also have a handle, so that it stays in place. You can, of course, also use a steamer basket. Place the veggies over the boiling water, cover, and steam away!

- If for some reason you don't want to use my super-special steaming method, just steam however you normally do and proceed with the recipe.

LENTIL-A-RONI

serves 8 · total time: 30 mins · active time: 30 mins

1 pound fusilli

½ cup cashews, soaked for at least 2 hours (see "ABS: Always Be Soaking," page 14, and Notes below)

1 cup vegetable broth

1 tablespoon olive oil

1 small yellow onion, finely chopped

1 teaspoon salt, plus a pinch

3 cloves garlic, minced

2 teaspoons dried thyme

Pinch of freshly ground black pepper

1½ cups cooked brown lentils (or one 15-ounce can, rinsed and drained)

1 (28-ounce) can crushed tomatoes with basil

NOTES:

• The cashews are soaked here, as usual, to get nice and creamy. But once in a while, if I get home and can't wait to soak cashews or just plain want to eat right away, I skip the soaking step and just get them as creamy as possible in the blender. A little texture in this recipe doesn't seem to hurt; it actually adds something of a Parmesan quality, so it's all about what you're in the mood for or have time for.

• If you'd like to add a few handfuls of greens, choose quick-cooking ones, like spinach or chard leaves (not the stems), and simply stir them in at the end. They'll wilt right away and become a healthy addition to your 'roni.

I don't know—it seems that childhood food that comes from a can is my weakness! This is an homage to that canned childhood favorite Beefaroni, but of course lentils are my beef of choice. Fusilli is the perfect pasta here; the meaty sauce manages to find its way into every twist. I think that kids will dig it, too. Even if you sneak in some chopped greens at the end, which I often do. This makes a lot and it tastes great as leftovers!

Bring a large pot of salted water to a boil for the pasta. When it's boiling, cook the pasta according to the package directions. Drain and set aside until ready to use.

Drain the cashews and add them to a blender along with the broth. Blend until very smooth; this could take 1 to 5 minutes depending on the strength of your blender (see Notes).

Preheat a large heavy-bottomed saucepan over medium heat and add the oil. Sauté the onion in the oil with a pinch of salt for about 3 minutes, until translucent. Add the minced garlic and sauté for 30 seconds or so.

Add the thyme, remaining 1 teaspoon salt, and black pepper, and sauté for another 30 seconds or so. Add the lentils and toss to coat. Use a small masher or a fork to partially mash a few of the lentils. You don't want them puréed, just a few mashed ones and some left whole; it should just take a minute or so.

Add the tomatoes and cover the pot, letting it cook for about 5 minutes. Pour in the cashew mixture and let thicken for about 3 minutes, stirring occasionally. Taste for seasoning. Add the fusilli and toss to coat and reheat. Serve.

GODDESS NOODLES

with Tempeh & Broccoli

serves 4 • total time: 30 mins • active time: 30 mins

8 ounces whole-wheat linguine

½ cup tahini

½ cup warm water

3 tablespoons fresh lemon juice

½ teaspoon salt, plus a couple of pinches

2 tablespoons nutritional yeast flakes

2 tablespoons plus 1 teaspoon olive oil

8 ounces tempeh, diced into ½-inch pieces

6 cups broccoli florets and thinly sliced stems

4 cloves garlic, minced

1 cup chopped fresh chives

Freshly ground black pepper

SWITCH IT UP:

If you're not up for tempeh, then you may use 1½ cups cooked chickpeas instead. No need to sauté; just toss them in with the linguine to heat through. And if you can't find fresh chives, then chopped scallions make for a great dish, too.

NOTES:

• The consistency of tahini can vary greatly from brand to brand. Some are thin and smooth, and others are firm and clumpy. Even the temperature of your tahini can make a difference. Depending on what your tahini is like, you may need to add more warm water to get it smooth. And if it is really clumpy, you may even need to transfer it to a small blender to smooth it out. For the best results, let your tahini come to room temperature before using for this recipe.

• I ask that you reserve some pasta water for thinning the sauce. Here's what I do: When the water stops boiling, tip a mug in (watch that you don't burn yourself!) and fill it up as much as possible, then just set aside and drain the pasta.

I almost didn't include this recipe for a very silly reason. "It's too easy! I make it all the time!" I thought. Followed shortly by "Hey, dummy, that is exactly what this book is about." Here's the idea: whole-wheat linguine, sautéed broccoli and tempeh, in a garlicky, lemony tahini sauce, tossed with fresh chives. Simple but sublime flavors that you will gravitate toward again and again. I know I do.

Bring a large pot of salted water to a boil for the pasta. When it's boiling, cook the pasta according to the package directions. Drain and set aside, reserving a cup or so of the cooking water.

In a liquid measuring cup, use a fork to stir together the tahini, warm water, lemon juice, and ½ teaspoon of the salt. Depending on the consistency of your tahini, you may need to add more water to get it to be relatively smooth (see Notes). Mix in the nutritional yeast. Set aside.

Preheat a large pan over medium-high heat and add 1 tablespoon of the oil. Sauté the tempeh in the oil with a big pinch of salt for about 7 minutes, tossing frequently, until lightly browned. Transfer to a plate and set aside.

In the same pan, cook the broccoli in another 1 tablespoon oil with a pinch of salt for about 5 minutes. The broccoli should be bright green and still have a snap to it.

Push the broccoli over to the side of the pan, and add the garlic, along with the remaining 1 teaspoon oil. Toss together and let the garlic cook for about 15 seconds; then mix it in with the broccoli.

Now add the pasta, and use a pasta fork to mix together the pasta and broccoli. Turn off the heat, add the tahini, and stir to coat. Now add the reserved pasta water as needed to thin the sauce and get everything coated.

Stir in the tempeh, chives, and some black pepper. Serve.

TEMPEH ORZILLA

serves 4 · total time: 35 min · active time: 35 mins

Brothy orzo with velvety ribbons of spinach, succulent bites of sun-dried tomatoes, and garlic. Lots and lots of garlic! I especially love the texture and flavor contrast with the sausage-y bites of crumbled tempeh on top and the soft, saucy orzo below. I call it "Orzilla" because Orzo with Spinach and Sun-Dried Tomatoes with Crumbled Anise Tempeh is just too long to type. And because it destroys cities. If you find tempeh to be particularly bitter, you can steam it for this recipe, but that is optional.

For the tempeh and orzo:

1 tablespoon olive oil

8 ounces tempeh, cut into bite-size pieces

½ teaspoon dried coriander

½ teaspoon anise seeds or chopped fennel seeds

1 tablespoon soy sauce

8 ounces orzo

For the sauce:

2 teaspoons olive oil

1 small red onion, thinly sliced

½ teaspoon salt, plus a pinch

4 cloves garlic, minced

½ teaspoon dried rosemary

1 cup dry white wine

½ cup sun-dried tomatoes (dry, not the oil-packed kind)

Several pinches of freshly ground black pepper

1 cup vegetable broth

2 tablespoons nutritional yeast flakes

3 cups baby spinach

PREPARE THE TEMPEH AND ORZO:

Bring a large pot of salted water to a boil for the orzo.

Meanwhile, for the tempeh, preheat a small pan over medium heat and add the oil. Sauté the tempeh in the oil for about 10 minutes, mashing the tempeh into crumbles with your spatula as you go. Add the coriander, anise seeds, and soy sauce and sauté for 2 more minutes, then turn off the heat and cover until ready to use.

Cook the orzo according to the package directions, and drain.

PREPARE THE SAUCE:

Preheat a large pan over medium heat and add the oil. Sauté the onion in the oil with a pinch of salt until soft, about 5 minutes. Add the garlic and sauté for 30 more seconds.

Add the rosemary, wine, and sun-dried tomatoes. Season with the remaining ½ teaspoon salt and pepper and turn the heat up to bring the sauce to a simmer. Let simmer until reduced by about half, 5 minutes or so.

Add the broth and nutritional yeast and warm through. Add the spinach in handfuls, letting each batch wilt before adding the next. Cook until the spinach is thoroughly wilted, then turn off the heat, add the orzo, mix well, and serve topped with the tempeh crumbles.

NOTE:

There's a photo of this recipe opposite the Contents page.

PESTO RISOTTO
with Roasted Zucchini

serves 6 · total time: 45 mins · active time: 45 mins

The pesto is added in stages, building the flavor, and there's lots of white wine, resulting in a really sensual dish that makes you feel pretty fancy and accomplished. The zuke is very simple, which is just how I like it. Still kind of crunchy, but roasty and toasty with lots of garlicky flavor. You can toss it over the top or mix it in—whatever floats your zucchini boat. Then top with extra toasted pine nuts for added fanciness and nutty texture.

For the risotto:

4 cups vegetable broth

1 tablespoon olive oil

1 medium yellow onion, finely chopped

½ teaspoon salt, plus a pinch

1½ cups Arborio rice

1 cup dry white wine

Several pinches of freshly ground black pepper

¾ cup Bestest Pesto (page 140)

For the zucchini:

1 pound zucchini, cut into chunky half-moons

1 tablespoon olive oil

3 cloves garlic, minced

½ teaspoon salt

Several pinches of freshly ground black pepper

For the garnish:

Extra pesto

Toasted pine nuts

Warm the vegetable broth in a saucepan or in the microwave (see "Real World Risotto," page 140).

Preheat the oven to 425°F for the zucchini and line a large rimmed baking sheet with parchment paper.

Now, let's make the risotto! Preheat a heavy-bottomed 4-quart pot over medium heat and add the oil. Sauté the onion in the oil with a pinch of salt until translucent, 4 to 5 minutes.

Add the rice and use a slanted wooden spoon to stir and coat with oil. Add the white wine and stir occasionally until the wine is mostly absorbed, 4 minutes or so. Add a few pinches of black pepper and ¼ teaspoon of the salt. Turn the heat down just a bit, to medium-low.

Add the warm broth by the cupful, stirring the risotto after each addition until the broth is mostly absorbed (6 to 8 minutes per cupful). After 2 cupfuls, add about half of the pesto and stir well, then continue to cook, adding broth by the cupful, stirring, and letting the liquid absorb.

PREPARE THE ZUCCHINI:

At some point in here, your oven will be preheated for the zucchini. Toss the zucchini with the oil, garlic, salt, and pepper. Roast for about 6 minutes on each side, or until softened and lightly browned. Remove from the oven and set aside.

Along with your last addition of broth, add the remainder of the pesto. Taste for salt and add the remaining ¼ teaspoon if needed. The risotto is ready when the rice is chewy but still firm and the sauce is very creamy. For a firmer risotto, just cook a few minutes extra to absorb more of the liquid.

To serve, scoop the risotto into bowls and top each with some zucchini. Drizzle with extra pesto and garnish with a few toasted pine nuts.

(recipe continues)

¼ cup walnut halves
¼ cup pine nuts
2 cloves garlic, peeled
2 ½ cups fresh basil
½ cup fresh cilantro
2 tablespoons fresh thyme
2 tablespoons nutritional yeast flakes
1 teaspoon salt
¼ cup water
¼ cup olive oil
1 tablespoon fresh lemon juice

Bestest Pesto
makes 2 cups

First toast the nuts. I will let you in on my secret hybrid nut toasting method. Preheat a large, heavy-bottomed skillet (preferably cast iron) over medium-low heat. First toast the walnuts for about 5 minutes, tossing them often. Then add the pine nuts for an additional 5 minutes. They should turn a few shades darker and smell warm and toasty.

Transfer the toasted nuts to a food processor. Add the garlic and pulse everything into fine crumbs. Add the basil, cilantro, thyme, nutritional yeast, salt, and water and purée until relatively smooth, scraping down the sides at least once to make sure you get everything. Stream in the olive oil and blend until well combined. Blend in the lemon juice.

Refrigerate in a tightly sealed container until ready to use.

REAL WORLD RISOTTO

Risotto and I have always been fairly simpatico. We have an understanding: I stir you, you get creamy. No big deal. But that was before reality cooking shows.

After one episode of *Hell's Kitchen*, you'll be pretty much convinced that risotto is the biggest, most backstabbingest heartbreaker there is. It will stop at nothing to betray you. Risotto makes Gordon Ramsay kick the trash can on the regular. It breaks. It burns. It refuses to cook. It jumps out of the pot and shivs you if given half the chance. Sleep with one eye open.

To add to the anxiety, an episode of *Food Network Star* featured Wolfgang Puck storming the kitchen to show a cheftestant how to make a proper risotto. She was, of course, in tears. The kind of tears reserved only for failed risotto. And most risottos are failures. Too stiff, too loose, too everything. It must be true because the canned soup guy says so!

But, wait, there's a better way: Make the risotto the way you prefer. If you're not on reality TV, it probably won't break or burn. If you add warm broth and stir it every few minutes, it will probably get deliciously creamy. And if you prefer a stiffer risotto, that's okay. If you want it to be a little more soupy and creamy, that's okay, too. Just add more broth. I'm okay. You're okay. Your risotto is okay.

And you can even step away while the risotto cooks. Yes, you need to stir often, but you're not chained to the stove. Go ahead, check your e-mail, start a load of laundry, watch some Internet cat videos. Just keep a close eye and stir when the liquid is absorbed.

There is one golden rule: The broth needs to be warm when you add it. I usually keep my broth warming in a pot on the stovetop like a good girl, but if I've got too much going on I'm not against keeping it in a microwave-safe bowl and nuking it every now and again. You gotta do what you gotta do! In any case, keep the broth warm for the best results. At least it will help to ward off the Gordons and Wolfgangs of the world.

ACORN SQUASH RISOTTO
with Cranberries

serves 4 · total time: 1 hour 30 mins · active time: 45 mins

I'm a sucker for autumn farmers' markets, especially when there are piles and piles of squash in every shape and size. I love to rummage through the acorn squash and pick out the ones with just the right amount of orange that seems to bloom from the rest of the deep-green skin. In this risotto recipe, the squash is roasted whole (well, halved) and then scooped into the pot, making it a pretty easy way to fill your winter squash quota for the evening. If you'd like even more squash on the menu, try stuffing the squash. Pick up two extra and roast them along with the others, then serve each half-filled with risotto. Fancy and easy! This risotto is made creamy with coconut milk and tart with lime juice and cranberries.

3 pounds acorn squash (2 medium squash)

2 tablespoons olive oil

1 small yellow onion, finely chopped

3 cloves garlic, minced

1 tablespoon minced fresh ginger

½ teaspoon crushed red pepper flakes

1½ cups Arborio rice

⅓ cup dry white wine

5 to 6 cups vegetable broth, warmed

½ teaspoon salt

½ cup dried cranberries

½ teaspoon ground nutmeg

¼ teaspoon ground cinnamon

2 tablespoons fresh lime juice

¾ cup coconut milk

1 teaspoon pure maple syrup (optional)

First prepare the squash. Preheat the oven to 425°F. Line a rimmed baking sheet with parchment paper and lightly oil the paper.

Hack the squash in half and remove the seeds and stringy bits with a tablespoon. Place the squash on the baking sheet cut side down. Bake for about 35 minutes, or until easily pierced with a fork but not completely mushy. Remove from the oven and let cool to the touch. Once cooled, peel off the skin and chop the squash into bite-size pieces.

In the meantime, start the risotto. Preheat a heavy-bottomed pot over medium heat and add the oil. Sauté the onion, garlic, ginger, and red pepper flakes in the oil for about 7 minutes, stirring often so that it doesn't burn. A slanted wooden spoon is the perfect tool for stirring. Add the rice and stir to coat with the oil. Add the wine to deglaze the pot, then add the first cup of broth, along with the salt. Stir until most of the water is absorbed. You don't have to stir the entire time; just do it as frequently as you can.

Continue adding broth, stirring a few more times, until only 1 cup of broth is left. It should take about 45 minutes, and by this point your squash should be ready to add. When you add the last cup, add the squash and cranberries too, and repeat stirring. When most of the liquid is absorbed, add the nutmeg, cinnamon, and lime juice. Stir in the coconut milk. Cook for about 5 more minutes, stirring occasionally. Taste and adjust the salt. At this point, you may add the maple syrup, if desired. This doesn't make it sweet per se, but it enhances the natural sweetness of the squash. It's now ready to serve!

MAKE AHEAD:
You can roast the squash a day in advance, wrap in plastic wrap, and refrigerate until ready to use.

WHITE WINE RISOTTO
With Peas & Shiitake Bacon

serves 6 · active time: 40 mins (plus 2 hours to soak the cashews) ·
total time: 40 mins

For the shiitake bacon:

1 tablespoon tamari or soy sauce

1 teaspoon olive oil

1 teaspoon liquid smoke

½ pound shiitake mushrooms, sliced
  ¼ inch thick

For the risotto:

½ cup cashews, soaked in water for
  2 hours or up to overnight

1 cup water

4 cups or so vegetable broth

1 tablespoon olive oil

1 medium yellow onion, finely chopped

3 cloves garlic, minced

1 teaspoon dried thyme

1½ cups Arborio rice

1½ cups dry white wine

Several dashes fresh black pepper

½ teaspoon salt

2 tablespoons fresh lemon juice

For garnish:

1 cup green peas, fresh or frozen

NOTES:

- If fresh peas aren't available to you,
  then mix in some frozen ones at the end.

- If you'd like to bulk the risotto up
  with some protein, either Classic
  Baked Tofu (page 238) or Garlicky
  Thyme Tempeh (page 236) would be a
  wonderful accompaniment.

This fancy-sounding risotto is deceptively simple. It's wine-scented and creamy, topped with salty, smoky shiitakes and bursts of fresh peas. It's a perfect beginner's risotto and actually lends itself to any produce you might have around.

Make the shiitake bacon: Preheat the oven to 425°F and line a rimmed baking sheet with parchment. In a small cup, mix together the tamari, olive oil, and liquid smoke.

Place the sliced mushrooms on the baking sheet and drizzle with the liquid. Toss to coat, and spread into an even layer. Bake for 12 to 15 minutes, until crispy at the edges. The texture should range from crispy to meaty in each mushroom. Set aside.

Now make the risotto: Drain the cashews and add them to a blender along with the water. Blend until very smooth. Set aside.

Warm the broth in a saucepan or in the microwave (see tips on page 140).

Preheat a heavy-bottomed 4-quart pot over medium heat. Sauté the onion in oil and a pinch of salt until translucent, 4 to 5 minutes. Mix in the garlic and thyme and sauté for 1 more minute.

Add the rice and use a slanted wooden spoon to stir and coat with oil. Add the white wine and stir occasionally, until the wine is mostly absorbed, 4 minutes or so. Add a few dashes fresh black pepper, and half of the salt. Turn the heat down just a bit, to medium-low.

Add the broth by the cupful, stirring the risotto after each addition until the broth is mostly absorbed (6 to 8 minutes per each addition).

With your last addition of broth, add the cashew cream and lemon juice. Taste for salt and add the remaining ¼ teaspoon if needed. The risotto is ready when the rice is chewy but still firm, and the sauce is very creamy. At this point you can toss in the peas to warm through, or gently heat them in a separate small pan with a few tablespoons water.

For a firmer risotto, cook a few minutes extra to absorb more of the liquid.

To serve: scoop risotto into each bowl and top with peas (if you haven't mixed them in) and shiitake bacon.

STEWS, CHILIS & curries

Here's where you can get WILD with your spice rack.

Stew is the ultimate downtime dinner, and the recipes in this chapter run the gamut. From classic American flavors, like an herby gravy topped with biscuits, to Indian favorites, like a tangy and spicy chana masala working its saucy way over some basmati rice, stew is one of the best ways to get creative at your stovetop. Here's where you'll be able to add a little more of this or that, experiment with curry blends, and figure out what you're really made of as you test your chili for spicy heat. Even if the recipes call for a few more ingredients than you feel like pulling out, they are all low-key enough to come together easily on a Tuesday evening. With stew, it's all about the downtime. Building flavor ingredient by ingredient, then letting the heat do the rest. And the best comes last—leftovers!

SEITAN & WILD MUSHROOM STEW

serves 6 to 8 • total time: 45 mins • active time: 20 mins

1 tablespoon olive oil

1 large yellow onion, quartered and thickly sliced

1 teaspoon salt, plus a pinch

4 cloves garlic, minced

3 medium carrots, peeled and sliced on the bias ½ inch thick

1 cup dry red wine

1 teaspoon dried rosemary

1 teaspoon dried thyme

1 teaspoon sweet paprika

½ teaspoon fennel seeds, crushed (or ground fennel)

Freshly ground black pepper

1 ounce dried wild mushrooms

3 cups vegetable broth

1½ pounds potatoes (any type), lazily peeled, cut into 1½-inch chunks

¼ cup all-purpose flour

½ cup water

2 tablespoons tomato paste

3 vegan sausages (store-bought or homemade; see page 237), sliced into chunky half-moons

Chopped fresh flat-leaf parsley or thyme sprigs for garnish (optional)

NOTES:

• Gluten-free option: Sub chickpea flour for the all-purpose flour. Sub thawed extra-firm frozen tofu with the water pressed out for the sausages (this was my second favorite "meat" while experimenting). Slice the tofu into ½-inch-thick triangles. Add an extra ½ teaspoon crushed fennel seeds to the stew for sausage-y flavor.

• If you can't find a wild mushroom mix, then just porcinis work beautifully. Shiitakes or portobellos will work as well, but chop them up a little finer before adding.

I've been on a mission to build a better vegan beef stew. Anyone can throw some wine and tomatoes into a pot, but even with all the right ingredients, it's still too easy to make a flat-tasting stew. I wanted deep, complex flavors, a thick and silky base, chunky carrots and potatoes cooked just right. And of course, *beefiness.* And I wanted it to all happen in one pot. A simple, filling stew shouldn't destroy the entire kitchen.

Put plainly, I wanted the *"DAAAAYAMN!"* factor. Nothing too fussy, but a bowl that not only comforts you on a cold winter's night but also straight-up makes you look forward to the snowiest, windiest, all-the-roads-shut-downiest night possible, just so you can make stew.

And here it is! The seitan sausage provides flavor and hearty texture without needing to be sautéed, while the mushrooms create a sultry broth and a falling-off-the-bone meatiness (that phrase isn't gross when you consider that there aren't any actual bones here, right?) that just sings "beef stew." Bring it on, winter.

Preheat a 4-quart pot over medium-high heat and add the oil. Sauté the onion in the oil with a pinch of salt until translucent, about 5 minutes. Add the garlic and sauté for 30 seconds, until fragrant.

Add the carrots, wine, rosemary (crushed in your fingers), thyme (crushed in your fingers), paprika, fennel seeds, remaining 1 teaspoon salt, and black pepper, and bring to a boil. The liquid should reduce in about 3 minutes.

Add the dried mushrooms and broth, cover, and cook at a full boil for 5 minutes or so to quickly hydrate the mushrooms. Now add the potatoes, lower the heat, and simmer just until fork-tender, about 10 minutes.

In a measuring cup, mix the flour into the water with a fork until no lumps are left. Slowly add the broth-flour mixture to the pot, mixing well. Mix in the tomato paste. Let thicken for 5 minutes or so. Add the sausages and continue to cook. After about 5 more minutes it should be perfectly thick but still smooth. Taste for seasoning, and serve. Sprinkle individual servings with fresh parsley or thyme if you want to be all '70s food chic.

LENTIL-QUINOA STEW

with Lots of Kale

serves 6 · total time: 1 hour · active time: 20 mins

1 tablespoon olive oil

1 medium yellow onion, diced

1 teaspoon salt, plus a pinch

3 cloves garlic, minced

1 teaspoon dried tarragon

1 teaspoon dried thyme

6 cups vegetable broth

1 bay leaf

1 cup diced carrots

3 ribs celery, thinly sliced

¾ cup brown lentils

1 cup quinoa (red quinoa looks prettiest)

Several pinches of freshly ground black pepper

1 pound kale, thick stems trimmed and leaves torn into bite-size pieces

Splash of balsamic vinegar (1 to 2 tablespoons)

Hot sauce, for serving (optional; I suggest Frank's RedHot)

The holy trinity of lentils, quinoa, and kale—all the classics in one pot! There may be some of you out there who don't have a recipe like this, and so it's important to spread the gospel. This is the easiest stew in the world, a meal unto itself, and so very beautifully inviting, too. Quinoa and lentils provide heartiness and plenty of protein, and a whole bushel of kale completes the meal and gives you vegan superpowers. After a few spoonfuls of this stew you'll be able to lift buses (filled with biodiesel, of course) and move entire food co-op bulk bins with just your pinkie.

Preheat a 4-quart soup pot over medium-high heat and add the oil. Sauté the onion in the oil with a pinch of salt until translucent, about 3 minutes. Add the garlic and sauté for 15 seconds or so, then add the thyme and tarragon and mix them in with the onions.

Add the broth, bay leaf, carrots, celery, lentils, quinoa, remaining 1 teaspoon salt, and pepper. Cover and bring to a boil. Once boiling, lower the heat to medium and cook for about 40 minutes, stirring occasionally, until the lentils are tender. Add the kale and stir frequently until the kale is wilted and velvety. Add the splash of balsamic vinegar, taste for salt, and let the stew sit for 10 minutes or so off the heat. Thin with water or broth if necessary, and serve (with a bottle of hot sauce, if desired).

BELGIAN BEER & SEITAN STEW

serves 6 to 8 · total time: 1 hour 15 mins · active time: 30 mins

This was my take on *carbonnade à la flamande,* the classic Belgian beef and beer stew. I had to research the hell out of this one because I had never had it in my pre-vegetarian days. But I love big old stews and I love cooking with beer, so the idea just wouldn't get out of my mind. Well, what followed was an amazing stew of caramelized onions, and a sweet tartness from a surprise ingredient . . . apples! The beer gives it a hoppy backdrop. To thicken it, a two-day-old baguette is put to work, making the stew satisfyingly rustic (and also a pretty clever way to use up stale bread).

I loved every spoonful! And so did my recipe testers. However, it was basically unanimous that it was nothing like a traditional carbonnade. And I, having never had the original, was not going to argue with my worldly and knowledgeable testers. A simple name change, and voilà—a deliciously satisfying Belgian stew inspired by the original.

2 tablespoons olive oil

2 medium yellow onions, diced (about 4 cups)

1 teaspoon salt, plus a pinch

1 pound seitan, sliced into chunky bite-size strips

8 ounces cremini mushrooms, thinly sliced

2 teaspoons dried thyme

2 bay leaves

Several pinches of freshly ground black pepper

1 cup Belgian ale (see Notes)

1½ pounds Yukon Gold potatoes, cut into ¾-inch chunks

4 cups vegetable broth

2 cups cubed day-old baguette

2 Granny Smith apples, peeled and diced into ½-inch pieces

1 tablespoon whole-grain mustard

Chopped fresh flat-leaf parsley, for garnish (optional)

Preheat a 4-quart pot over medium-low heat. Add the onions and 2 teaspoons of the oil. Mix well and cover the pot, leaving a little room for steam to escape, and cook for about 15 minutes, stirring occasionally. What you're doing here is sweating the onions, getting them nice and plump and coaxing all the sweetness out of them. They should turn a slightly mellow amber color. Lift the lid, turn the heat to medium, add a pinch of salt, and cook for 5 more minutes, until the onions are golden.

While the onions are going, brown the seitan in a separate pan. Preheat a large pan over medium heat. Sauté the seitan in 1 tablespoon of the oil for about 5 minutes, just to brown. Set aside.

To the onions add the mushrooms, thyme, bay leaves, remaining 1 teaspoon salt, pepper, and remaining 1 teaspoon oil. Cook for about 5 minutes.

Add the beer and turn up the heat to bring to a boil. Let boil for a minute or two to reduce. Now add the potatoes and broth. Cover the pot and bring back to a boil. Once boiling, lower the heat to a simmer and cook for about 5 minutes. The potatoes should be just about tender enough to eat but still very firm.

Add the bread and apples. Cook uncovered for about 20 more minutes, stirring occasionally. The bread and apples should be broken down and the stew should be thickened. Add the seitan, turn off the heat, and let sit for 10 minutes or so, to let the flavors meld. Remove the bay leaves before serving. Serve garnished with parsley, if desired.

NOTES:

- If you'd like to skip the seitan sautéing step, you may use 3 steamed seitan sausages cut into chunky half-moons instead.

- Belgian ale is the preferred beer to use here, but if you can't find any, then any good-quality pale ale will do.

DILLY STEW
with Rosemary Dumplings

serves 6 to 8 • total time: 1 hour • active time: 30 mins

You can think of this as a play on vegan chicken and dumplings or just take it for what it is—a soul-satisfying, thick, hearty stew with chunky potatoes and carrots and creamy white beans, all laced through with dilly yumminess. The dumplings soak up all that goodness on the outside and stay deliciously doughy in the center. The best part is spooning on the squashy-squishy dumpling dough, only to reveal beautifully firm and plump dumplings when you lift the lid minutes later. Makes you feel like a kitchen god. Or maybe that's the winter cabin fever setting in.

PREPARE THE STEW:

First we will make a lower-fat roux.

Preheat a large, heavy-bottomed pot over medium-low heat. Add the oil and sprinkle in the flour. Use a slanted wooden spatula to stir pretty consistently for 3 to 4 minutes, until the flour is clumpy and toasty. Add the onion and salt, and toss to coat the onions completely in the flour mixture. Cook for 5 minutes, stirring often. Add the garlic and stir for about 30 more seconds.

Stream in the broth, whisking constantly to prevent clumping. Add the celery, potatoes, carrots, dill, thyme, paprika, and black pepper, then turn the heat up and cover to bring to a boil. Keep a close eye on it and stir often so that it doesn't clump or boil over.

Once boiling, lower the heat to a simmer and let cook uncovered for 20 to 25 minutes, stirring occasionally, until the stew is nicely thickened and the potatoes and carrots are tender. In the meantime, prepare the dumplings.

PREPARE THE DUMPLINGS:

Sift the flour, baking powder, and salt together in a large bowl. Mix in the rosemary. Make a well in the center and add the milk and olive oil. Use a wooden spoon to mix together until a wet dough forms.

When the stew is ready, mix in the beans and plop spoonfuls of dough right on top of the stew. You should get about 14 dumplings. Cover the pot tightly and cook for about 14 more minutes. The dumplings should be nice and firm. Use your ladle to dunk them into the stew to coat them.

Ladle the stew into bowls, and top with the dumplings. Garnish with additional herbs and serve.

For the stew:

3 tablespoons olive oil

¼ cup all-purpose flour

1 medium yellow onion, quartered and thinly sliced

1 teaspoon salt

3 cloves garlic, minced

6 cups vegetable broth, at room temperature

2 ribs celery, sliced ¼ inch thick

1½ pounds Yukon Gold potatoes, cut into ¾-inch chunks

1 cup carrots peeled and sliced into chunky half-moons

2 tablespoons chopped fresh dill

1 tablespoon chopped fresh thyme

½ teaspoon sweet paprika

Several pinches of freshly ground black pepper

1 (15-ounce) can navy beans, rinsed and drained (1½ cups)

For the dumplings:

1½ cups all-purpose flour

2 teaspoons baking powder

½ teaspoon salt

1 tablespoon dried rosemary, finely chopped

¾ cup unsweetened almond milk (or non-dairy milk of your choice)

2 tablespoons olive oil

NOTE:

I use a Le Creuset Dutch oven for this. You don't need to use cast iron, but the wider the pot the better, because you need lots of surface area to make the roux and cook the dumplings later. If you don't have a wide pot, then a large, deep pan will work, too. Make sure, whatever vehicle you use, that it has a lid that fits securely. This will ensure that your dumplings steam all the way through and come out deliciously fluffy.

LEMON-GARLIC FAVA BEANS & Mushrooms

serves 4 • total time: 30 mins • active time: 30 mins

2 teaspoons olive oil

1 small red onion, thinly sliced into half-moons

½ teaspoon salt, plus a pinch

3 cloves garlic, minced

1 tablespoon chopped fresh thyme

8 ounces cremini mushrooms, sliced in half

2 tablespoons fine dry bread crumbs (plain or seasoned)

2 cups vegetable broth

Several pinches of freshly ground black pepper

Juice and zest of ½ lemon

2 (15-ounce) cans fava beans, rinsed and drained (3 cups)

Slivered scallions, for garnish (optional)

Fava is a bean's bean—big, meaty, and toothsome. They're epic, really. And so I like to use strong, bold flavors when I cook with them. This dish is savory and saucy, with lots of garlic, thyme, and lemon. I left the mushrooms nice and big, too, so that they can go toe to toe with the fava beans. A sprinkle of bread crumbs adds a nice toasty flavor and thickens the sauce for maximum deliciousness.

To play up the earthiness, I love to serve this with a wild rice blend and Garlicky Thyme Tempeh (page 236).

Preheat a large pan over medium heat and add the oil. Sauté the onion in the oil with a pinch of salt for 5 to 7 minutes, until slightly browned. Add the garlic and thyme and sauté for 1 minute. Add the mushrooms and cook to release their moisture, about 5 minutes.

Add the bread crumbs, toss to coat everything, and toast the crumbs for 3 to 5 minutes. Add the broth, remaining ½ teaspoon salt, black pepper, lemon zest and juice, and fava beans. Bring to a boil. Let reduce and thicken for 7 minutes or so. Taste for seasoning and serve topped with scallions, if desired.

WHITE BEANS
in Sherry–Bread Crumb Gravy

serves 4 · total time: 25 mins · active time: 15 mins

Gravy is pure comfort for me, and if I can make a gravy into a meal, so much the better. This is one of my favorite ways to have a rich, comforting, and filling dinner in less than half an hour. It also contains one of my favorite methods to get a toasty gravy base with lots of depth—toasting bread crumbs. After caramelizing the onions, you sprinkle in the bread crumbs and toss them around a bit until golden brown. Then, when you add the liquid ingredients, the bread crumbs thicken and flavor the gravy. It's wonderful served with grilled or sautéed kale, and over mashed potatoes (see page 231).

Preheat a large pan over medium-high heat and add the oil. Sauté the onion in the oil for 7 to 10 minutes, until lightly caramelized. Add the garlic and cook until fragrant, about 15 seconds. Add the bread crumbs and toss to coat the onions.

Now let the bread crumbs toast, tossing occasionally, for about 2 minutes, or until they are a few shades darker.

Add the sherry and mix so that the bread crumbs absorb the sherry. Cook for about 1 minute.

Add the thyme, salt, black pepper, and broth. Mix well, cover the pan, and turn the heat up to a boil. Once boiling, uncover the pan, lower the heat, and let the gravy simmer, bubble, and reduce. Once it's thickened to a gravy consistency, add the white beans and heat through. Add the lemon juice and taste for seasoning. Serve hot.

2 teaspoons olive oil

1 medium yellow onion, thinly sliced

3 cloves garlic, minced

¼ cup fine dry plain bread crumbs (see Notes)

¼ cup sherry

2 tablespoons fresh thyme

½ teaspoon salt

Several pinches of freshly ground black pepper

1½ cups vegetable broth

1 (15-ounce) can white beans, rinsed and drained (1½ cups)

2 tablespoons fresh lemon juice

NOTES:

- I use store-bought bread crumbs here, and they (for whatever reason) act a lot differently than homemade ones. You can make your own if you like, but use about ⅓ cup and make sure they are very fine and dry.

- Either great northern or navy beans would be great here. I think cannellini are a bit too big for this recipe, but you can use those if you like!

COCONUT CHANA SAAG

serves 6 · total time: 30 mins · active time: 20 mins

2 tablespoons refined coconut oil

1 medium yellow onion, diced

3 cloves garlic, minced

2 tablespoons minced fresh ginger

2 tablespoons mild curry powder

1 teaspoon salt

Several pinches of freshly ground black pepper

½ teaspoon anise seeds (or crushed fennel seeds)

¼ teaspoon garam masala

½ teaspoon ground cumin

¼ teaspoon cayenne (or more or less depending on how spicy you like it)

1 (24-ounce) can whole tomatoes

2 (15-ounce) cans chickpeas, rinsed and drained (3 cups)

8 ounces kale, chopped

1 (14-ounce) can regular or lite coconut milk

2 tablespoons fresh lime juice

For serving:

Cooked basmati rice

Mango chutney (store-bought)

Chopped fresh cilantro

NOTE:

Spinach is often used in saag, but I prefer sturdier greens that stay a bit more intact. Chard or collards will both work here (although collards will be a bit more rugged), but if you'd like to use spinach, you can add a few extra cups since it will break down more than its less delicate cousins.

Chickpeas and greens! I love the mix of plump chickpeas and cooked-down greens swimming in sultry spices. The versions I've had have typically been made in a tomato base, but I've seen it made with cream as well. I just decided to pair the two to make for a rich coconut-creamy tomato concoction that hits all the right notes. I love the hint of mystery that anise seeds bring to Indian-inspired food. Serve over basmati rice, and don't be ashamed to pick up a jar of mango chutney as well.

Preheat a 4-quart pot over medium heat and add the coconut oil. Sauté the onion in the oil for 5 to 7 minutes, until lightly browned.

Add the garlic and ginger and sauté until fragrant, about 30 seconds. Add the curry powder, salt, pepper, anise seeds, garam masala, cumin, and cayenne and toss to coat the onions, letting the spices toast a bit (for a minute or so).

Add the tomato juice from the can, scraping the bottom of the pan to deglaze. Simply hold the tomatoes and let the juice strain through your fingers. Now add the tomatoes from the can, squishing them with your fingers as you put them in the pot, to mash them up. Add the chickpeas and mix well.

Cover the pan and bring the heat up a bit. Let simmer for about 10 minutes, stirring occasionally. Add the kale and stir until wilted, then let simmer for 5 more minutes, uncovered, to cook it down even further.

Add the coconut milk and heat through. Add the lime juice, then taste for seasoning. It tastes best if you let it sit for 10 minutes or so, but if you can't wait, then just dig in!

Serve over basmati rice with a little mango chutney and cilantro on top.

CHANA MASALA

serves 8 to 10 · total time: 1 hour · active time: 30 mins

For the Masala Spice Blend:

1 tablespoon plus 1 teaspoon ground cumin

1 tablespoon ground coriander

1 teaspoon ground turmeric

½ teaspoon fennel seeds, chopped

½ teaspoon ground cardamom

¼ teaspoon ground cinnamon

¼ teaspoon ground cayenne (optional, and more or less to taste)

⅛ teaspoon ground cloves

For everything else:

3 tablespoons refined coconut oil

1 large yellow onion, sliced into medium pieces

2 jalapeños, seeded and thinly sliced

5 cloves garlic, minced

1 heaping tablespoon minced fresh ginger

¼ cup finely chopped fresh cilantro, plus extra for garnish (optional)

3 pounds tomatoes, diced

1 teaspoon salt

Freshly ground black pepper

2 (15-ounce) cans chickpeas, rinsed and drained (3 cups)

1 teaspoon agave nectar

Juice of 1 lime, or 1 teaspoon tamarind concentrate

Cooked basmati rice, for serving

As a teenage vegetarian, one of the very first dishes I ever tried to re-create at home was chana masala. This was before the invention of vegetables, so when I went out for Indian food in my neighborhood, it was usually chana masala, a samosa, and basmati rice. I probably started out with a recipe from somewhere, but I would just adjust, adjust, and adjust until it tasted like what I would get on Coney Island Avenue. Spicy, tangy, and fragrant, almost perfumed, with sweet spices like cardamom and cinnamon. The jalapeños probably have no place in chana masala, but hey, tell that to me twenty years ago.

This is one of those recipes that will help fine-tune your taste buds. Look for the spicy, the sour, the salty, and adjust until you're thoroughly pleased. Even after all this time, I'm still adding a little of this or that.

Preheat a large pan over medium heat. I prefer a pan to a pot, because it encourages the tomatoes to cook down faster.

PREPARE THE SPICE BLEND:

Meanwhile, mix together all of the ingredients for the spice blend in a small bowl.

PREPARE EVERYTHING ELSE:

When the pan is hot add the coconut oil and sauté the onion in the oil for about 10 minutes, until nicely browned.

Add the jalapeños, garlic, and ginger, and sauté until fragrant, about 30 seconds. Add the cilantro and sauté until wilted. Add the spice blend and toss to coat the onions, letting the spices toast a bit (for a minute or so).

Add the tomatoes and mix well, scraping the bottom of the pan to deglaze. Add the salt, pepper, chickpeas, and agave. Cover the pan and bring the heat up a bit. The tomatoes should take about 10 minutes to break down and get saucy. Remove the lid and cook for about 20 more minutes on low heat, so that the flavors meld and the sauce thickens. It shouldn't be too thick (like a marinara), but it shouldn't be watery, either.

Add the lime juice. Taste for seasoning. You might want to add a little of this or that. Let sit for 10 minutes or so off the heat before serving. Serve with basmati rice and garnish with extra cilantro, if you like!

DOWN-HOME CURRY

with Tofu & Broccoli

serves 6 · total time: 30 mins · active time: 30 mins

I crave this one-pot curry, loaded with lots of broccoli, tender potatoes and carrots, and bites of chunky tofu. Of course, tofu and broccoli are hardly traditional curry ingredients, but that's okay. This recipe is more about a few of my favorite things all thrown together to create a homey, filling, stick-to-your ribs meal that's easy enough to throw together anytime the feeling strikes you. Serve with some basmati rice for an extra dose of aromatherapy.

1 medium yellow onion, thinly sliced

1 tablespoon refined coconut oil

4 cloves garlic, minced

1 tablespoon fresh minced ginger

2 tablespoons curry powder

¼ teaspoon red pepper flakes

3 cups vegetable broth

2 tablespoons soy sauce or tamari

2 tablespoons pure maple syrup

2 tablespoons tomato paste

¾ pound Yukon Gold potatoes, cut in ¾-inch pieces

1 large carrot, peeled and sliced on a bias, ¼ inch thick

4 cups large broccoli florets

14 ounces tofu, cut into little triangles (see page 18)

1 cup regular or lite coconut milk

Cooked basmati rice, for serving

¼ cup finely chopped fresh cilantro, plus extra for garnish (optional)

Sriracha, for serving (optional)

Preheat a 4-quart pot over medium heat. Sauté the onion in the coconut oil for 5 to 7 minutes, until lightly browned.

Add the garlic and ginger, and sauté until fragrant, about 30 seconds. Add the curry powder, red pepper flakes, vegetable broth, soy sauce, maple syrup, and tomato paste, and stir. The tomato paste may not dissolve just yet but that's okay, it will when it heats through.

Add the potatoes and carrots, cover the pot, and bring to a boil. Once boiling, immediately lower the heat to a simmer and leave the lid ajar so that steam can escape. Let the potatoes cook just until tender, about 5 more minutes.

Once the potatoes are tender, add the broccoli, tofu, coconut milk, and cilantro. Stir gently to incorporate, being careful not to break up the tofu. Leave the lid ajar again and bring to a simmer. Let simmer just until the broccoli is tender; it should only take a few minutes.

Turn off the heat and taste for salt. It tastes best if you let it sit for 10 minutes or so, but if you can't wait, then just dig in!

Serve over basmati rice with fresh cilantro on top, if you like, and some sriracha on the side if you'd like more heat.

NOTES:

- If you want to compete on a cooking show or impress a date, you'll probably want to make your own curry powder. But if you simply want something comforting that tastes scrumptious and aromatic, then all you need is to find a curry powder that you love! There are premade curry blends out there that are perfectly delicious. One that is widely available and very dependable is Penzey's Sweet Mild Curry Powder.

- If you don't feel like tofu, then 1½ cups cooked chickpeas are a great substitute. Of course, there are already two other chickpea curry recipes here, but come on. Can you ever have enough chickpeas? And if you'd rather cauliflower than broccoli, you can make that substitution as well.

BHINDI MASALA
with Black-Eyed Peas

serves 6 · total time: 1 hour 10 mins · active time: 20 mins

For the longest time, the only way I enjoyed okra was in curry, and I thought it was high time I tried to re-create my favorite dish at home. Since I already loved to make gumbo, I essentially used that method, replacing the flour roux with a gluten-free chickpea flour. The result is a thick and saucy bowlful of curry, studded with black-eyed peas and juicy bites of okra. Serve with basmati rice to sop up all of its goodness, and dollop with some coconut-milk yogurt.

3 tablespoons refined coconut oil

2 teaspoons cumin seeds

⅓ cup chickpea flour

1 medium yellow onion, diced

1 teaspoon salt

3 cloves garlic, minced

2 tablespoons minced fresh ginger

1 (28-ounce) can whole tomatoes

2 tablespoons mild curry powder

1 cup vegetable broth, plus extra for thinning

2 cups sliced okra (about 10 ounces)

2 (15-ounce) cans black-eyed peas, rinsed and drained (3 cups)

For serving:

Cooked basmati rice

Plain unsweetened coconut milk yogurt

Fresh cilantro

Preheat a 4-quart pot over medium-low heat. Add 1 tablespoon of the coconut oil and toast the cumin seeds in the oil for a minute or so, until fragrant. Add the remaining 2 tablespoons oil and sprinkle in the chickpea flour. Use a wooden spatula to toss the flour in the oil, and stir pretty consistently for 3 to 4 minutes, until the flour is clumpy and toasty.

Add the onion and salt, and toss to coat the onion completely in the flour mixture. Cook this way for 5 minutes, stirring often. Add the garlic and ginger and stir for 1 more minute.

Drain the tomatoes, reserving the liquid. Crush up the tomatoes with your hands and add them to the pot, along with the curry powder, mixing for a few minutes until the tomatoes break down a bit and the mixture appears thick and saucy.

Stream in the broth, stirring constantly to prevent clumping. Now do the same with the remaining tomato juices. Add the okra and black-eyed peas, then turn the heat up and cover to bring to a boil. Stir occasionally.

Once boiling, reduce the heat to a simmer and let cook uncovered for 30 to 45 minutes, stirring occasionally, until the stew is nicely thickened and the okra is tender. If it's too thick, thin with a bit of vegetable broth. If it's not as thick as you like, just cook it a bit longer. Serve with basmati rice and topped with yogurt and cilantro.

RED SWEET POTATO CURRY

with Cauliflower & Adzuki Beans

serves 4 · total time: 90 mins · active time: 20 mins

This is a sweet and rich Thai-style curry. What makes it unique is that the base is created with mashed sweet potatoes instead of relying solely on coconut milk. Not only is it healthier than your average curry, it's also deliciously creamy and sweet. And of course bright orange! I love cauliflower in curry, but you can use broccoli or even Brussels sprouts. For protein, adzuki beans are a wonderful addition. They have a sweetness all their own and soak up lots of flavor. Serve over plenty of jasmine rice!

For the curry:

2 cups mashed sweet potatoes (about a pound, directions given below)

3 cloves garlic, minced

1 tablespoon minced ginger

2 teaspoons peanut oil

3 tablespoons red curry paste

2 cups vegetable broth

2 star anise

1 (15-ounce) can lite coconut milk

2 tablespoons soy sauce

½ teaspoon salt

Sriracha

Lime juice

For the veggies:

1½ cups thinly sliced shallots

1 tablespoon peanut oil

1 red bell pepper, seeded, thinly sliced

½ pound green beans, cut into 1-inch pieces

1 pound cauliflower, cut into small florets

½ cup water

1 (15-ounce) can adzuki beans, rinsed and drained (1½ cups)

For serving:

Jasmine rice

Chopped fresh cilantro

Lime wedges

First, you'll need baked sweet potatoes. Just preheat the oven to 350°F and place the sweet potatoes right on the oven rack, no poking or wrapping necessary (although, you might want to put a tray lined with tin foil under the rack to collect any juices that leak from the sweet potatoes). It takes about an hour for your average sweet potato to cook adequately. Make sure it's very soft and easily mashable without being chunky. Once cooled, peel and mash and set aside.

Preheat a 4-quart pot over medium-low heat. Sauté the garlic and ginger in the oil for about a minute, stirring often and being careful not to burn. Mix in the curry paste and get it warm, about a minute or so. Add the veggie broth and star anise, cover, and turn the heat up to bring to a boil. Let boil for about 5 minutes, to get the flavor out of the star anise.

Uncover, remove the star anise, and lower the heat to simmer. Add the sweet potato, coconut milk, soy sauce, and salt, and mash well. Try to get it as smooth as possible. You can use a immersion blender to make it completely smooth, although that may not be totally necessary, depending on how mushy your mashed potatoes are. Add sriracha and lime juice to taste.

PREPARE THE VEGGIES:

Preheat a large pan over medium-high heat. Sauté the shallots in the oil with a pinch of salt for about 5 minutes, until browned. Add the red pepper and green beans and sauté another 5 minutes. Have a cover ready and waiting, and add the cauliflower along with ½ cup water. Immediately cover the pan so that the cauli gets a burst of steam. Cook for about 3 minutes, covered. The cauliflower should be soft enough to eat but still firm.

Add the veggies and beans to the curry pot. Let sit for about 10 minutes so the flavors can marry. Serve over jasmine rice, garnished with cilantro and lime wedges.

NOTE:

You can prepare the veggies and the curry base at the same time. Get the shallots going for the veggies and then start the curry base. For some reason, the directions are really long! But it's not really a difficult recipe, I promise. All that's happening is you're preparing the saucy curry base in one pot and the veggies in a separate pan, then just throwing them together.

MUSHROOM HOT POT

serves 6 · total time: 1 hour · active time: 30 mins

Autumn in Omaha is slightly magical. The light seems to come in two varieties, silver or gold, and sometimes the glow makes it feel like the prairies are threatening to take over; like at any moment the concrete will start falling away and luscious grasses will spring up everywhere, wildflowers and meadow spreading out as far as the eye can see.

It was on a day like this that these flavors seemed to possess me. I was planning on a simple soup for lunch, standing in the produce aisle, examining some veggie or other, when seemingly out of nowhere my senses were overtaken by star anise, lemongrass, and ginger. Then the words formed on my lips: *hot pot.* The name alone should win you over on a rainy autumn day.

I first had hot pot at a Vietnamese restaurant, and you often see it called "Mongolian Hot Pot" on menus. But I'm not going to get into the history, primarily because I only have a GED, but also because I want to get to the fun part: the experience!

The idea is similar to fondue: a simmering vessel of rich broth surrounded by delicious tidbits that you can mix and match in your own bowl. You can totally dip, too, but I think it's more satisfying (and perhaps neater) to have your own little serving.

And if you're not going in for the whole ceremony of serving it with lots of accompaniments, that's fine, too. At its most basic, this is just a really delicious stew that will warm you right up. I'd say that the only necessary serving suggestions are some fresh herbs; everything else is up to you in terms of what you have time for, how many people you're serving, and how hungry everyone is.

1 tablespoon toasted sesame oil

1 tablespoon organic cornstarch

4 cups mushroom or vegetable broth

1 medium red onion, thinly sliced

1 red bell pepper, thinly sliced

Big pinch of salt

3 cloves garlic, minced

2 tablespoons minced lemongrass

1 tablespoon minced fresh ginger

½ teaspoon crushed red pepper flakes

2 whole star anise pods

¼ teaspoon ground cinnamon

1 ounce dried shiitake mushrooms

2 tablespoons tamari or soy sauce

1 medium tomato, coarsely chopped

Pinch of freshly ground black pepper

1 (15-ounce) can lite coconut milk

Juice of ½ lime

For serving (optional):

Cooked rice noodles or jasmine rice

Fresh cilantro leaves

Fresh basil leaves (Thai basil if you can find it)

Fresh mint leaves

Grilled Tofu (page 163)

Sriracha

Preheat a 4-quart pot over medium heat and add the oil. Mix the cornstarch into the broth and set aside (this is easiest if you just mix it into about a cup of the broth, then pour the rest of the broth in). Sauté the onions and red pepper in the oil with a big pinch of salt until the onions are soft, about 5 minutes.

Add the garlic, lemongrass, ginger, and red pepper flakes, and mix. Cook until fragrant, about 1 minute, then stream in the broth-cornstarch mixture and add most of the other ingredients: the star anise, cinnamon, shiitakes, tamari, tomatoes, and black pepper. Cook, stirring often for the first 10 minutes or so, until the cornstarch has thickened the broth a bit. Now cover the pot and bring to a boil. Once boiling, lower the heat and simmer, covered, for a good 30 minutes, until the mushrooms are completely softened.

Add the coconut milk and lime juice, and taste for salt. Heat through and serve with fresh herbs and other accoutrements.

(recipe continues)

Grilled Tofu

This is a really basic grilled tofu, with subtle hints of sesame. The real star is the charred flavor. Use a thin metal spatula to flip the tofu so that you can really get under it and have the charred bits stick to the tofu instead of the pan.

Preheat a large grill pan over medium-high heat.

Slice the tofu into triangles (see page 19). Drizzle the tamari and sesame oil on a dinner plate. Dredge the tofu triangles in the tamari-oil mixture.

When the pan is hot, brush or spray it with vegetable oil. Grill the triangles on each side for 3 to 5 minutes, until grill marks appear. Remove from the pan and serve!

14 ounces extra-firm tofu (you can press it first to remove excess moisture, but that's optional)

3 tablespoons tamari

1 tablespoon toasted sesame oil

Vegetable oil, for the pan

MORE SERVING SUGGESTIONS:

Roasted cashews, cooked adzuki beans, thinly sliced sautéed seitan, steamed broccoli or cauliflower, finely sliced bok choy, extra wedges of fresh lime.

NOTES:

· I don't actually have a fondue pot or anything, as tempting as they always look in thrift stores. You can just place the pot on a trivet in the middle of the table. It won't have a chance to get cold!

· I use dried shiitakes because they have an even more concentrated flavor than fresh, and they're also much cheaper. And since hot pot is often served with thinly sliced meats, these meaty morsels really do the job. If dried shiitakes aren't available, then fresh will work. But instead of simmering them in the stew, add them for the last 2 minutes of cooking, just to get them softened.

· Speaking of prairie grasses, have you cooked much with lemongrass? It adds a sultry perfume to stews, and it's really just a fun ingredient to work with. Who doesn't want to walk around the grocery store with tall stalks of grass poking out of the cart? You use only the inner core of the bulb at the very bottom of the stalk. Peel away the outer leaves until you get to the smooth, cool core. Cut off a sliver of the bottom and mince. You'll probably need 3 stalks for this recipe. You can also reserve the rest of the stalk for making a broth.

SMOKY INCAN STEW

serves 6 to 8 · total time: 45 mins · active time: 20 mins

If you put quinoa in something it automatically becomes Incan. Did denizens of Mesoamerica sit around eating stew day and night? Probably not, but I really needed to shorten the name, because Quinoa, Black Bean & Chipotle Stew with Sweet Potatoes & Corn would spill off the page! This stew gets its smokiness from chipotles. Quinoa and black beans make it hearty and filling, and sweet potatoes add a naturally sweet touch. If you can, use fresh corn instead of frozen because it's really worth it here. Since it's added at the end, you get a fresh, snappy bite from each kernel.

Preheat a 4-quart pot over medium heat and add the oil. Sauté the onion in the oil with a pinch of salt for about 5 minutes, until translucent. Add the garlic and sauté until fragrant, about 30 seconds. Add the chipotles, quinoa, broth, remaining ¾ teaspoon salt, and pepper. Cover the pot and bring to a boil. Let boil for 7 minutes, until the quinoa is almost ready.

Lower the heat to a simmer and add the sweet potatoes. Cover the pot and simmer for about 12 minutes. The sweet potatoes should be tender and the quinoa fully cooked. Add the corn, tomatoes, black beans, and cilantro and simmer for about 7 minutes, just until everything is heated through. It tastes best if you let it sit for a few minutes before serving, allowing the flavors to marry. You may need to add some of the reserved tomato juice to thin it out to your liking. Serve hot.

1 tablespoon olive oil

1 medium yellow onion, diced

¾ teaspoon salt, plus a pinch

3 cloves garlic, minced

¼ cup chopped chipotles in adobo sauce, seeded

¾ cup quinoa (red quinoa looks prettiest)

4 cups vegetable broth

Freshly ground black pepper

1½ pounds sweet potatoes, peeled and cut into ¾-inch chunks

1½ cups corn kernels, preferably fresh (see page 181; but frozen is okay)

1 (15-ounce) can whole tomatoes, drained and juice reserved, tomatoes crushed into pieces (see Note)

1 (15-ounce) can black beans, rinsed and drained (1½ cups)

½ cup loosely packed fresh cilantro, chopped

Heat of the Moment

Working with chipotles can be a serious pain in the butt, but they're worth it! Slice them lengthwise with a paring knife, then scrape the seeds out with the back of the knife and discard. It's okay if you don't get absolutely every single seed out; just do your best. The less seeds, the less heat, which means you can add more chipotles for maximum smokiness and flavor, keeping the spiciness pleasant.

You're bound to have extra chipotles. You can store them in a plastic bag in the fridge and use within a week, but it's unlikely that you'll be using chipotles twice in one week. What I like to do is store them in plastic and freeze. That way, whenever a dish could use a little spicy kick, I just break off a little frozen piece of chipotle.

NOTES:

- The recipe calls for a can of whole tomatoes, but only the tomatoes are used at first. The juice in the can may be used to thicken the stew, or maybe you want to make a Bloody Mary or something? For prepping the tomatoes, you can just crush them with your hands. I do this right over the pot when it comes time to add them. Just grab one out of the can and squeeze between your fingers. It's messy fun! Fresh tomatoes may be subbed, but add them along with the quinoa so that they have time to break down. About 1½ cups chopped fresh tomatoes ought to do it.

- One more thing: Touching hot peppers can really burn you, so handle them briefly and carefully, and wash your hands with soapy water immediately after. You can even wear rubber gloves if you want to be extra careful.

OKRA GUMBO
with Chickpeas & Kidney Beans

serves 6 · total time: 1 hour · active time: 25 mins

3 tablespoons olive oil

¼ cup all-purpose flour

1 medium yellow onion, coarsely chopped

1 teaspoon salt

3 cloves garlic, minced

2 ribs celery, thinly sliced

1 heaping cup diced sweet red bell peppers

2 cups chopped tomatoes

Freshly ground black pepper

2 bay leaves

2 teaspoons smoked paprika

8 sprigs fresh thyme, plus extra for garnish

2½ to 3 cups vegetable broth, at room temperature

2 cups okra (about 10 ounces), sliced ¼ inch thick or so

1 (15-ounce) can kidney beans, rinsed and drained (1½ cups)

1 (15-ounce) can chickpeas, rinsed and drained (1½ cups)

1 tablespoon fresh lemon juice

Cooked rice, for serving

Oh, how lucky I feel when there's finally okra at the farmers' market. I immediately know what I must do, I mean, no brainer. *Gumbo.* Thick and tangy and filled to the brim with veggies straight from the garden and two kinds of beans. A toasty roux, fresh tomatoes, plenty of onion and garlic, fresh thyme, and, of course, okra. If you're an okra newbie, or maybe just afraid to cook with it, this is a great recipe to start with. I use lots of veggie broth to thin the roux and cook the okra, and then I reduce it with a long simmer, making for a thick and velvety sauce that is not at all slimy.

First we're going to make a roux, but it has a little less fat than a traditional roux, which means it doesn't get as goopy. If you'd like a more traditional roux, just add 3 additional tablespoons vegetable oil.

Preheat a large, heavy-bottomed pot over medium-low heat. The wider the pot, the better, so that you have lots of surface area to make your roux. Add the oil and sprinkle in the flour. Use a wooden spatula to toss the flour in the oil, and stir pretty consistently for 3 to 4 minutes, until the flour is clumpy and toasty.

Add the onions and salt, and toss to coat the onions completely in the flour mixture. Cook for 5 minutes, stirring often. Add the garlic and stir for 30 seconds or so.

Add the celery, peppers, and tomatoes and cook for about 10 more minutes. As the tomatoes break down, the mixture should become thick and pasty.

Season with black pepper, add the bay leaves, smoked paprika, and thyme, and mix well.

Stream in the 2½ cups vegetable broth, stirring constantly to prevent clumping. Add the okra and both kinds of beans, then turn the heat up and cover to bring to a boil, stirring occasionally. Once boiling, reduce the heat and simmer, uncovered, for 30 to 45 minutes, stirring occasionally, until the stew is nicely thickened and the okra is tender. If it's too thick, thin with up to ½ cup additional vegetable broth. If it's not as thick as you like, just cook it a bit longer.

Add the lemon juice and taste for seasoning. Remove the bay leaves and thyme stems (if you can find them), then serve in a big, wide bowl, topped with a scoop of rice and garnished with fresh thyme sprigs.

RED LENTIL
THAI CHILI

serves 8 to 10 · total time: 40 mins · active time: 15 mins

You know those food magazines that you flip through while in the checkout line at the supermarket? The ones you put back on the rack, all the better for knowing that you can make a casserole out of a can of soup and thirty-five egg whites? Yeah, well, I buy those magazines. All of them. It is my secret shame.

But every once in a while you get a great idea, and for this recipe it was a magazine cover that gave me the chutzpah to do what I've always wanted to—put Thai red curry paste in everything. Or at least in chili!

This isn't their exact recipe; I just ripped off the idea (I do have *some* integrity). It's just as awesome as you would imagine if you threw together a Thai curry and a chili. Okay, fine, maybe that doesn't sound awesome, but it was! I used red lentils for texture and kept the main ingredients as is: sweet potatoes and big, meaty kidney beans. It's really satisfying and blessedly easy, so make it the next time you want to switch up your chili repertoire. It makes a lot, too, so freeze the leftovers and have chili whenever you want.

1 tablespoon olive oil

1 large yellow onion, diced

1 red bell pepper, diced

1 teaspoon salt, plus a pinch

3 cloves garlic, minced

1 1/2 pounds sweet potatoes, cut into 3/4-inch chunks

1 cup red lentils

4 cups vegetable broth

2 tablespoons chili powder

2 (15-ounce) cans kidney beans, rinsed and drained (3 cups)

2 tablespoons Thai red curry paste

1 (15-ounce) can lite coconut milk

1 (28-ounce) can diced tomatoes

1/2 cup chopped fresh cilantro, plus extra for garnish

Lime wedges, for garnish (optional)

Preheat a 4-quart pot over medium heat and add the oil. Sauté the onion and bell pepper in the oil with a pinch of salt for 5 to 7 minutes. Add the garlic and sauté for 1 more minute.

Add the sweet potatoes, lentils, broth, chili powder, and remaining 1 teaspoon salt. Cover and bring to a boil. Let boil for 15 to 20 minutes, stirring occasionally to prevent burning. When the lentils are soft and mushy and the sweet potatoes are tender, add the kidney beans, curry paste, coconut milk, tomatoes, and cilantro, and heat through.

Taste for seasoning, top with cilantro and lime wedges, if desired, and serve.

MEATY BEANY CHILI

serves 8 to 10 • total time: 1 hour • active time: 20 mins

1 tablespoon olive oil

1 medium yellow onion, diced

1 green bell pepper, diced

2 jalapeños, thinly sliced (seeded if you want it less spicy)

1½ teaspoons salt, plus a pinch

6 cloves garlic, minced

3 to 4 tablespoons mild chili powder

1 tablespoon dried Mexican oregano

2 teaspoons ground cumin

Several pinches of freshly ground black pepper

⅛ teaspoon ground cloves

4 cups water, plus more as needed

1 cup brown lentils

1 (28-ounce) can crushed tomatoes

1 (15-ounce) can kidney beans, rinsed and drained (1½ cups)

1 (15-ounce) can black beans, rinsed and drained (1½ cups)

2 tablespoons fresh lime juice

1 tablespoon pure maple syrup

NOTES:

• If you don't want to futz with two different kinds of whole beans, either kidney or black beans could go solo, instead.

• Start with 4 cups of water and thin it from there as needed. There's no telling how much it will cook down, and it's easier to thin a chili than it is to thicken it.

I'm no Texas chili expert, but I am a culinary reality TV expert, and one thing that's for sure is that if chefs on a cooking competition talk about Texas, they talk about chili. And if they talk about chili, they have to state no fewer than ten times that Texas chili has no beans in it. They'll say it in slo-mo and with echo and dubbed over techno music. Texas chili has no beans. Did you hear that? *No beans!* So this is my reverse homage to Texas chili. A mean pot of stew filled with all my favorite beans! It's thick and stick-to-your-ribs and super-duper meaty, thanks to the cooked-down lentils. Serve with Cornbread Muffins (page 264) and Pepe's Secret Guacamole (page 233) or avocado.

Preheat a 4-quart pot over medium-high heat and add the oil. Sauté the onion, green pepper, and jalapeños in the oil with a big pinch of salt for 5 to 7 minutes, until the onion is translucent.

Add the garlic and sauté until fragrant, about 30 seconds. Add the chili powder (start with 3 tablespoons and go from there), oregano, cumin, remaining 1½ teaspoons salt, black pepper, and cloves and toss to coat the onions, letting the spices toast a bit (for a minute or so).

Add the 4 cups water and scrape the bottom of the pan to deglaze. Add the lentils, cover the pot, and turn the heat up to bring to a boil. Let boil for about 20 minutes, stirring every now and again. The lentils should still be firm but almost tender enough to eat.

Add the tomatoes, kidney beans, and black beans. Cover the pot and turn the heat down to a simmer. Let cook for about 30 more minutes, stirring occasionally. The lentils should be quite mushy, almost melting into the chili. You may also need to add more water, depending on how much the chili has cooked down. Adding up to 2 cups more would not be unheard of.

Add the lime juice and maple syrup, and then taste for seasoning. It tastes best if you let it sit for 10 minutes or so before serving, but if you can't wait, then just dig in!

STIR-FRIES & SAUTÉS

I think it's important to know what 'AUTHENTIC' food is,

but I definitely don't let the idea box me in. Especially as a vegan chef, I'm constantly playing with traditions and concepts, creating vegan translations of classics and breathing new life into old favorites. But the bottom line is that no matter what culinary roads I travel, my food will always be a reflection of the world as seen by a Jewish-American woman from Brooklyn. As obsessed as I am with how things are *really* done, I will never be able to do them that way. Will I ever be able to make a stir-fry like a Cantonese chef? Of course not! The only way for me to get a stir-fry the way I like is to cook things separately, in a cast-iron pan, at a very high heat and very quickly. It doesn't have to be as fussy as it sounds—as each ingredient cooks you can prep the next, so everything should be ready quickly. This chapter starts off with the scrumptious flavors of Asia, but it doesn't end there. Sautés employ similar methods, and once you've got these stovetop techniques mastered, you'll start tossing around all manner of veggies and grains, transforming them into dinner in no time at all.

BEEFY ASPARAGUS STIR-FRY

with Fresh Herbs

serves 4 · total time: 30 mins · active time: 30 mins

For the sauce:

½ cup vegetable broth, chilled

2 teaspoons organic cornstarch

6 tablespoons soy sauce

1 to 2 tablespoons sriracha (see Notes)

2 tablespoons fresh lime juice

2 tablespoons agave nectar

2 tablespoons finely chopped fresh mint

2 tablespoons finely chopped fresh Thai basil or regular basil

For everything else:

2 tablespoons toasted sesame oil

1 pound seitan, cut into thin strips

Several pinches of freshly ground black pepper

1 cup thinly sliced shallots

8 ounces asparagus, bottom stems removed, cut into 1½-inch pieces

2 tablespoons minced fresh ginger

2 cloves garlic, minced

½ cup toasted cashews (see Notes)

1 cup bean sprouts

For serving:

Cooked jasmine rice

Extra fresh mint and/or basil

NOTES:

- You can buy roasted cashews, in which case no need to toast them. But if you'd like to toast raw cashews, I think they taste extra special. Just preheat a small pan over medium-low heat, add the cashews, and dry-toast them for about 5 minutes, flipping often. You can do this while your seitan is cooking.

- For the sriracha, I love 2 tablespoons in the sauce, but that is a little too spicy for some people's palates. Start with 1 tablespoon and see how that suits you, then go ahead and add the other if you like.

I think that beef and asparagus from a Chinese takeout in Brooklyn was my first introduction to that beautiful floral spear of a veggie, and I haven't looked back. This version is brightened up with the influence of Southeast Asian flavorings, like mint and Thai basil. And of course a healthy dose of my favorite spicy rooster friend, sriracha. The end result is a peppery and herbaceous brown gravy that clings to the seared seitan and asparagus like a best buddy. Some toasted cashews add a fun, decadent bite, and bean sprouts add a fresh crunch!

Sometimes stir-fry ingredient lists can look daunting (the good ones, anyway), but all you're doing is tossing some stuff around in a skillet and mixing up a sauce to pour in at the end. No big whoop.

PREPARE THE SAUCE:

You can do this while everything else is cooking or do it beforehand. Mix together the broth and cornstarch until well dissolved. Add the soy sauce, sriracha, lime juice, and agave and mix well, then mix in the mint and basil. Set aside.

PREPARE EVERYTHING ELSE:

Preheat a large, heavy pan over medium-high heat and add 2 teaspoons of the sesame oil. Sauté the seitan in the oil, along with a few pinches of black pepper, until seared on both sides, 5 to 7 minutes. Transfer to a plate and set aside.

Sauté the shallots in the pan with 2 more teaspoons of the oil and a pinch of salt until browned, about 5 minutes. Add the asparagus and 1 more teaspoon of the oil. Toss often for about 3 minutes, or until they are bright green. You want them to have some snap to them, so be careful not to overcook (although if you do, no biggie, just remember for next time).

Push the veggies to the side, and add the ginger and garlic to a clear spot. Drizzle the remaining 1 teaspoon oil into the pan and toss for about 15 seconds, just until fragrant, and then toss it together with the veggies.

Add the seitan back to the pan. Now add the sauce and turn up the heat to bring it to a boil. It should thicken and reduce in about 3 minutes. Once thick, add the cashews and bean sprouts and toss to coat. Serve immediately over rice, topped with fresh herbs if desired.

CAST-IRON STIR-FRY
with Avocado, Basil & Peanuts

serves 4 • total time: 30 mins • active time: 30 mins

This, my favorite weeknight stir-fry, typifies what I love about stir-frying. Broccoli, some red onion and bell pepper, and beautifully browned tofu. It's delicious enough, for sure, but what really makes it are the garnishes. I love the California flavors here: peanut, avocado, and fresh basil are the bestest besties in the world, and perfect for cooling off the stir-fry, adding creaminess, crunch, and a burst of freshness.

Preheat a cast-iron pan over high heat. Mix together all of the sauce ingredients and set aside.

Have at the ready a baking pan or large bowl to hold the ingredients as they finish cooking. I like to use a 9 x 13–inch pan so that there's plenty of room and things aren't sitting on top of each other and steaming.

Once the cast-iron pan is good and hot, apply 2 teaspoons of the oil. Add the cubed tofu and sprinkle with ¼ teaspoon of the salt and some black pepper. The ingredients should immediately sizzle when they hit the pan; otherwise, turn the heat up. Cook for about 7 minutes, tossing often and spraying with oil as necessary, until the tofu is nicely browned. Not all sides have to be evenly browned; just as long as a few of them are, you're good to go.

Transfer the tofu to the baking pan or bowl and proceed with the broccoli. Apply 2 teaspoons of the oil, toss in the broccoli, and add ¼ teaspoon of the salt and some black pepper. Cook until the broccoli is charred and bright green, about 5 minutes. Cover the pan between tosses so that it cooks faster. Transfer to the pan with the tofu.

Now proceed with the onion and bell pepper. Apply the remaining 2 teaspoons oil and toss in the onion and pepper. Sprinkle with the remaining ¼ teaspoon salt and some black pepper. Cook for about 3 minutes; they should be charred but still crisp. Transfer to the pan with the tofu. Now we'll finish it off with the sauce.

Add the garlic, ginger, and crushed red pepper flakes to the cast-iron pan and sauté until fragrant (about 1 minute) being careful not to burn (add more oil if necessary). Add the sauce and mix together until heated through and bubbly, about 2 minutes.

Add back all the veggies and the tofu and toss to coat. Taste for seasoning.

Serve over quinoa or brown rice, top with the avocado, peanuts, and basil, and serve hot.

For the sauce:

2 tablespoons hoisin sauce

2 tablespoons mirin (Japanese rice wine for cooking)

2 tablespoons water

1 tablespoon plus 1 teaspoon soy sauce or tamari

1 tablespoon agave nectar

For everything else:

2 tablespoons toasted sesame oil

14 ounces tofu, cubed or cut into tiny triangles (press it if you have the time; otherwise, just blot with a paper towel to remove moisture)

¾ teaspoon salt

Several pinches of freshly ground black pepper

1 pound broccoli, cut into florets, stems sliced ¼ inch thick

1 small red onion, sliced into half-moons

1 bell pepper (red, yellow, or orange), sliced ¼ inch thick

4 cloves garlic, minced

2 teaspoons minced fresh ginger

1 teaspoon crushed red pepper flakes (use less if you're a spice wimp)

Cooked quinoa or brown rice, for serving

For the garnish:

1 avocado, pitted, peeled and diced

½ cup roasted salted peanuts

2 big handfuls fresh basil leaves, cut into chiffonade (or thinly sliced)

OMAHA YAKISOBA

with Red Cabbage & Corn

serves 2 · total time: 20 mins · active time: 20 mins

1 tablespoon plus 1 teaspoon toasted
   sesame oil

3 cups broccoli florets

2 cups thinly sliced red cabbage

4 ounces shiitake mushrooms, cut into
   ¼-inch slices

1 cup fresh corn kernels (from 2 ears
   of corn; see page 181)

2 cloves garlic, minced

1 tablespoon minced fresh ginger

3 tablespoons soy sauce

3 tablespoons vegetable broth

2 tablespoons mirin (Japanese rice
   wine for cooking)

2 teaspoons sriracha

1 (12-ounce) package precooked udon
   noodles (see Notes)

1 cup chopped scallions

NOTES:

- Make sure the pan is plenty hot!
  Everything should sizzle as it touches
  down. Flick a little water from your
  fingers into the pan to test once it's
  been preheated; the water should
  evaporate almost immediately.

- You can buy ready-to-eat udon noodles
  in the refrigerated section of many
  supermarkets. They are so convenient! I
  run them under warm water for a minute
  just to get them to separate, and then
  toss 'em right into the pan. But read the
  package directions and follow them, just
  in case they're a little different.

- You can also, of course, boil your own
  noodles—4 ounces ought to do it. Since
  udon comes in many varieties, make sure
  you get the thick kind. Otherwise, I feel
  you'd be missing out.

- This recipe serves two—any more
  ingredients than that won't fit in the pan
  at the same time. If you'd like to double
  the recipe, it's so incredibly fast that
  you can just make two separate batches.
  If you prep all the veggies for both
  batches together, I bet you can still get
  everything on the table in 30 minutes.

Honestly, I had never had yakisoba until I moved to Omaha. Why not? Because I've been a spoiled New Yorker for most of my life and there are a zillion vegan options at NYC Japanese restaurants. In Omaha, not so much. And the thing is, nine times out of ten when I go out to eat here in the Big O, I end up at a sushi place. But woman cannot live on cucumber rolls alone! Luckily, there's always a stir-fried noodle dish on the menu, so yakisoba it is.

You'd think that I'd get tired of the one thing I always order, but instead I began to crave it. It's pretty twisted, but really, how could you not? Big, fat udon noodles are so satisfying, all coated in a salty-gingery soy sauce. Lots and lots of veggies make it not only beautiful but also a gigantic bowl of noodles that's a feast for the eyes. Broccoli, red cabbage, a handful of shiitakes, and to make it even more Nebraska, you can't forget the fresh corn. If you'd like to bulk it up, some cubes of tofu or Sesame Tofu (page 239) should do the trick. You could also toss in some roasted cashews.

Preheat a large pan over medium heat and add 1 tablespoon of the oil. Sauté the broccoli in the oil for about 5 minutes, until bright green. Add splashes of water if it seems to get dry. Add the cabbage and mushrooms, and cook for about 3 minutes, until the cabbage is wilted but still a little snappy. Add the corn and toss to warm through.

Push all the veggies aside and add the garlic and ginger to the pan. Quickly drizzle the remaining 1 teaspoon oil over the garlic and ginger and toss for a few seconds, until fragrant; then mix in among the rest of the veggies.

Add the soy sauce, broth, mirin, and sriracha to the pan and toss to coat. Let that cook down for about 1 minute. Add the noodles and toss again to coat. Last, toss in the scallions, and then serve.

EVERYDAY PAD THAI

serves 4 · total time: 30 mins · active time: 30 mins

The quintessential sweet-and-sour Thai noodle. Also, the key to my heart. If I didn't think it would leave me with some sort of vitamin deficiency, I'd probably eat Pad Thai for every meal. This recipe introduces my super top-secret ingredient. Um, as usual, it's miso. It adds a bit of fermented depth that mimics traditional fish sauce. Usually pad thai is made to order, one at a time. But if I have no one to impress, I'm not going through that trouble. This isn't exactly authentic, but it gets the job done with common ingredients and has a great balance of sweet, sour, spice, and salt.

You'll need a large cast-iron pan for the tofu, or something nonstick that can take very high heat. Preheat the pan over high heat. Once the pan is good and hot, apply 1 tablespoon of the oil. Add the cubed tofu and sprinkle with about ¼ teaspoon of the salt. The tofu should immediately sizzle when it hits the hot pan; otherwise, turn up the heat. Cook for about 7 minutes, tossing often, until it's nicely browned.

PREPARE THE SAUCE:

In the meantime, mix together all of the ingredients for the sauce and set aside. The miso may not completely dissolve, but that's okay; just get it as smooth as possible.

When the tofu is browned, transfer it to a plate and cover loosely with aluminum foil to keep warm. In the same pan, cook the broccoli in 2 teaspoons of the oil with the remaining ¼ teaspoon salt. Cover the pan in between stirring to get it to cook faster. It should take about 5 minutes and be lightly charred in some places. Transfer to the same plate as the tofu.

Now we'll cook the sauce. Lower the heat to medium. Cook the garlic in the remaining 1 teaspoon oil very briefly, about 15 seconds. Add the scallions and cilantro and toss just to get it wilted. Now pour in about half the sauce and heat it through.

Add the noodles and toss to coat. Then add back the tofu and broccoli, the bean sprouts, and the remaining sauce, and toss to coat.

Serve immediately, topped with peanuts and lime wedges, plus extra cilantro if desired.

2 tablespoons vegetable oil

14 ounces tofu, cut into ½-inch cubes

½ teaspoon salt

For the sauce:

2 tablespoons tomato paste

5 tablespoons soy sauce

6 tablespoons light brown sugar

¼ cup fresh lime juice

2 tablespoons sriracha

2 tablespoons mellow white miso

¼ cup water

For everything else:

4 cups broccoli florets and thinly sliced stems

4 cloves garlic, minced

2 cups scallions chopped into 1-inch pieces

1 cup loosely packed fresh cilantro, chopped, plus more for garnish (optional)

8 ounces pad thai rice noodles, cooked according to package directions, immediately rinsed with cold water and cooled

4 ounces mung bean sprouts

¾ cup chopped roasted peanuts

Lime wedges, for serving

NOTES:

- Rice noodles come packed in different quantities, and nothing seems to be consistent. I think that 8 ounces is just about perfect. If you have a package that is more than that, I would suggest making all of the noodles and using the leftovers in a salad the next day. Perhaps with some leftover curried peanut sauce (see page 199)? But more than 8 ounces in this dish makes it really difficult to stir the noodles properly.

- I make this all in one pan. While the tofu browns, I prep everything else. You might save a little time by using two pans, but this method has served me well.

MANGO FRIED RICE

serves 4 to 6 · total time: 30 mins · active time: 30 mins

3/4 cup cashews

6 ounces green beans, trimmed and sliced into 1-inch pieces (about 1½ cups)

3 tablespoons peanut or canola oil

Several pinches of salt

1 medium red onion, diced

3 cloves garlic, minced

1 tablespoon minced fresh ginger

2 teaspoons coriander seeds, crushed

¼ teaspoon crushed red pepper flakes

6 cups cooked jasmine rice, chilled

3 tablespoons tamari or soy sauce

1 tablespoon sriracha

1 medium tomato, diced into ½-inch pieces

2 mangos, peeled, pitted, and sliced into ½-inch pieces (about 1½ cups)

15 fresh basil leaves, cut into chiffonade

2 tablespoons fresh lime juice

For serving:
Fresh cilantro (optional)
Sriracha

NOTES:

- I'm no mango-slicing aficionado by any stretch of the imagination. But this is what I do: peel off the skin with a veggie peeler, stand it on its head, and use a chef's knife to slice off one side along the pit. Once you've got that side sliced off, you can lay the mango on its flat side for balance and slice off the rest of the fruit, getting as close to the pit as possible. Then just cut into manageable pieces. They don't have to be perfectly uniform; you're not on *Top Chef*. But there are many tutorials online about how to slice a mango perfectly.

- The rice has to be cold for this recipe to work correctly; otherwise it will get mushy and sticky. Many supermarkets carry frozen bags of rice for reasonable prices. I created this recipe with a standard 20-ounce bag of rice in mind. But you can certainly chill or freeze your own (see page 12)!

This rice is tangy and spicy, panfried with lots of ginger, garlic, and a little crushed coriander seeds, then punctuated with seared but still snappy green beans, toasty cashews, and juicy bits of sweet fruit. Then you finish it off with some lime and fresh basil leaves, making the dish so fragrant and heavenly that you might be inspired to start a Mango Fried Rice food cart. I didn't make it too oily, but the frying is definitely a part of its addictiveness (although you can feel free to cut the oil by half or so).

I think this is a meal in itself, what with the cashews for protein and the fiber from the veggies and rice. But if you want, you can sauté up some tofu (see page 175) and toss it in, or try the Sesame Tofu (page 239). If using roasted cashews, you can skip the toasting step and save yourself a few minutes.

Preheat a large, heavy-bottomed pan over medium heat. Toss in the cashews and dry-toast them for about 5 minutes, flipping occasionally. They should be slightly browned in some spots, but it's okay if they're unevenly browned; you don't have to be too precise about it. Transfer the cashews to a large plate.

Now we're going to sear the green beans. Turn the heat up to medium-high. Add the green beans, a scant 1 tablespoon of the oil, and a pinch of salt. Cook for 3 to 5 minutes, until the beans are bright green and seared. Transfer the beans to the same plate as the cashews.

Add the onion to the pan, along with another 1 tablespoon of the oil, and a pinch of salt. Toss for about 3 minutes, until slightly charred but still firm. Add the garlic, ginger, coriander, and crushed red pepper flakes, and toss for 30 seconds or so, being careful not to burn.

Add the remaining 1 tablespoon oil and about half of the cold rice. Toss to coat, then add in the remaining rice, tossing once again. Cook for about 3 minutes, tossing often, until warmed through.

Add the tamari, sriracha, and tomato, and toss. Cook for another 3 minutes, until the rice has browned sufficiently and the tomato is slightly broken down.

Add the green beans and cashews, mangos, basil leaves, and lime juice. Cook just until the mangos are heated through and the basil is wilted, a minute or two. Taste for salt (don't add more tamari, just add salt if it needs it) and serve, garnished with cilantro, if you like, and with a bottle of sriracha close by.

SUMMER SEITAN SAUTÉ
with Cilantro & Lime

serves 4 • total time: 30 mins • active time: 30 mins

I got turned on to this combination as a burrito filling when I was cooking in a café in Brooklyn, and I've been hooked ever since! I don't go too crazy with the spices, instead letting the bright and fresh flavors shine through. Mushrooms, cilantro, and lime have an affinity for each other, and the fresh corn adds a wonderful summery pop, while the seared seitan, of course, provides meatiness. But no need to serve in a tortilla. I love it over rice with a nice big scoop of guacamole. Oh, and make my margarita salted!

2 tablespoons olive oil

1 medium red onion, thinly sliced into half-moons

1 jalapeño, thinly sliced (seeded if you want less heat)

½ teaspoon salt, plus a pinch

8 ounces seitan, thinly sliced

1 cup fresh corn kernels (from 2 ears of corn; see Notes)

8 ounces cremini mushrooms, sliced into thin strips

¼ cup chopped fresh cilantro, plus more for garnish (optional)

Several pinches of freshly ground black pepper

3 cloves garlic, minced

3 tablespoons fresh lime juice

Preheat a large, heavy-bottomed pan over medium-high heat (cast iron, as always, is ideal) and add 2 teaspoons of the oil. Sauté the onion and jalapeño in the oil with a pinch of salt until translucent, 3 to 5 minutes.

Add the seitan and corn and an additional 1 tablespoon of the oil and cook for about 5 minutes, until the seitan is lightly browned, stirring often.

Add the mushrooms, cilantro, remaining ½ teaspoon salt, and pepper and cook for about 5 minutes.

Push everything to one side of the pan so that you have space to quickly sauté the garlic. Put the remaining 1 teaspoon oil in the pan and toss in the garlic, stirring as it sizzles for about 15 seconds. Then mix everything together, and add the lime juice as well.

Taste for seasonings, and serve. Garnish with fresh cilantro, if desired.

NOTES:

- To cut down on prep time, you can often find shucked corn on the cob at the supermarket. It's a great shortcut that doesn't compromise on flavor. If you absolutely must, then frozen corn will work. But really try for fresh. It adds a wonderful snap to the dish that just screams "summer." Without the sunburn.

- If you do go for the fresh, it's easy to get those kernels off quickly and neatly. Place the shucked corn stem side down in a wide bowl. Hold it steady by the tip top and use your knife to slice from top to bottom, letting the kernels fall into the bowl. Continue on all four sides, and voilà! Fresh, delicious corn.

- For time-management purposes, prep the corn and mushrooms while the seitan is cooking. Everything should come together in a breezy 30 minutes.

STICKY ORANGE
CHICKY STIR-FRY

serves 4 · total time: 30 mins · active time: 30 mins

2 tablespoons toasted sesame oil

2 Steamed Chicky Seitan cutlets, sliced ¼ inch thick

For the sauce:

1 cup fresh orange juice

¼ cup agave nectar

2 teaspoons grated orange zest

3 tablespoons soy sauce

2 tablespoons mirin (Japanese rice wine for cooking)

1 tablespoon plus 1 teaspoon organic cornstarch

For everything else:

1 cup thinly sliced shallots

1 red bell pepper, thinly sliced

2 teaspoons minced fresh ginger

3 cloves garlic, minced

½ teaspoon crushed red pepper flakes

6 ounces green beans, trimmed and cut into 1-inch pieces (about 1½ cups)

Cooked rice, for serving

Thinly sliced scallions, for garnish

Toasted sesame seeds, for garnish

Mmm, there was a time in my life when I practically lived on stir-fries with sticky-sweet orange sauce. This version tastes pretty classy, with undertones of sesame, ginger, a little spice, and of course plenty of orange goodness coating strips of chicken-style seitan. For best results, used freshly squeezed OJ, from about 3 navel oranges. Serve over basmati rice and let it soak up the extra sauce. Orange heaven!

If you'd like to use tofu instead of the Steamed Chicky Seitan (page 241), just follow the tofu directions for the cast-iron stir-fry method (see page 175).

Preheat a large pan over medium-high heat and add 1 tablespoon of the oil. Sauté the sliced Chicky Seitan cutlets in the oil until lightly browned, about 5 minutes.

PREPARE THE SAUCE:

In the meantime, vigorously mix together all of the ingredients for the sauce until the cornstarch is dissolved, and set aside.

PREPARE EVERYTHING ELSE:

When the Chicky Seitan slices are browned, transfer to a plate and cover with aluminum foil to keep warm.

Now, in that same pan, over medium heat, sauté the shallots in the remaining 1 tablespoon oil for 3 minutes or so, until lightly browned. Add the red bell pepper and cook for 2 minutes, just until softened. Add the ginger, garlic, and crushed red pepper flakes and sauté for 30 seconds or so, just until fragrant. Add the green beans and sauté for 2 minutes or so. You want them to retain their crispness.

Pour in the sauce and toss to coat everything. When it begins to bubble and thicken (after about 5 minutes), toss in the Chicky Seitan. Let cook for another few minutes, until thick and dark. Serve immediately over rice, topped with scallions and sesame seeds.

SEITAN & BROCCOLI

with Pantry BBQ Sauce

serves 4 · total time: 30 mins · active time: 20 mins

I find most store-bought barbecue sauce to be cloyingly sweet, so when I want barbecue, I head for my pantry. The great thing about this sauce is that you can customize it to your heart's content. Want more spice? Add extra sriracha. More sweetness? Add more mapley goodness. For more tang, well, there's the mustard—have at it! It's really as easy as can be.

I used to call it 2x2 BBQ Sauce because it took 2 minutes and everything was 2 tablespoons (except for the liquid smoke), so it was easy to memorize, but I have since refined it down to these measurements.

Still, I never have to actually measure anything, I just eyeball it. The peanut butter is my secret ingredient—it doesn't make the sauce very peanutty, but it gives excellent texture and a flavor that will keep people guessing. In a good way. Unless they are allergic. So ask.

Serve over rice or mashed potatoes, and if you'd like to include Cornbread Muffins (page 264), I'm sure no one would argue. And don't forget the lemonade!

For the Pantry BBQ Sauce:

½ cup vegetable broth

2 tablespoons pure maple syrup

2 tablespoons molasses

2 tablespoons tomato paste

2 tablespoons peanut butter

1 tablespoon soy sauce

1 tablespoon apple cider vinegar

1 tablespoon mustard (I use Dijon)

½ teaspoon liquid smoke

½ teaspoon sriracha

For everything else:

1 tablespoon olive oil

1 small yellow onion, thinly sliced

Big pinch of salt

1 pound seitan, thinly sliced

3 cloves garlic, minced

Several pinches of freshly ground black pepper

3 to 4 cups broccoli florets and stems sliced ¼ inch thick

PREPARE THE SAUCE:

Mix all of the barbecue sauce ingredients together in a small bowl and set aside.

PREPARE EVERYTHING ELSE:

Preheat a large pan over medium-high heat and add the oil. Sauté the onion in the oil with a big pinch of salt for about 5 minutes, until lightly browned. Add the seitan and cook for 7 to 10 minutes, until the seitan is browned. Add the garlic and black pepper and sauté for about 1 minute, until fragrant. Add a tiny bit more oil if needed.

Mix in the broccoli and cover the pan; cook, lifting intermittently to stir, until softened, about 5 minutes.

Add the barbecue sauce, toss to coat, and cook for about 5 more minutes. The sauce should become thick and bubbly. Taste for seasoning and serve.

VARIATION:

Grill the seitan instead of sautéing it, using the directions on page 241. Then proceed with the recipe.

TEMPEH GIARDINO

serves 4 · total time: 25 mins · active time: 25 mins

2 tablespoons plus ¼ teaspoon olive oil

8 ounces tempeh, cut into little rectangles

½ teaspoon salt, plus a few pinches

1 small red onion, thinly sliced into half-moons

1 average-size yellow squash (about 8 ounces), sliced lengthwise and into ¼-inch-thick half-moons

Freshly ground black pepper

5 cloves garlic, minced

1½ cups chopped tomato (one average-size tomato)

½ teaspoon crushed red pepper flakes

⅓ cup loosely packed fresh basil leaves

Little rectangles of tempeh get sautéed up with garden veggies and lots of garlic and basil. In 25 minutes you can transport yourself to an Italian garden. Or something like that. I love the yellow squash here, cooked not to oblivion but just until soft and coated in all of the garlicky yumminess. Serve over mashed potatoes or rice, or even soft polenta. You can sub zucchini for the yellow squash if you like, or you can use thinly sliced pattypan squash. Really, any summer squash will do here.

Preheat a large, heavy-bottomed pan over medium-high heat and add 1 tablespoon of the oil. Sauté the tempeh in the oil with a pinch of salt. Cook for about 5 minutes, tossing frequently, until lightly browned.

Add the onion to the pan and drizzle an additional 1 teaspoon oil over it, as well as another pinch of salt. Sauté for another 3 minutes, just until translucent, then transfer the tempeh and onion to a large bowl.

Drizzle another 2 teaspoons of the oil into the pan and add the squash, tossing to coat. Sprinkle with another pinch of salt and some black pepper. Cook for 5 to 7 minutes, tossing frequently, until lightly browned. You want it to be still firm and not cooked to death.

Move the squash to one side and add the remaining ¼ teaspoon oil to a clear spot in the pan, along with the minced garlic. Working quickly so that the garlic doesn't burn, add the chopped tomato to the garlic, along with the red pepper flakes and remaining ½ teaspoon salt, and toss to coat.

Cook the tomato-garlic mixture for about 1 minute, just to blend the flavors, then toss with the squash and add back the tempeh and onion. Mix everything together, add the basil leaves, and cook for another 2 minutes or so, just to wilt the basil leaves. Taste for seasonings, and serve.

TRUMPET MUSHROOM & TOFU SAUTÉ with Asparagus

serves 4 · total time: 30 mins · active time: 30 mins

2 tablespoons olive oil

14 ounces extra-firm tofu, cut into ¼-inch-thick strips

½ teaspoon salt, plus a couple of pinches

Freshly ground black pepper

1 small yellow onion, quartered and thinly sliced

8 ounces trumpet mushrooms, sliced ¼ inch thick

2 tablespoons chopped fresh thyme

4 ounces asparagus, tough stems removed, cut into 1½-inch pieces

5 cloves garlic, minced

1 cup dry white wine

NOTE:

Trumpet mushrooms aren't available year-round. Portobello caps make a good replacement, but for this recipe, you should scrape out the gills with a spoon so that they don't color the entire dish. Also, sauté them for only 3 minutes, since they cook down much faster than trumpets. If your portobello caps are especially large, I'd also suggest cutting them in half before slicing.

Woodsy mushrooms, verdant asparagus, garlic, white wine—there is so much to love here! Trumpet mushrooms have this amazing ability to be firm and succulent all at once, and I love how they match up with the seared strips of tofu. I keep the asparagus nice and crisp so that you really get that garden / forest contrast between the veggies and the mushrooms. Serve over mashed potatoes or rice, or you can even make it into a pasta dish by tossing in 8 ounces cooked pasta at the end.

Preheat a large, heavy-bottomed pan over medium-high heat and add 1 tablespoon of the oil. Sauté the tofu strips in the oil, with a pinch of salt and a few pinches of black pepper. Cook for about 5 minutes, tossing frequently, until lightly browned. Use a thin metal spatula when flipping the tofu, to make sure you can get under the pieces and flip them without tearing them and losing their brown surface to the bottom on the pan. If a few tear here and there, no big deal. Transfer to a plate and set aside.

Sauté the onion in another 2 teaspoons of the oil with a pinch of salt until translucent, about 3 minutes. Add the mushrooms, the remaining ½ teaspoon salt, and thyme and sauté for 3 minutes, so that the mushrooms release some of their moisture. Add the asparagus and cook for 3 more minutes.

Move the veggies to one side and add the remaining 1 teaspoon oil to a clear spot in the pan, along with the minced garlic. Let it sizzle for 10 seconds or so, then mix it in with the rest of the veggies.

Add the wine and turn up the heat so that it comes to a boil for about 30 seconds. Lower the heat and toss the tofu back in to coat. Taste for seasoning and serve.

CHICKPEAS & ESCAROLE

in White Wine Broth

serves 2 to 4 • total time: 20 mins • active time: 20 mins

Escarole might look like lettuce, but it's totally deceiving you. It cooks up more like a leafy green, with silky upper leaves that soak up tons of flavor and a firmer base that retains its crunch. I used to get sautéed escarole at Italian restaurants growing up, but it's harder to find outside of the Northeast, so when I see it, I'm sure to snatch it up! This sauté is somehow rustic and elegant all at once. I love to serve it with roasted potatoes, but mashed potatoes would be a great choice, too. Also, include some bread to round out the meal. If huge appetites are in play and you aren't planning on serving anything else, then it's going to be more like two servings than four.

1 tablespoon olive oil

1 small red onion, thinly sliced into half-moons

½ teaspoon salt, plus a pinch

4 cloves garlic, minced

1 teaspoon dried thyme

½ cup dry white wine

Several pinches of freshly ground black pepper

½ cup vegetable broth

1 pound escarole (1 large head), coarsely chopped into large pieces

1 (15-ounce) can chickpeas, rinsed and drained (1 ½ cups)

2 tablespoons capers

1 tablespoon fresh lemon juice

½ teaspoon crushed red pepper flakes (optional)

Preheat a large pan over medium heat and add the oil. Sauté the onion in the oil with a pinch of salt until lightly browned, about 5 minutes. Add the garlic and thyme and sauté for another minute or so.

Add the wine, remaining ½ teaspoon salt, and black pepper and turn up the heat so that it comes to a boil for about 30 seconds. Add the broth, escarole, chickpeas, and capers and cover the pan to cook the escarole down, stirring occasionally, for about 5 minutes. Sprinkle in the lemon juice, taste for seasonings, and serve. I sprinkle mine with some red pepper flakes, too.

CHAPTER 7

BOWLS

(& A FEW PLATES)

My idea of a
HEAVENLY
DINNER

is a large bowl of grains, veggies, a little protein, and a killer sauce. Although I've written these recipes to showcase combinations that I love, they leave a lot of room for improvisation and self-expression. Feel free to mix and match, using whatever grain you love or whatever veggies appeared in your CSA box that week. That's what a bowl is all about! The sauces can be used in multiple ways, too. If you're having a roasted veggie side, serve it with Miso-Tahini Dressing. Use the sauce from the pizza bowl on—wait for it—actual pizza! And not surprisingly, the *queso* makes a fabulous addition to nachos or tacos. Even though this chapter is relatively slim, it still speaks to what I love about vegan cuisine. A shift in the paradigm of meat as the center of the plate, and instead a diverse bowlful of a few simply prepared ingredients that together form something extraordinary.

ROASTY SOBA BOWL
with Miso-Tahini Dressing

serves 4 · total time: 30 mins (45 mins if you don't have
prepared lentils) · active time: 15 mins

1 medium head cauliflower, cut into
large florets

8 ounces buckwheat soba noodles

1 tablespoon olive oil

¼ teaspoon salt

Several pinches of freshly ground
black pepper

**For the Miso-Tahini
Dressing:**

½ cup to ¾ cup water

¼ cup mellow white miso

¼ cup tahini

1 clove garlic

2 cups cooked brown or green lentils

Sprouts or fresh herbs, for garnish
(optional; dill, cilantro, and flat-
leaf parsley are all good choices)

Let's start this chapter off right, with the mother of all bowls! Or at least, the bowl I eat more often than any other. Nutritious and delicious soba noodles made with eye-catching buckwheat, a few healthy handfuls of lentils, roasty-toasty cauliflower, and plenty of miso-tahini dressing. Even though there are a few components, they are all very simple to prepare. This recipe is a primo reason always to have cooked lentils in the fridge. I like to top this bowl off with something fresh and green. Sunflower or radish sprouts or any fresh herb will do!

Preheat the oven to 425°F. Bring a pot of water to a boil for the soba noodles. While you're waiting for the water to boil, chop the cauliflower into large florets. It's easy to do this by chopping it in half lengthwise, pulling off the leafy base, and then pulling off the florets with your hands.

When the water boils, cook the soba according to the package directions. Drain, rinse with cold water to prevent sticking, and set aside.

Line a large, rimmed baking sheet with parchment paper. Toss the cauliflower on the sheet with the olive oil, salt, and pepper. Roast for about 20 minutes, flipping once, until aromatic and nicely toasted.

PREPARE THE DRESSING:
In the meantime, place all of the dressing ingredients in a small blender and purée. Start with ½ cup water and then add another ¼ cup to thin, if you like.

TO ASSEMBLE:
Divide the soba noodles among big bowls. Top with the lentils, cauliflower, and plenty of dressing. Garnish with sprouts or herbs and serve.

GOOD GRAVY BOWL
with Broccoli & Seitan

serves 4 · total time: 30 mins · active time: 30 mins

Oh lentils, what can't you do? Here they join forces with miso to create a flavorful, silky gravy that you'll want to pour over everything. You have my permission to do so, but let's start here: with quinoa, sautéed seitan, and broccoli that's steamed perfectly, still crispy and bright. For a more organic feel, tear the seitan into bite-size pieces with your hands instead of slicing it with a knife. You'll have more gravy than you need, but reserve the rest for sopping up with toast or biscuits for breakfast.

For the Lentil-Miso Gravy:

2 teaspoons olive oil

1 medium yellow onion, diced

3 cloves garlic, chopped

Pinch of salt

1 ½ tablespoons organic cornstarch

1 ½ cups vegetable broth

3 tablespoons chopped fresh thyme

½ teaspoon dried sage

Several pinches of freshly ground black pepper

1 ½ cups cooked brown lentils

2 tablespoons mellow white miso

For the seitan:

2 teaspoons olive oil

2 cups thinly sliced seitan (store-bought or homemade; see page 240), in bite-size pieces

Several pinches of freshly ground black pepper

For everything else:

4 cups broccoli florets

4 cups cooked quinoa

Prepare the gravy: Preheat a 2-quart saucepan over medium heat and add the oil. Sauté the onion and garlic in the oil with a pinch of salt for 5 to 7 minutes, until lightly browned.

In the meantime, mix the cornstarch with ½ cup of the vegetable broth, stirring with a fork to dissolve, and set aside.

When the onions have browned, add the thyme, sage, and pepper and sauté for 30 seconds or so. Add the lentils, miso, and the remaining 1 cup broth (not the broth mixed with the cornstarch just yet) and heat through. Once warm, use an immersion blender to purée until relatively smooth. If you don't have an immersion blender, transfer to a blender or food processor to purée, and then transfer back to the pot.

Stream in the broth-cornstarch mixture, stirring constantly, and heat for another 7 minutes, until thick and silky. Taste for seasoning and keep warm until ready to serve.

Prepare the seitan: Preheat a large, heavy pan over medium-high heat (as usual, cast iron is preferred) and add the oil. Sauté the seitan in the oil, along with a few pinches of black pepper, until seared on both sides, 5 to 7 minutes. Set aside until ready to serve.

Steam the broccoli: Get your steaming apparatus ready. Place the broccoli in the steamer and sprinkle on a pinch of salt. Steam for 5 to 7 minutes, until brilliantly bright green. Remove from the steamer immediately.

To assemble: Place the quinoa in bowls, then add the broccoli and seitan. Smother in gravy, and serve!

VARIATIONS:

- **Meet & Potatoes Bowl:** Serve over mashed potatoes (see page 231) instead of quinoa.
- **Thanksgiving Bowl:** Serve over mashed sweet potatoes (see page 160) instead of quinoa.
- **Breaded Tofu Gravy Bowl:** Replace the seitan with the breaded tofu from the Pesto-Cauliflower Pasta with Breaded Tofu (page 126).

SPINACH & BLACK BEAN
BURRITO BOWL

serves 4 · total time: 20 mins · active time: 20 mins

For the spinach:

1 tablespoon olive oil

1 small yellow onion, quartered and thinly sliced

¾ teaspoon salt, plus a pinch

4 cloves garlic, minced

1 medium tomato, chopped

1½ teaspoons ground cumin

½ cup dry white wine

8 ounces baby spinach (about 6 cups)

2 (15-ounce) cans black beans, rinsed and drained (3 cups)

For serving:

4 cups cooked brown rice or quinoa

Pepe's Secret Guacamole (page 233)

Chopped fresh cilantro (optional)

Hot sauce (optional)

I swear I was spilling burritos into bowls before it was fashionable! This is one of those combinations that is so simple and so satisfying. The spinach absorbs all the white wine and garlic, punctuated by yummy black beans. Mush it all up with the brown rice and guac and you've got yourself one hell of a reason for living. Or, if you prefer, dinner. I like to use baby spinach here, just because it's so easy and no prep is required. If you don't have baby spinach, then just use fresh spinach leaves torn into bite-size pieces. You can serve with corn tortillas or just crumble some tortilla chips over the top for that taqueria feel.

PREPARE THE SPINACH:

Preheat a large, heavy-bottomed pan over medium-high heat and add the oil. Sauté the onion in the oil with a pinch of salt for 5 minutes, until translucent. Add the garlic and sauté until fragrant, about 30 seconds.

Add the tomato, cumin, and remaining ¾ teaspoon salt, and sauté for 1 minute, so that the tomatoes release some of their moisture.

Add the white wine and turn up the heat to bring to a boil for a minute or so. Lower the heat and add the spinach in batches, tossing to get it to cook down. Add the black beans and heat through, about 2 minutes.

TO ASSEMBLE:

Taste for seasoning and serve over rice, topped with guac and cilantro, if you like. Oh, and you may want some hot sauce, too.

CURRIED PEANUT SAUCE BOWL

with Tofu & Kale

serves 4 · total time: 25 mins · active time: 25 mins

This is the peanut sauce of the gods: a gingery peanut sauce with curry powder that will have you licking the spoon, then licking the plate, and, once everything is totally gone, sniffing around your kitchen like an addict wondering if maybe you spilled a little somewhere. I love it with some flash-steamed kale and simply prepared seared cubes of tofu. Serve over rice, quinoa, or rice noodles.

PREPARE THE TOFU:

You'll need a cast-iron pan, or something nonstick that can take very high heat. Preheat the pan over high heat. Once the pan is good and hot, apply the olive oil in a thin layer. Add the cubed tofu and sprinkle with the salt. The tofu should immediately sizzle when it hits the hot the pan; otherwise, turn up the heat. Cook for about 7 minutes, tossing often, until it's nicely browned.

PREPARE THE SAUCE:

Preheat a 2-quart saucepan over medium-low heat and add the oil. Sauté the ginger and garlic in the oil for about 30 seconds. Add the water and deglaze the pan, then turn up the heat a bit. Once the water is warm, add the peanut butter, curry powder, rice vinegar, tamari, agave, and sriracha. As the ingredients heat up, the peanut butter will blend smoothly into the water as you stir. It should take 5 minutes or so, stirring often. Taste for seasonings, especially to see if you like the level of curry, and add more if you like.

PREPARE THE KALE:

Get your steaming apparatus ready. Place the kale in the steamer and sprinkle on a pinch of salt. Steam for about 5 minutes, until soft but still with a little spring to it.

TO ASSEMBLE:

Spoon the rice into bowls. Add the kale, then the tofu, and smother in the peanut sauce. Top with sriracha and cilantro, if you like.

For the tofu:

1 tablespoon olive oil

14 ounces extra-firm tofu, cut into ¾-inch cubes

¼ teaspoon salt

For the sauce and kale:

2 teaspoons olive oil

1 tablespoon minced fresh ginger

3 cloves garlic, minced

1 cup water

½ cup smooth peanut butter

2 teaspoons curry powder (see Note)

2 tablespoons rice vinegar

2 tablespoons tamari

2 tablespoons agave nectar

1 teaspoon sriracha

1 bunch kale, stems removed, torn into pieces

Pinch of salt

For serving:

4 cups cooked brown rice, quinoa, or rice noodles

Sriracha (optional)

Fresh cilantro (optional)

NOTE:

I use S&B Oriental Curry Powder for this, the kind that comes in a red-and-yellow container. It has star anise in it, and I love the matchup of star anise and peanut. It will still be good with any curry powder, but if you can find some of this brand, snatch it up.

CUCUMBER RANCH BOWL

with Breaded Tofu

serves 4 · total time: 30 mins (plus time for soaking the cashews) · active time: 30 mins

For the breaded tofu and broccoli:

3 tablespoons tamari or soy sauce

½ cup fine dry bread crumbs (I use whole wheat)

¼ cup nutritional yeast flakes

½ teaspoon dried thyme, crushed between your fingers

1 tablespoon garlic powder

14 ounces extra-firm tofu, cut into ½-inch cubes

1 tablespoon olive oil, plus more as needed

4 cups broccoli florets

For the Ranch Dressing:

½ cup cashews, soaked for at least 2 hours (see "ABS: Always Be Soaking," page 14)

½ cup vegetable broth

¼ cup fresh lemon juice

2 cups chopped cucumber

¼ cup chopped white onion

2 cloves garlic, peeled

2 tablespoons nutritional yeast flakes (optional)

½ teaspoon salt

¼ cup chopped fresh dill, plus extra for garnish (optional)

For serving:

4 cups cooked brown rice or quinoa

NOTES:

- The nutritional yeast adds another dimension of rich creaminess to the dressing, so I love to use it. But it's okay to leave it out.

- When the creamy sauce and crispy breading meet, it's *Romeo and Juliet* forbidden passion stuff. But if you're feeling especially lazy (or not very romantic), you can also use the sautéed tofu from the Curried Peanut Sauce Bowl with Tofu & Kale (page 199) and still have a ton of flavor.

Omaha doesn't have a million vegan options, but there's one restaurant nearby that makes a scrumptious cucumber ranch dressing that I always get with my steamed veggies. And thus the cucumber ranch bowl was born! My version is made with cashews, a healthy dose of fresh lemon juice, fresh dill, and, of course, a heap of refreshing cucumber. It's so zesty and mouthwatering! I love it with seasoned breaded tofu.

To prepare the breaded tofu, preheat a large nonstick pan (cast iron is my preference, as usual) over medium-high heat.

Get two dinner plates. Pour the tamari onto one. On the other, use your fingertips to mix together the bread crumbs, nutritional yeast, thyme, and garlic.

Place a handful of tofu cubes in the soy sauce and toss to coat. Then dredge them in the bread crumbs, tossing to coat. (Use your dry hand to handle the tofu in the bread crumbs; otherwise you'll get a crumb mitten on your hand.) Put the coated tofu off to the side of the plate and continue until all the tofu is coated.

Add the oil to the preheated pan in a thin layer, and then cook the tofu cubes. Be careful not to crowd the pan; if your pan isn't big enough, do it in two batches. Let cook for a few minutes, then flip, using a thin metal spatula so that you don't scrape off the breading. Cook for about 7 minutes total, drizzling in extra oil as needed and flipping occasionally until browned on most sides.

For the broccoli, preheat your steaming apparatus. Place the broccoli in the steamer and sprinkle on a pinch of salt. Steam for 5 to 7 minutes, until brilliantly bright green. Remove from the steamer immediately.

PREPARE THE RANCH DRESSING:

Drain the cashews and add them to a blender along with the vegetable broth, lemon juice, cucumber, onion, garlic, nutritional yeast (if using), and salt. Purée until relatively smooth. There will still be some texture from the veggies. Scrape down the sides with a rubber spatula to make sure you get everything. Pulse in the dill until it makes the ranch a pretty green, all flecked with dill. Taste for seasoning.

TO ASSEMBLE:

Scoop rice into each bowl, arrange the broccoli and tofu over the rice, and smother in sauce. Serve garnished with extra dill, if you like.

COZY HUMMUS BOWL

serves 4 • total time: 15 mins (if tofu and rice are already made) • active time: 15 mins

There's something quintessentially vegan about hummus, and perhaps our adoration of it makes vegans the butt of jokes at times, but the thing is, hummus is delicious. For my money, there is nothing more comforting and cozily vegan. And, truthfully, as a cliché vegan, I eat it a few times a week. So a book about my favorite weeknight meals would be dishonest if it didn't include this: the fabulously classic hippie vegan hummus bowl. Baked tofu, brown rice, a bunch of salady stuff, and a big ladle of hummus to smother it all with. The baked tofu is best if homemade, but you can use store-bought in a pinch.

For the hummus:

1½ cups cooked chickpeas (see Notes)

1 clove garlic

¼ cup tahini

3 tablespoons fresh lemon juice

2 tablespoons olive oil

½ teaspoon salt

¼ cup pitted Kalamata olives

For everything else:

4 cups cooked brown rice

8 cups mixed salad greens

1 recipe Classic Baked Tofu (page 238) or store-bought baked tofu

1 large tomato, diced

1 cup diced cucumber

1 cup alfalfa sprouts

In a blender or food processor, pulse together the chickpeas and garlic to get them chopped up. Add the tahini, lemon juice, olive oil, and salt and blend, adding a few tablespoons of water and/or reserved chickpea cooking liquid until the hummus is smooth. It should be just pourable and not stiff, for the purpose of slathering over everything in the bowl.

Once you've reached the desired consistency, add the olives and pulse until they are chopped up. You don't want them to be puréed. Taste for salt and seasoning and mix in any additional ingredients with a fork. Don't blend again or you will chop the olives up too much.

Keep sealed and refrigerated until ready to use.

TO ASSEMBLE:

Place a scoop of brown rice in your bowl and nudge it over to one side. On the other side, add the lettuce. Place the tofu on top of the rice, and add a big scoop of hummus. Garnish with diced tomato and cucumber and some sprouts.

NOTES:

• Using a little bit of the cooking liquid, whether homemade or from a can, is a great way to add body to your hummus, so reserve a couple of tablespoons for thinning.

• I like the contrast of warm and cold with the salad, but you can replace the raw veggies with steamed greens or roasted cauliflower if you like.

CITRUS-TAHINI BOWL

with Bok Choy & Grilled Tofu

serves 4 · total time: 20 mins (plus time for pressing
and marinating the tofu) · active time: 20 mins

For the marinade:

½ cup fresh orange juice

2 tablespoons fresh lime juice

2 tablespoons soy sauce

2 teaspoons toasted sesame oil

2 cloves garlic, minced

1 tablespoon minced fresh ginger

1 teaspoon agave nectar

½ teaspoon crushed red pepper flakes

For everything else:

1 (14-ounce) block extra-firm tofu,
  drained and pressed

Olive oil, for the grill

4 bunches baby bok choy, tough stems
  removed

¼ cup tahini

4 cups cooked red quinoa

2 cups fresh orange segments (from
  about 2 navel oranges; see Notes,
  page 70)

For the garnish (optional):

Chopped scallions

Fresh cilantro

Toasted sesame seeds

VARIATION:

You can grill the baby bok choy instead
of steaming it. Simply slice in half,
brush with oil, and sprinkle with salt.
Grill cut side down for about 5 minutes,
until dark grill marks appear.

Tofu flavored with delicate notes of orange, lime, and ginger with crisp, clean, and oh-so-bright-green baby bok choy, plus fresh orange segments, all smothered in a citrusy tahini sauce. What I love about this bowl is that nothing goes to waste—the leftover marinade is mixed with tahini to create the sauce. Oh, and I also love how delicious it is! Tahini and orange are an unexpectedly irresistible surprise, with a hint of spice from the red pepper flakes.

PREPARE THE MARINADE:

In a large bowl, mix together all of the marinade ingredients.

Slice the tofu into 8 slabs, widthwise. Now slice each of those in half to make squares. Marinate the squares for about 1 hour or up to overnight, flipping at least once.

Now grill the squares. Preheat a large cast-iron grill pan over medium-high heat. Brush or spray the grill with oil. Place the tofu squares on the grill (reserve the marinade) and let cook for 3 to 5 minutes, until grill marks form. Flip the tofu pieces, spraying or brushing the pan again before placing the tofu pieces back down. Grill for 3 to 5 more minutes, and remove from the pan.

While the tofu cooks, get your steaming apparatus ready. Place the bok choy in the steamer and steam for 5 minutes or so, until crisp-tender and bright green.

Meanwhile, transfer the leftover marinade to a blender. Add the tahini and blend until smooth. Taste for seasoning. You may need to adjust with a little extra orange juice if the tofu sucked up too much marinade.

Place the quinoa in bowls. Overlap the bok choy, tofu, and orange segments over the quinoa. Drizzle with sauce, sprinkle with any or all of the optional garnishes, and serve!

HOW TO BE THE MAGILLA GRILLA:
Grilling Tips for the Indoor Grill

Don't work hard for those char marks only to lose them when flipping the tofu!
Here are a few tips for keeping your grill marks intact.

- Make sure the grill is good and hot before applying the oil and grilling the tofu. Let it preheat for a good 5 minutes to be sure.

- Use a thin metal spatula for flipping (see page 7). Wooden or plastic can be too thick; you need to effectively scrape under the tofu in order to keep your grill marks.

- Spray oil is perfect for coating the grill pan. Pouring oil on will result in a lot of grease in the crevices without coating the ridges effectively. You can also brush the oil on with a heat-resistant brush.

- Smoking is okay! In fact, that's how you know it's working. Don't worry about a little smokiness. Turn up the exhaust fan, open a window, and have at it. Although your fire alarm and your neighbors might disagree.

PIZZA BOWL

with Greens, Sausages & Olives

serves 4 · total time: 30 mins (plus time for soaking the cashews) · active time: 30 mins

For the kale and sausages:

2 tablespoons olive oil

8 cloves garlic, thinly sliced

1 small red onion, thinly sliced

¼ teaspoon salt, plus a pinch

4 vegan sausages (store-bought or homemade; see page 237), sliced into chunky half-moons

1 bunch kale (about 8 ounces), tough stems removed, chopped into large pieces

For the sauce:

½ cup cashews, soaked for at least 2 hours (see "ABS: Always Be Soaking," page 14)

2 cloves garlic, peeled

3 tablespoons tomato paste

1 roasted red pepper (store-bought or homemade; see page 118)

½ cup vegetable broth

1 tablespoon fresh lemon juice

¼ teaspoon salt

For serving:

4 cups cooked brown rice

½ cup sliced oil-cured black olives (or any high-quality olive)

2 tablespoons fresh thyme leaves

Crushed red pepper flakes

NOTE:

The basic recipe is plenty amazing, but you might want to add any number of your favorite pizza toppings: toasted pine nuts, fresh basil leaves, sautéed mushrooms, even chunks of pineapple if you swing in the tropical way. And of course you can change up the grain. Soft polenta would be a fun Italian choice, as would farro.

There are so many amazing vegan pizzas out there. This bowl, however, is for those times when you've got a pizza craving yet want to fill up on more meaningful carbs and lots of veggies. A bowl of sautéed kale, onions, big garlic slices, and chunky sausages over hearty brown rice, all doused in an easy, creamy, cheezy, and dreamy pizza-inspired sauce. Dotted with black olives and topped with thyme, this is a true pizza feast and more satisfying than something that comes in a delivery box. But if you want, feel free to serve it in a delivery box. I'm not judgin'.

PREPARE THE KALE AND SAUSAGES:

Preheat a large pan over low heat and add 2 teaspoons of the oil. We're going to do the garlic first. Sauté the garlic cloves in the oil just until they are lightly browned. It should take only a minute or so. Transfer them to a plate. Now we'll sauté everything else in that same pan.

Turn up the heat to medium. Sauté the onion in another 2 teaspoons of the oil, along with a pinch of salt. When translucent, after about 3 minutes, add the sausages and remaining 2 teaspoons oil. Lightly brown the sausages, about 4 minutes.

Now add the kale and remaining ¼ teaspoon salt. It won't all fit in one shot, so add large handfuls of kale, along with splashes of water, and toss to cook it down for a minute or so, then add the next batch. This should only take two or three batches, so about 5 minutes total. Mix the garlic back in. Taste for salt.

PREPARE THE SAUCE:

While the kale is cooking, simply add all of the sauce ingredients to a blender and purée until completely smooth. This can take anywhere from 1 to 5 minutes depending on the strength of your machine. Scrape down the sides with a rubber spatula to make sure you get everything. Taste for salt and lemoniness. Keep refrigerated until ready to serve. It does thicken as it chills, so thin out with a little water if necessary.

TO ASSEMBLE:

Scoop the rice into bowls. Arrange the kale and sausages over the rice. Drizzle with a generous amount of sauce. Top with the olives, thyme, and red pepper flakes, and serve.

CHIMICHURRI-
PUMPKIN BOWL

total time: 1 hour · active time: 20 mins

Roasted pumpkin comes alive when smothered in chimichurri, an Argentinian sauce usually reserved for steak. The idea for chimichurri is similar to pesto in that it's full of fresh puréed herbs. In this version, I've combined parsley and cilantro with pepitas and a healthy dose of red wine vinegar for a thick, nutty sauce with a hit of acidity that is perfect for waking the dead, or mixing into a nice wholesome bowl. I love the contrast of the sweet autumnal pumpkin with the intensely herbal chimichurri. And black beans are a natural addition that pulls everything together. If sugar pumpkins aren't available, then any sweet winter squash will do. I love red kuri squash, but other nice options are dumpling squash or butternut. I also dig soba noodles as the starch, but, as usual, quinoa would be a great choice as well.

For the pumpkin and noodles:

1 (3-pound) sugar pumpkin, sliced in half and seeded

8 ounces soba noodles (I used spelt soba in the photo)

For the Chimichurri:

2 cloves garlic, peeled

½ cup pepitas

2 cups chopped fresh flat-leaf parsley, plus more for garnish (optional)

1 cup chopped fresh cilantro, plus more for garnish (optional)

¼ cup red wine vinegar

¼ cup water

1 tablespoon olive oil

1 teaspoon salt

½ teaspoon crushed red pepper flakes

For serving:

2 (15-ounce) cans black beans, rinsed and drained (3 cups), warmed

¼ cup pepitas

PREPARE THE PUMPKIN AND NOODLES:

First bake the pumpkin. Preheat the oven to 425°F. Line a rimmed baking sheet with parchment paper and lightly grease.

Place the pumpkin halves, cut side down, on the baking sheet. Bake for about 45 minutes, or until very tender.

In the meantime, bring a pot of salted water to a boil. Cook your noodles according to the package directions. Drain, place back in the pot, and set aside.

PREPARE THE CHIMICHURRI:

While the pumpkin bakes, place the garlic in a blender or food processor and pulse to get it chopped up. And the pepitas and pulse into fine crumbs. Add the rest of the chimichurri ingredients and purée. It should be thick, with a gritty texture from the nuts. Taste for seasoning.

TO ASSEMBLE:

Toss the noodles with about ⅓ cup of the chimichurri and divide among bowls. Scoop cooked pumpkin into each bowl, and add some black beans. Top with additional chimichurri and pepitas. Garnish with additional herbs, if you like, and serve.

WARM POTATO SALAD
with Grilled Seitan & Asparagus

serves 4 · total time: 30 mins · active time: 30 mins

For the potato salad:

2 pounds red potatoes, cut into ¾-inch chunks

¼ teaspoon salt, plus a few pinches

1 tablespoon olive oil

1 medium yellow onion, quartered and thinly sliced

2 cloves garlic, minced

½ cup low-fat vegan mayo

½ cup whole-grain mustard

½ cup vegetable broth

Freshly ground black pepper

For the seitan and asparagus:

8 ounces seitan, cut into ¼-inch-thick slices

2 tablespoons olive oil

¼ teaspoon salt

Several pinches of freshly ground black pepper

8 ounces asparagus, tough ends removed

NOTES:

- This would be fastest on a large, two-burner grill pan or an outdoor grill, but it still works if you're using a smaller one. It just takes a bit longer because your grilled components need to be done in batches. If you're using a smaller grill pan, you'll be looking at 40 minutes instead of 30. No biggie.

- If you don't have a grill pan or just don't want to futz with it on a weeknight, then you can simply sauté the seitan in a pan for 5 minutes or so and then do the same with the asparagus.

I'm not sure that warm potatoes with grilled seitan is a salad anymore, but let's not fight about it. This is a wonderfully (wheat) meat-and-potatoes meal with a bit of a French influence. The potatoes are the star here, and they act as a sauce as well. It's not that they're overwhelmingly saucy, but the tangy mustard adds lots of flavor to the accompanying seitan. It's important to get the onions as thin as possible and well caramelized so that they add sweet notes throughout the potato salad.

Prepare the potatoes: Place the potatoes in a medium pot and submerge in water by 2 inches or so. Add a generous amount of salt to the water. Bring to a boil, and then lower the heat immediately and let simmer for about 10 minutes, or until the potatoes are fork-tender. Keep a close eye on them and be careful not to overcook; you want them to retain some firmness. Drain and set aside.

While the potatoes are boiling, prepare the sauce. Preheat a heavy-bottomed pan over medium heat and add the oil. Sauté the onion in the oil with a pinch of salt for about 10 minutes, until nicely browned. Add the garlic and sauté until fragrant, about 30 seconds.

Add the mayo, mustard, and broth and stir to combine. Once warm, add the cooked potatoes, remaining ¼ teaspoon salt, and pepper and toss to coat. Turn off the heat and cover to keep warm. Before serving, taste for seasoning. If it gets a little less saucy while you cook everything else, just add a drizzle of water.

Prepare the seitan and asparagus: Preheat a grill pan over medium-high heat. Place the seitan slices on a plate, drizzle with 1 tablespoon of the olive oil, sprinkle with some of the salt and some black pepper, and toss to coat. When the grill pan is very hot, lightly grease and then grill the seitan for about 3 minutes each side, until dark grill marks form. You may have to do this in two batches. Keep finished slices on a plate covered with aluminum foil until ready to serve.

While the seitan is cooking, place the asparagus on the plate where you prepared the seitan and drizzle with the remaining 1 tablespoon olive oil, a sprinkle of the salt, and some black pepper. Toss to coat. When you're done grilling the seitan, grill the asparagus for about 4 minutes, until bright green and charred in some spots, turning occasionally.

Arrange everything prettily on dinner plates and serve!

TEMPEH AGRODOLCE
over Grilled Polenta

serves 4 to 6 • total time: 45 mins (plus time for marinating the tempeh) • active time: 45 mins

Agrodolce means "sour-sweet" in Italian. This is *salsa agrodolce*, a sweet-and-sour tomato sauce. And that is about where my Italian language skills end. This sauce is really surprising; the sweetness is caramely and complex from slow cooking the onions and then caramelizing them with brown sugar. The sour comes from vinegar, two types: red wine vinegar sets the stage with a mellow acidity, and a splash of balsamic vinegar adds a sharp bite. A hint of cinnamon brings mystery, and fresh basil makes you feel like you're in an Italian bistro. Or at least an Italian chain restaurant. But a really good one.

I chose tempeh as the meat because I wanted a nutty and succulent contrast. It's marinated with red wine vinegar as well, so there's lots of harmony here. I serve over grilled polenta, but it would be good over soft polenta, too, if you just can't be bothered. It needs something that can suck up sauce. As a rule, roasted cauliflower is a wonderful accompaniment to *agrodolce*.

This is another dish with a lot of components, but they do come together easily!

STEAM AND MARINATE THE TEMPEH:

Set up your steaming apparatus. Place the tempeh in the steamer and steam for 15 minutes. In a shallow bowl, mix together all of the marinade ingredients. When the tempeh is done, immediately submerge it in the marinade for at least 1 hour and up to overnight. The longer you marinate it, the more flavor it will absorb. When the tempeh is done marinating, make the sauce.

PREPARE THE SALSA:

Preheat a saucepan over medium-low heat and add the oil. Cook the onion in the oil for about 10 minutes, covering the pan and lifting the lid occasionally to stir. You're steaming the onion so that it gets very juicy. Then, uncover and turn up the heat to medium-high. Let the onion brown for 5 minutes or so. Add the garlic and stir for about 30 seconds.

Add the brown sugar and cook for about 5 minutes, so that the sugar gets melty, dark, and smooth. Stir pretty consistently.

For the tempeh:
1 pound tempeh, sliced ½ inch thick

For the marinade:
½ cup red wine vinegar
2 tablespoons soy sauce
1 tablespoon pure maple syrup
1 tablespoon olive oil, plus more for cooking the tempeh

For the Salsa Agrodolce:
1 tablespoon olive oil
1 large yellow onion, quartered and thickly sliced (about ½ inch)
3 cloves garlic, minced
3 tablespoons light brown sugar
1 (24-ounce) can whole tomatoes
2 tablespoons red wine vinegar
1 tablespoon balsamic vinegar
1 teaspoon salt
¼ teaspoon ground cinnamon
Several pinches of freshly ground black pepper
Pinch of crushed red pepper flakes
8 fresh basil leaves, torn into pieces

To assemble:
1 batch Polenta Grilled, Broiled, or Soft (page 212)

MAKE AHEAD:

Steam the tempeh in the morning and then let it marinate all day. When you're ready for dinner, it should come together very quickly.

(recipe continues)

Now use your hands to crush the tomatoes and add them to the pot. Once all the whole tomatoes are crushed and added, pour in the remaining juice. Stir in both vinegars, the salt, cinnamon, black pepper, and red pepper flakes, and cook, uncovered, for about 20 minutes. It needs that much cooking time for the sauce to thicken and the flavors to develop. In the last few minutes, add the basil leaves. Taste for seasoning.

WHILE THE SAUCE IS THICKENING, COOK THE TEMPEH:

Heat a heavy-bottomed pan over medium heat. Drizzle a little olive oil into the pan and cook the tempeh for about 15 minutes, flipping often, until browned on both sides. Sprinkle with a tiny bit of salt as it cooks.

Serve the tempeh over the polenta, topped with lots and lots of sauce.

Polenta Grilled, Broiled, or Soft
serves 4

4 cups vegetable broth
½ teaspoon salt
1¼ cups polenta
Several pinches of freshly ground black pepper
Olive oil, for brushing

Polenta is a bright, fresh, and homey canvas for any number of saucy, delicious things. Here are three different ways to prepare it.

Line an 8-inch square pan with parchment paper if broiling or grilling.

Bring the vegetable broth and salt to a boil in a 2-quart pot. Lower the heat to a simmer. Add the polenta in a slow, steady stream, stirring constantly with a whisk for about 5 minutes, until the polenta is thickened. Add a few pinches of black pepper. Keeping the heat low, cover and let cook for 10 more minutes or so, stirring occasionally. If you are serving soft polenta, it's ready now! If grilling or broiling, please proceed.

Pour into the prepared pan and use a spatula to spread it evenly. When the polenta stops steaming, cover with aluminum foil and chill for several hours, until firm and chilled all the way through.

Turn the polenta pan over onto a cutting board to unmold the polenta. Peel away the parchment. Slice the polenta into 4 squares, and then slice each square corner to corner to make triangles.

To grill: Lightly brush a cast-iron grill pan with oil and preheat over medium heat. Lightly brush each piece with olive oil, and grill for 6 to 8 minutes on each side. Most grill pans will fit about 4 triangles at a time. Use a thin metal spatula to flip the pieces over, and make sure you don't lose the grill marks.

To broil: Preheat the broiler and place a rack about 3 inches from the heat. Place the polenta pieces on a lightly oiled rimmed baking sheet. Brush each piece lightly with oil. Place in the broiler and cook for about 5 minutes on each side, until golden brown.

QUESO BLANCO BOWL

with Crispy Kale

serves 4 · total time: 30 mins (plus time for soaking the cashews) · active time: 20 mins

The inspiration for this bowl is nachos! Kale is baked in the oven until crispy like a chip, then served with rice and pinto beans. Over the top goes an oozy, spicy *queso blanco* with yummy bites of onion and jalapeño. If you're not dining with polite company, you can use the kale to grab up nibbles of everything and eat with your hands. Otherwise, a fork should do.

This recipe is more than the sum of it parts: the kale chips come in really handy as a snack all on their own. And the *queso*, of course, can be used for nachos (see page 232) or tacos or as a luscious dip at your next soirée. Luckily the *queso* recipe makes more than you'll need for the bowl, so leftovers become nice and thick when refrigerated—you can even spread it on crackers!

PREPARE THE KALE:

Preheat the oven to 325°F. Line two rimmed baking sheets with parchment paper.

Make sure that the kale is totally dry; otherwise it could turn out soggy. Divide the kale between the baking sheets. Spray lightly or drizzle with olive oil and sprinkle each sheet with ¼ teaspoon salt. Toss to coat and spread into a single layer as best you can. Bake for about 15 minutes, until crispy, rotating the pans about halfway through.

PREPARE THE QUESO:

Drain the cashews and add them to a blender along with the broth, miso, nutritional yeast, garlic, cumin, salt, and lemon juice. Purée until completely smooth; this can take anywhere from 1 to 5 minutes depending on the strength of your machine. Scrape down the sides with a rubber spatula to make sure you get everything.

Preheat a 2-quart saucepan over low heat and add the oil. Sauté the onion and jalapeños in the oil with a pinch of salt for 3 minutes, just until soft. Add the blended cashew mixture and turn the heat to medium. Cook for about 10 minutes, using an angled wooden spoon to stir occasionally, until the *queso* is hot and thickened. Keep warm until ready to serve.

TO ASSEMBLE:

Place a scoop of rice in each bowl. Scoop on some beans, place some crispy kale in each bowl, and pour *queso* over everything. Top with the avocado, tomato, and cilantro (if desired), and serve.

For the kale:

1 large bunch kale (about 1 pound), torn into large pieces (about 4 inches)

Spray olive oil, or 2 teaspoons olive oil

½ teaspoon salt

For the Queso Blanco:

¾ cup cashews, soaked for at least 2 hours (see "ABS: Always Be Soaking," page 14)

1¼ cups vegetable broth

1 tablespoon mellow white miso

3 tablespoons nutritional yeast flakes

2 cloves garlic, peeled

2 teaspoons ground cumin

¼ teaspoon salt, plus a pinch

2 tablespoons fresh lemon juice

2 teaspoons oil

1 small white onion, finely diced

2 jalapeños, seeded and chopped

For everything else:

4 cups cooked brown rice or quinoa

2 (15-ounce) cans pinto beans, rinsed and drained (3 cups), warmed

1 avocado, pitted, peeled, and diced

1 large tomato, chopped

Fresh cilantro for garnish (optional)

SUNDAY NIGHT SUPPERS

Sunday nights are all about COMFORT FOOD

. . . and big, filling casseroles. The idea here is to take a dish that is typically labor-intensive and make it less so. Perhaps not simplified to the point that you're going to walk in the door after work and whip it up, but certainly perfect for a Sunday evening, when you've got an hour or so to spare and a burning desire to branch out and create something super-duper special. It's especially perfect for an evening of cooking together, with friends or family. Get out a second cutting board, put on some fun music, have the kids peel carrots or your best friend measure out ingredients, or simply put someone on dish duty! I find that Sundays are the best time to create positive kitchen moments that will make you want to be in that room the rest of the week. A few notes on tools: An amazing ceramic casserole dish will go a long way toward making your food more delicious, and there's also just something so feel-goody about it. Yes, you can line a metal baking pan with foil, and that's cool, but there's something very comforting about putting on the oven mitts and lifting this big sturdy casserole out of the oven, steaming deliciously, and setting it on a trivet. The presentation is breathtaking. Maybe it makes you feel like the casserole: You, too, are strong, dependable, capable, and delicious.

CHANDRA MALAI KOFTA

serves 4 · total time: 1 hour (plus time for soaking the cashews) ·
active time: 30 mins

For the kofta:

½ of a 15-ounce can chickpeas, rinsed and drained (¾ cup)

½ cup slivered almonds

1½ teaspoons cumin seeds

8 ounces zucchini, shredded (see Notes, page 218)

¼ cup finely chopped fresh cilantro

1 tablespoon minced fresh ginger

2 cloves garlic, minced

½ teaspoon salt

Several pinches of freshly ground black pepper

1¼ cups panko bread crumbs

For the sauce:

1 cup cashews, soaked for at least 2 hours (see "ABS: Always Be Soaking," page 14)

2 cups vegetable broth

1 tablespoon refined coconut oil

1 medium yellow onion, very finely diced

3 cloves garlic, minced

1 tablespoon minced fresh ginger

1 tablespoon mild curry powder

1 teaspoon garam masala

1 teaspoon ground cumin

1 (14-ounce) can lite coconut milk

3 tablespoons tomato paste

1 teaspoon salt

1 cup frozen peas

For everything else:

Refined coconut oil, for frying (2 tablespoons or so)

Cooked basmati rice, for serving

Fresh cilantro, for garnish (optional)

Kofta, if you don't know, is an Indian meatball, in this case a vegan one. *Malai* means "cream." And Chandra is my middle name. This is my story.

For fifteen years, my mom lived in this shoe box on the Upper East Side. It wasn't even an adult-size shoe box; it was, like, for baby booties. The living room was the dining room was the bedroom. And somehow, when I'd visit, sometimes for days, we'd manage to cohabitate and have enough space to do our own things. We'd each huddle down on our own side of the futon, she perhaps paying bills or practicing Sanskrit, me reading a food magazine or doing my nails. Of course, *Law & Order* was on the TV, providing us with ambience. As you can imagine, the kitchen was no large affair. And although we created some fabulous meals with that Holly Hobbie stove, more often than not we'd order in from the pile of food-stained paper menus in the silverware drawer.

One of our favorites was an Indian restaurant, and one of the best things to share was a kofta, the description of which read, "It's impossible to describe but you will love it." Okay, it's impossible, but let me try. A football-shape dumpling, covered in thick, creamy curry sauce. Each forkful was just a feast of flavor and texture. Dip into the sauce to hunt for the soft dumpling with its crisp coating, sink your fork in, and inside you'd find the toasted almonds and little bits of zucchini. Plenty of basmati rice to soak up the cream made everything just perfect.

So here is my attempt re-create the experience at home, without all of the aluminum containers.

PREPARE THE KOFTA MIXTURE:

In a medium bowl, mash the chickpeas until they're mushy but not quite puréed.

Preheat a large, heavy pan over medium heat. Toast the almonds for about 7 minutes, tossing frequently, until they are golden and browned in some spots. Transfer them immediately to the bowl. Next, toast the cumin seeds for 3 minutes or so, until fragrant and a shade or two darker. Transfer those to the bowl as well.

Add the zucchini, cilantro, ginger, garlic, salt, and black pepper, and mix well.

Now add the bread crumbs and use your hands to mix and mush until it holds together. Cover with plastic wrap (or a plate) and place in the fridge for at least 30 minutes.

(recipe continues)

MAKE AHEAD:

You can prepare the kofta mixture a day ahead if you like. Refrigerate until ready to use.

NOTES:

- This recipe serves 4, with 3 kofta apiece. It's plenty of food when served with rice, but I like to bulk it up with extra veggies, like sautéed cauliflower and zucchini. So it makes more sauce than you'll need if you're just serving it with the kofta. You'll be happy for the extra sauce, though, I promise! Later in the week, you can steam up some veggies and thin the sauce out with some vegetable broth for a fabulous korma-style curry. Or just pour it over a baked potato!

- It's easy to shred the zucchini by hand using the big holes on a box grater. I prefer the shorter strands of zuke that this produces, as opposed to the longer strands you might get in a food processor. Since it's not that large an amount, it's not too much of a chore to do it by hand.

- I love the convenience of this recipe because the kofta ingredients don't need any sautéing before you throw them together; you just need to do a little toasting for the cumin and almonds. Those few minutes of work are worth it! You can toast them while you're assembling the other ingredients. And what's even better is that you can use that same pan for panfrying the kofta later on; no need to wash it first.

PREPARE THE SAUCE:

Drain the cashews and add them to a blender along with the broth. Blend until very smooth. This could take anywhere from 1 to 5 minutes depending on the strength of your machine, so give your blender a break every minute or so and test the sauce for smoothness. It should be very smooth, with only a slight graininess. Scrape down the sides with a rubber spatula to make sure you get everything.

Preheat a 4-quart pot over medium heat and add the coconut oil. Sauté the onion in the oil for about 3 minutes, until translucent. Add the garlic and ginger, and cook just until fragrant, 15 seconds or so. Add the curry powder, garam masala, and cumin and toss for a minute or so, just to toast the spices a bit.

Add the coconut milk, tomato paste, blended cashews, and salt. Bring to a low simmer and let cook for 15 minutes or so. It should thicken up nicely. Add the peas and let them warm through. Taste for seasonings, then turn off the heat and cover until ready to serve.

COOK THE KOFTA:

Preheat a large cast-iron pan over medium heat, or any pan that is nonstick and good for frying. Line the counter with some parchment paper to keep the formed kofta from sticking. Scoop up a scant ¼ cup of the mixture. Roll between your hands to pack it well, and then roll into a football shape. Set on the parchment and continue to form all 12 kofta.

When the pan is hot enough, add some coconut oil and make sure it coats the bottom of the pan. Now add the kofta, rolling each one around in the pan when you add it, making sure to coat all sides. Use a little extra oil, if needed.

Fry them for about 7 minutes, rolling them around in the pan to get them browned on all sides. They don't have to be uniformly browned; just do your best. Once browned, turn off the heat.

TO ASSEMBLE:

Scoop some rice onto each plate, place 3 koftas on top of the rice, and cover with sauce. Garnish with cilantro, if you like, and serve.

PHYLLO POT PIE

serves 8 · total time: 45 mins · active time: 30 mins

Pot pie has got to be some sort of American dinner-table warrior; after all, there aren't many iconic dishes that survived the '70s! But the pot pie is still standing. And what is left to say about it? If you have ever walked in from the cold, into a warm kitchen in which one was baking, then you understand that pot pie needs no words. But here are some anyway: tender pastry with a savory grav-ory filling; chock-full of potatoes, carrots, celery, and peas. And where do you get your protein? Well, in this case, chicky seitan! A delicious chickpea wheat meat that is perfect to cube up where one might use chicken. Speaking of which, this is one of those dishes that you need not fear feeding to an omnivore. Bring it to any family gathering and plunk it down right in the center of the table with confidence and authority.

To simplify things, I've also forgone the traditional pastry crust in favor of a super-easy phyllo. I know phyllo can be a fussy fellow, so instead of brushing each papery piece, one by one, we're slicing a stack into ribbons, tossing them around with some olive oil, and bunching up handfuls on top, as sloppy and beautiful as can be! What's more, everything is cooked in the cast-iron skillet, which can go right into the oven when topped with the phyllo. Meaning fewer dishes, and more time for leafing through '70s cookbooks.

2 tablespoons olive oil

1 medium yellow onion, diced

1 teaspoon salt, plus a pinch

¾ cup peeled diced carrots (½-inch dice)

2 ribs celery, diced into ½-inch pieces

3 cloves garlic, minced

2 tablespoons fresh thyme

2 teaspoons dried rubbed sage

3 tablespoons sherry or white wine

Several pinches of freshly ground black pepper

2 medium russet potatoes, peeled and diced into ½-inch pieces

3 cups vegetable broth

¼ cup all-purpose flour

1 cup water

2 Chicky Seitan cutlets (page 241), diced into ½-inch pieces

½ cup frozen peas

10 sheets phyllo dough, thawed

Spray olive oil, or 2 teaspoons olive oil

Preheat a large cast-iron or oven-safe pan over medium-high heat and add the oil (see Notes if you don't have either). Sauté the onion in the oil with a pinch of salt just until softened, about 3 minutes.

Add the carrots and celery and sauté for about 5 more minutes, until the onions are lightly browned. Add the garlic, thyme, and sage (crushed in your fingers). Sauté for a minute or so, then add the sherry to deglaze the pan, along with the remaining 1 teaspoon salt and the pepper. Let the sherry reduce for a few minutes.

Now add the potatoes and vegetable broth. Cover the pan and bring to a boil. Once boiling, lower the heat and let simmer until the potatoes are tender, about 5 minutes. Be careful not to overcook them; you don't want mushy potatoes.

Preheat the oven to 400°F.

(recipe continues)

- If you're like, "Isa, thank you for the easy pot pie, but I just gotta' have a bottom crust," well, first of all, you're welcome. Second of all, here's an idea. Purchase two 9-inch premade piecrusts. Par-bake them for 10 minutes at 350°F. Then fill each with half of the pot pie filling, top with phyllo bunches, and bake!

- If you don't have a large cast-iron pan, or any pan that can go from stovetop to oven, don't worry. You can still totally do this. Simply cook everything in a large pan and then transfer to a 9-inch square casserole or baking pan. Then top with the phyllo and proceed.

- If you have a spray bottle of oil, now is the time to break it out. It works really well to lightly coat the phyllo in oil just right. If not, just drizzle in little bits at a time.

- If you don't want to mess with the Chicky Seitan, then 2 cups of chickpeas will work instead. Or navy beans.

In a measuring cup, mix the flour into the water with a fork until no lumps are left. Slowly add the water-flour mixture to the pot, mixing well. Let thicken for 5 minutes or so. Add the seitan and peas and continue to cook. After about 5 more minutes it should be perfectly thick but still smooth. Taste for seasonings.

While the oven is preheating and the stew is thickening, prepare the phyllo. Cut the stack into ribbons that are about 1 ½ inches wide and 6 inches long, give or take an inch depending on the size of your sheets. Toss the ribbons into a bowl and use your hands to separate them as best you can. Now spray or drizzle with oil and toss to coat.

When the stew is ready, smooth it down with your spatula and top with bunches of phyllo. Place in the oven and bake for about 12 minutes, until lightly browned. And serve!

SWEET POTATO GNOCCHI

with Seared Brussels Sprouts & Tarragon Cream

serves 4 · total time: 1 hour 30 min (plus time for soaking
the cashews) · active time: 30 mins

Oh, those addictive, fluffy pillows of pasta. You'd think that the kind of person who makes her own gnocchi would be a world apart from us mere mortals. But you totally can be that person! Sweet-potato gnocchi, in particular, is easier to master because of how effortless it is to achieve a creamy, fluffy potato texture, no special skills or equipment necessary.

This version is a real restaurant-style dish that I think will impress anyone. The combination of fragrant licorice-y tarragon cream complements the earthy autumnal gnocchi just right. Add the seared Brussels sprouts and well, you're just simply killin' it at the dinner table tonight.

Don't worry too much about getting the shapes and sizes of the gnocchi perfect. This isn't about perfection—it's about love. And be it love or gnocchi, we shouldn't have to think too hard about either one.

For the gnocchi:
1 pound garnet yams
1 tablespoon olive oil
1 tablespoon mellow white miso
½ teaspoon salt
1½ to 1¾ cups all-purpose flour
2 tablespoons organic cornstarch

PREPARE THE GNOCCHI:

Preheat the oven to 375°F. Place the yams right on the rack, with a large baking sheet on the rack below to collect any juices that fall. Bake for 40 minutes, or until very tender. Remove from the oven and let cool.

Once cool, bring a large pot of salted water to a boil.

Scoop the yam insides out of their skins into a large bowl and mash well, along with the olive oil, miso, and salt. Mix in the flour, along with the cornstarch, ½ cup at a time, until you've added 1½ cups flour. The dough should be soft and smooth and slightly tacky, but not so sticky that it's clumping on your hands and difficult to work with. If needed, add a little extra flour by the tablespoon until that texture is achieved.

Lightly flour a clean work surface. Divide the dough into four balls and roll each ball into a snake that is about 1 inch in circumference.

Use a floured knife to cut the snakes into about 1-inch pieces. If you like, roll each gnocco across the back of the tines of a fork to make grooves. This takes some practice and isn't wholly necessary, so at this point you can simply proceed to cook.

(recipe continues)

Turn the heat down slightly so that the water is at a simmer, not at a full rolling boil. Use a slotted spoon to lower the gnocchi into the water. Once all the gnocchi have been added, wait for them to float to the surface. Let them bob for a minute or so, then remove with a slotted spoon and transfer to a large plate until ready to serve. If you need to heat them through before serving, simply sauté for a minute or so.

PREPARE THE SAUCE AND THE BRUSSELS SPROUTS:

Drain the cashews and add them to a blender along with the vegetable broth. Blend until very smooth. This could take anywhere from 1 to 5 minutes depending on the strength of your machine. Scrape down the sides with a rubber spatula occasionally to make sure you get everything. It should be very smooth, with only a slight graininess.

In the meantime, sear the Brussels sprouts. Preheat a large cast-iron pan over medium-high heat and add 1 tablespoon of the oil. Sauté the Brussels sprouts in the oil with ¼ teaspoon salt and some pepper for about 5 minutes, until lightly browned. Now add about ¼ cup water and immediately cover the pan with a tight-fitting lid to finish off the cooking. Let steam for about 1 minute. The water should be absorbed. Remove from the pan and set aside.

Lower the heat under the pan to medium, add the remaining 1 tablespoon oil, and sauté the onion and sliced garlic in the oil with a pinch of salt for about 7 minutes, until lightly browned.

Add the wine, remaining ½ teaspoon salt, and some pepper, stir, and turn the heat up to high. Let the wine reduce by about half. This should take 5 minutes or so. Turn the heat down to medium.

Stir in the tarragon leaves. Pour in the cashew mixture. Stir until well combined, and let cook and thicken for about 5 minutes. Thin with a little water or veggie broth if necessary; you want it to have a pourable consistency. Taste for seasoning. Add the Brussels sprouts back in and toss to coat.

Now divide the gnocchi among bowls. Cover with sauce and Brussels sprouts, and serve.

For the Tarragon Cream and Brussels sprouts:

½ cup cashews, soaked for at least 2 hours (see "ABS: Always Be Soaking," page 14)

1½ cups vegetable broth

2 tablespoons olive oil

8 ounces Brussels sprouts, trimmed and quartered

¾ teaspoon salt, plus a pinch

Several pinches of freshly ground black pepper

1 medium yellow onion, quartered and thinly sliced

¼ cup thinly sliced garlic

1 cup dry white wine

Scant ¼ cup loosely packed fresh tarragon leaves

NIRVANA ENCHILADA CASSEROLE

serves 8 • total time: 1 hour 10 mins
(plus time for soaking the cashews) • active time: 30 mins

The thing is, enchiladas can be a fussy production. A worth-it production, but a production nonetheless. This version, in casserole form, is a little less so. Don't get me wrong, it still requires more dishes than you want to clean, but it's a lot easier than stuffing each tortilla.

Now that I've scared all of you poseurs away with that foreboding introduction, I'll let you in on a little secret: This is ridiculously amazing. Shh! Layers of corn tortilla sopping up spicy, fragrant red sauce, then overstuffed with mushrooms, pinto beans, and roasted potatoes. On top is a voluptuous cashew cream that will have you rolling your eyes to the back of your head like a zombie. An enchilada zombie.

This is definitely a Sunday night supper, but if you want to enjoy it on a weeknight, it can happen. Make the enchilada sauce the night before and be sure to soak your cashews in advance. Everything will come together in a snap! Although there are four components, I tried to keep them all simple enough so that they work together well and don't cause too much grief.

PREPARE THE POTATOES:

Preheat the oven to 425°F. Line a large rimmed baking sheet with parchment paper.

Toss the potatoes with the oil right on the baking sheet. Sprinkle with salt and black pepper and toss to coat. Bake for 15 minutes, reduce the heat to 350°F, flip the potatoes, and bake for 10 more minutes. Remove from the oven and set aside. Leave the oven at 350°F because that is the temp at which the enchiladas need to bake.

PREPARE THE ENCHILADA SAUCE:

Preheat a 4-quart pot over medium heat. Dry-toast the cumin and coriander seeds in the pan for about 2 minutes, stirring frequently, until they're fragrant and a few shades darker. Just be careful not to burn. Add the oil and sauté the onion, jalapeño, garlic, oregano, and a pinch of salt for about 5 minutes, until the onions are translucent. Add the tomatoes, agave, and remaining 1 teaspoon salt, cover the pot, and turn the heat up to bring to a low boil. Let cook for about 20 minutes.

(recipe continues)

For the potatoes:

1½ pounds Yukon Gold potatoes, diced into ½-inch pieces

1 tablespoon olive oil

½ teaspoon salt

Freshly ground black pepper

For the enchilada sauce:

4 teaspoons cumin seeds

1 tablespoon coriander seeds

1 tablespoon olive oil

1 medium yellow onion, diced

1 jalapeño, seeded and chopped (use 2 if you like more heat)

6 cloves garlic, chopped

2 teaspoons dried oregano (Mexican, preferably)

1 teaspoon salt, plus a pinch

2 (28-ounce) cans whole tomatoes

1 teaspoon agave nectar

For the filling:

1 tablespoon olive oil

1 medium yellow onion, quartered and thinly sliced

½ teaspoon salt, plus a pinch

2 cloves garlic, minced

8 ounces cremini mushrooms, thinly sliced

2 (15-ounce) cans pinto beans, rinsed and drained (3 cups)

2 tablespoons fresh lime juice

For the white sauce:

1 cup cashews, soaked for at least 2 hours (see "ABS: Always Be Soaking," page 14)

¾ cup water

2 teaspoons organic cornstarch

½ teaspoon salt

For assembly:

18 (8-inch) corn tortillas

Pepitas (optional)

Chopped fresh cilantro (optional)

Once cooked, purée until smooth with either an immersion blender or by transferring to a blender or food processor. If using a blender, intermittently lift the lid to let steam escape so that it doesn't build up and explode and kill you. Also, note that if you use an immersion blender, you really have to blend a lot to get the seeds to smooth out. Taste for salt and set aside to cool.

PREPARE THE FILLING:

Preheat a large pan over medium heat and add the oil. Sauté the onion in the oil with a pinch of salt for about 5 minutes, until translucent. Add the garlic and sauté just until fragrant, 15 seconds or so. Add the mushrooms and remaining ½ teaspoon salt and cook until the mushrooms have released a lot of their moisture, about 5 minutes. Add the pinto beans and lime juice and cook just until heated through, 2 minutes or so.

Toss the roasted potatoes into the filling mix. Taste for seasoning and set aside.

PREPARE THE WHITE SAUCE:

Drain the cashews. Add all of the white sauce ingredients to the blender and purée until completely smooth, anywhere from 1 to 5 minutes depending on the strength of your machine. It's rather thick, so definitely scrape down the sides with a rubber spatula often to make sure you get everything. Refrigerate until ready to use.

TO ASSEMBLE THIS BAD BOY:

So we're just going to be adding layers of sauce, tortillas, and filling, then topping it all off. Let's begin:

Lightly grease a 9 x 13–inch casserole pan. Ladle in a thin layer of enchilada sauce, then layer 6 tortillas into the pan. Now things are going to get a bit messy! Ladle in another layer of enchilada sauce (about 1 cup), and flip each tortilla to smother in the sauce. Each one should be coated, but you should still be able to see the tortilla; that is to say, it shouldn't be drowning in the sauce. Next, arrange the tortillas so that they're slightly overlapping and covering the bottom of the pan.

Now add half of the filling and pour on ½ cup or so enchilada sauce. Layer in 6 more tortillas and repeat the process of smothering each of them in a cup of sauce. Cover with the remaining filling. Once again pour ½ cup enchilada sauce over the filling, and add the final layer of tortillas. Smother those in a cup of sauce. Reserve the rest of the sauce (if any) for serving.

Finally, top with the white sauce. I pour it directly out of the blender and try to ribbon it in thick globs over the top. It doesn't have to be neat; it will look cute pretty much no matter what.

Bake uncovered for about 30 minutes. The topping should be lightly golden.

Remove from the oven and sprinkle with a handful of pepitas and chopped fresh cilantro if you like. Now it's ready to serve!

WORK FLOW:

Here's the order of steps to get this done in just over an hour:

1. Preheat oven, prep potatoes, and begin your *mise en place*.
2. Roast the potatoes.
3. Start the enchilada sauce.
4. Start the filling.
5. While all that is cooking, blend the cashew sauce.
6. Assemble, bake, and go relax!

NOTES:

- If you're not feeding an army, you can halve this recipe and bake in an 8-inch square casserole dish. Just make sure it's a deep one or you'll have an overflowing enchilada monster on your hands.

- If you want to add extra heat, there are a couple of ways I can recommend doing it. Sauté a sliced and seeded jalapeño with the onion for the filling, or try adding an extra jalapeño to the sauce.

- The white sauce is not entirely necessary, but it's easy enough to do and it looks (and tastes) great. If, however, it's too much to finagle at the moment or you forgot to soak the cashews, then you can just serve the enchiladas topped with some guac. If you wanted to bake with your favorite meltable vegan cheese instead, then I will try to look the other way.

- I love the tenderness of pinto beans here, but feel free to use black beans. I bet lentils would be yummy, too. But that's no surprise, because I always think lentils would be yummy.

ROASTED & TOASTED THINGS
with Wild Rice

serves 4 to 6 · total time: 1 hour · active time: 20 mins

For the rice:
1½ cups wild rice blend, rinsed

3 cups water

¼ teaspoon salt

For the veggies:
1 pound eggplant, cut into ¾-inch chunks

8 ounces whole cremini mushrooms

¼ cup olive oil

1 teaspoon salt

Freshly ground black pepper

1½ pounds tomatoes, chopped

1 medium yellow onion, thinly sliced into half-moons

10 sprigs fresh thyme

4 cloves garlic, minced

For everything else:
⅓ cup pine nuts

1 (15-ounce) can cannellini beans, rinsed and drained (1½ cups)

Balsamic vinegar, for serving

NOTE:
About the mushrooms: I purchase small ones and keep them whole. This cuts down on prep time, obviously, but I also love the juicy texture of roasted whole 'shrooms. If any large ones sneak in, just slice them in half and proceed.

Sometimes I just want roasted and toasted things. It's the kind of meal I make when I crave something delicious but don't want to think too much about it and desperately want to warm up the house a bit. Not just with the heat of the oven but also with the amazing roasty aromas that generate while the veggies cook. Basically, you throw together a bunch of veggies on a couple of baking sheets, boil some rice, toast some pine nuts, mix everything together, and dinner is served. The rice is chewy and rustic, the veggies—mushrooms, eggplant, and onions—are satisfyingly caramelized, and the tomatoes make everything saucy and delicious. Some beans for protein and pine nuts for crunch and we're in business.

There are some important methods here that can really take your cooking to the next level. Roasting is a necessary skill, of course, but you'll also learn my patented method of roasting minced garlic without burning it. And cooking whole thyme sprigs with the tomatoes is a wonderful way to minimize your prep time and get herbalicious flavor infused into your veggies. So try it my way once, then take your new skills and run with them your way. It may not be incredibly fast the first time you make this, but it gets easier as you get into the roasting habit—which I promise you will!

PREPARE THE RICE:
Preheat the oven to 400°F. Then get the rice going. Place it in a 2-quart pot with the water and salt. Cover and bring to a boil, then lower the heat to a very low simmer. Let simmer for about 25 minutes, until tender. Remove from the heat and set aside, keeping warm.

PREPARE THE VEGGIES:
Now we'll roast the veggies on two large rimmed baking sheets. Line both sheets with parchment paper. Place the eggplant and mushrooms on one baking sheet and drizzle with 2 tablespoons of the olive oil, ½ teaspoon salt, and a few pinches of black pepper. Toss to coat and roast for about 30 minutes, tossing once. The tomatoes and onions require a shorter roasting time, so you can stick them in the oven about 5 minutes after the eggplant. Place the chopped tomatoes on one side of the baking sheet and the onions on the other. You'll need to keep them separate while roasting so that they cook evenly. Toss the tomatoes with 2 teaspoons of the oil, ¼ teaspoon salt,

and some black pepper, and tuck the thyme sprigs into them as well. Toss the onions with 2 teaspoons of the oil and ¼ teaspoon salt.

Now we'll use my patented method of roasting the minced garlic. Right on the cutting board where you minced it, drizzle it with the remaining 2 teaspoons olive oil. Then sprinkle it over the tomatoes, letting it rest on top without mixing it in.

Place the second baking sheet in the oven and roast for about 25 minutes, tossing once midway through cooking. It's cool to mix the garlic in at that point.

In the meantime, toast the pine nuts by preheating a heavy-bottomed pan over medium-low heat. Then toast the pine nuts for about 5 minutes, tossing frequently, until they're a few shades darker. Remove from the pan and set aside.

When everything is roasted and yummy, remove from the oven. Remove the thyme sprigs from the tomatoes. Some leaves should fall off naturally; if they're being stubborn you can coax them off and into the tomatoes. Discard the stems.

Transfer the tomatoes and onions to the eggplant pan, toss in the beans, and mix together. Scoop the rice into bowls, top with the veggies, sprinkle with a little balsamic vinegar (1 teaspoon should do it), top with the pine nuts, and serve.

TAMALE SHEPHERD'S PIE

serves 8 to 10 • total time: 1 hour • active time: 30 mins

Who among us doesn't love mashed potatoes? Add something spicy, savory, and stewy bubbling underneath and it pretty much takes that love over the top and into creepy obsession territory.

This dish has a creamy layer of lime-kissed mashed red potatoes over a succulent and spicy stew of black beans, mushrooms, tomatoes, poblano peppers, and corn, with a few of the usual Southwestern flavors thrown in. To give it true tamale flavor, a few handfuls of crumbled tortilla chips tossed into the stew do the trick. I love how the red potatoes look on top, adding flecks of pretty blush. It makes a ton, too, and leftovers taste just as good.

Place the potatoes in a pot, submerge in water, and add salt generously. Cover and bring to a boil. Once boiling, lower the heat and simmer for about 15 minutes, or until the potatoes are tender.

Drain the potatoes and immediately transfer them back to the pot. It's important to do this while everything is still hot. Give them a quick preliminary mash, and then add the milk, olive oil, lime zest, and salt. Mash until creamy, taste for salt, then cover and set aside.

While the potatoes are cooking, start the stew. Preheat a large, heavy-bottomed pan over medium-high heat and add the oil. Sauté the onion and poblano pepper in the oil with a pinch of salt until softened, about 7 minutes.

Add the garlic and sauté until fragrant, 30 seconds or so. Add the mushrooms and cilantro and cook until the mushrooms have released a lot of moisture, about 5 minutes. Add the tomatoes, corn, wine, cumin, remaining ¾ teaspoon salt, and red pepper flakes. Turn up the heat and cover the pan, stirring occasionally and cooking for 5 to 7 minutes. The tomatoes should break down and become saucy (if the corn was frozen it may take a bit longer).

Now take the tortilla chips and crush them into fine crumbs with your hands. It's okay if there are a few bigger pieces, but aim for crumbs. Add them to the stew and mix well. Since tortilla chips can be salty, wait until they're added to taste for salt. Mix in the lime juice and hot sauce, then fold in the black beans and heat through. Now taste for seasonings.

To assemble: Preheat the oven to 350°F. Lightly grease a deep 11 x 13–inch casserole dish (cooking spray works just fine). Transfer the stew to the casserole and even it out with a spatula. Add the potatoes in dollops and spread into an even layer.

Bake for about 25 minutes, until the potatoes are lightly browned. Serve hot, garnished with chile peppers, cilantro, and lime slices.

For the mashed potato layer:

- 2½ pounds red potatoes, cut into big chunks (1½ inches or so)
- ½ cup unsweetened non-dairy milk, room temperature
- 2 tablespoons olive oil
- 1 scant teaspoon grated lime zest
- ¾ teaspoon salt

For the stew:

- 2 tablespoons olive oil, plus more as needed
- 1 medium yellow onion, diced
- 1 poblano pepper, seeded and diced
- ¾ teaspoon salt, plus a pinch
- 4 cloves garlic, minced
- 8 ounces cremini mushrooms, cut in half and sliced ¼ inch thick or so
- 1 cup loosely packed fresh cilantro, chopped
- 1¼ pounds plum tomatoes (about 6), chopped
- ½ cup corn kernels (fresh or frozen; see page 181)
- ¼ cup dry red wine
- 1 teaspoon ground cumin
- ½ teaspoon crushed red pepper flakes
- 2 ounces tortilla chips (about 4 good-size handfuls)
- 2 tablespoons fresh lime juice
- 2 tablespoons Frank's RedHot sauce, plus extra for serving
- 2 (15-ounce) cans black beans, rinsed and drained (3 cups)

For the garnish:

Hot red chile peppers
Chopped fresh cilantro
Lime slices

NOTE:

You can adjust the spice level to your liking by (obviously) adjusting the amount of hot sauce and red pepper flakes. As is, I'd say it's a low-medium spicy.

NACHO NIGHT

serves 6 · total time: 45 mins
(plus time for soaking the cashews) · active time: 45 mins

For the *Queso Blanco:*

¾ cup cashews, soaked for at least 2 hours (see "ABS: Always Be Soaking," page 14)

1¼ cups vegetable broth

1 tablespoon mellow white miso

3 tablespoons nutritional yeast flakes

2 cloves garlic, peeled

2 teaspoons ground cumin

¼ teaspoon salt, plus a pinch

2 tablespoons fresh lemon juice

2 teaspoons olive oil

1 small yellow onion, finely diced

2 jalapeños, seeded and chopped

For the spice mix:

½ teaspoon dried oregano

2 teaspoons ground ancho chile

1 teaspoon ground cumin

½ teaspoon ground coriander

½ teaspoon salt

For the lentil meat:

2 teaspoons olive oil

1 small yellow onion, minced

2 cloves garlic, minced

Pinch of salt

2½ cups cooked brown lentils

3 tablespoons tomato paste

2 tablespoons hot sauce (preferably Cholula)

This recipe is actually a conglomeration of a few different recipes in the book. But I hate flipping back and forth through cookbooks to get all the components I need, so everything is listed here for your convenience. Now, let's get down to business. Nacho Night!

Creamy *queso* oozes all over spicy lentil meat, cool and creamy guacamole, juicy *pico de gallo,* and crisp lettuce. It's so fun to sit around the table (or, ya know, in front of the TV), eating with your hands and getting a different flavor every time you lift chip to mouth.

Let the chips be your palette here! You can pare this recipe down or up. If you'd rather go with something simple, use black beans instead of lentil meat and sliced avocado instead of guacamole. If you'd like to add more veggies, roasted zucchini makes a great topping, as do sautéed mushrooms or even small cubes of roasted butternut squash. You can also add pepitas for texture.

There's a photo of this recipe facing the title page.

PREPARE THE QUESO:

Drain the cashews and add them to a blender along with the vegetable broth, miso, nutritional yeast, garlic, cumin, ¼ teaspoon salt, and lemon juice. Purée until completely smooth. This could take anywhere from 1 to 5 minutes depending on the strength of your machine. Scrape down the sides with a rubber spatula to make sure you get everything.

Preheat a 2-quart saucepan over low heat and add the oil. Sauté the onion and jalapeños in the oil with a pinch of salt for 3 minutes, just until soft. Add the blended cashew mixture and turn the heat to medium. Cook for about 10 minutes, using an angled wooden spoon to stir occasionally, until the *queso* is hot and thickened. Keep warm until ready to serve.

PREPARE THE SPICE MIX AND LENTIL MEAT:

First combine all of the ingredients for the spice mix and set aside. Also, keep a cup of water within reach. You'll need to add splashes as you cook.

Preheat a large skillet over medium-high heat and add the oil. Sauté the onion and garlic in the oil with a pinch of salt for about 3 minutes, until lightly browned. Add the spice mix and toss for 30 seconds or so to toast.

Lower the heat to medium, add the lentils, a few splashes of water, the tomato paste, and hot sauce; use a spatula to mash them a bit as they cook, until they hold together. If your spatula isn't strong enough to accomplish this, just use a sturdy fork. Do this for about 5 minutes, adding splashes of water as necessary if it appears dry. Taste for seasoning; you may want to add more spices or hot sauce. Keep warm until ready to serve.

PREPARE THE PICO DE GALLO:

Simply mix all of the ingredients together in a bowl!

PREPARE THE GUACAMOLE:

Cut the avocado in half, remove the pit, and scoop into a bowl. Add the tomato, onion, and salt, and use an avocado masher to mash everything together. Add the orange juice, and taste for seasoning.

TO ASSEMBLE:

To serve, place all of components on the table for diners to make their own nacho plates. It's nacho night!

For the *Pico de Gallo*:
1 pound tomatoes, chopped
1 small red onion, finely diced
1 jalapeño, seeded and finely chopped
¼ cup chopped fresh cilantro
2 tablespoons fresh lime juice
Pinch of salt

For Pepe's Secret Guacamole:
2 ripe avocados
⅓ cup chopped tomato
3 tablespoons finely chopped white onion
½ teaspoon salt
¼ cup fresh orange juice

For serving:
1 large bag tortilla chips (preferably "restaurant style")
Shredded romaine lettuce
Chopped scallions
Chopped fresh cilantro

Building Better Nachos

Vegan nachos are just plain fun. I've taken quite a few trips to Kansas City for the express purpose of obtaining a big plateful at one of my favorite vegan restaurants, FüD. What I love about their nachos is that they understand that toppings don't have to start and end at the top. You should have oozy, gooey, cheezy goodness and nummy-yummy spiciness right down to the last chip! To get there, they do several layers of chips and toppings piled high. That is one way to do it. Another is to get humongous dinner plates and spread out one layer of chips, then throw all the toppings on, so that you have a guaranteed smorgasbord on each individual chip. Both ways are totally acceptable and totally fun. So long as you're not serving a pile of dry chips with a metric ton of toppings on those chips lucky enough to be at the summit, you are golden.

VARIATIONS:

- Not feeling like lentil meat? Try black beans instead: 1½ cups cooked (or a 15-ounce can, drained and rinsed).

- Seitan is also a great addition to nachos. Slice up about 2 cups and lightly sauté.

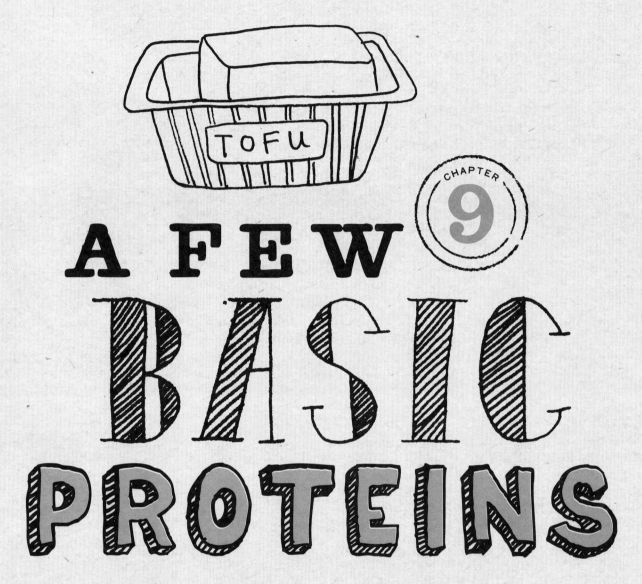

A FEW BASIC PROTEINS

CHAPTER 9

Here are a few SIMPLE PREPARATIONS

for some choice proteins that would be great for adding to salads, pastas, bowls, and so forth. And if any of these made their way into a sandwich, I don't think anyone would complain!

GARLICKY THYME TEMPEH

serves 2 to 4 · time: 1 hour 10 mins · active time: 15 mins

8 ounces tempeh

For the marinade:

2 tablespoons soy sauce or tamari

4 cloves garlic, smashed

½ cup vegetable broth

2 tablespoons white balsamic vinegar (or 1 tablespoon regular balsamic vinegar)

3 tablespoons fresh lemon juice

½ cup fresh thyme (leaves whole, soft stems chopped)

2 tablespoons olive oil

NOTES:

- Don't be scared by the total time, because most of it is just the tempeh marinating. You can let it sit overnight or all day, so go ahead and marinate, then do your shopping or protest on Washington or whatever, then come back and cook it.

- I slice the tempeh thinly, another way to help infuse flavor. Prep directions for rectangles and squares of tempeh are both given. Trapezoids and rhombuses need not apply.

This tempeh is great for topping pastas or salads, alongside mashed potatoes and gravy, or tucked into sandwiches.

If you're just a young soybean and have never cooked tempeh before, the gist is that you're steaming it first to take away the beaniness and get it ready to absorb lots of flavor. A long swim in the marinade and then it's ready to be cooked to succulent perfection, either on the grill or in the broiler.

For the fresh thyme, I just slide as much leaf as I can off the stems. If the stems are soft enough, they can be thrown in, too. Don't be alarmed at the quantities; remember, this is just the marinade, you won't be eating it in the final product, so you want to infuse as much flavor as possible.

Set up your steaming apparatus.

If your tempeh comes packaged as a rectangle: Slice it into 2 squares. Slice those squares into 2 thin squares across the middle, sort of like a clamshell. Now slice each square corner to corner, into triangles. You should have 8 thin triangles.

If your tempeh comes packaged as a square: Slice in half into 2 rectangles. Slice each rectangle across the middle, sort of like a clamshell. Then slice in half, into squares. You should have 8 thin squares.

Steam the tempeh for 10 minutes. It's going to smell like baking bread!

PREPARE THE MARINADE:

In the meantime, mix all of the marinade ingredients together in a big bowl. When the tempeh is ready, transfer it directly into the marinade. Let marinate for 1 hour or up to overnight, flipping occasionally.

TO GRILL:

Preheat a lightly oiled grill (indoor or outdoor) on medium-high heat. Cook the tempeh for 5 minutes on each side, flipping with a metal spatula so that it doesn't stick. Extra flavor tip: Rub the thyme and garlic from the marinade on each side. Some will fall off, but not all of it.

TO BROIL:

Preheat the broiler. Place the tempeh on a baking sheet and position 2 to 3 inches from the heat. Keeping a close eye, broil the tempeh for 3 to 5 minutes on each side. Baste with some of the marinade when you flip it.

STEAMY BEANY SAUSAGES

makes 4 sausages · total time: 50 mins · active time: 10 mins

Don't be intimidated by making your own seitan sausage. It can all happen right on your stovetop without any unknown ingredients or equipment. The process is simple: Mash some beans, throw in vital wheat gluten and some other flavorings, roll 'em up in aluminum foil like a Tootsie Roll, and steam! Just 40 minutes later, you've got incredible, versatile, scrumptious sausages to sauté, use in soups or stews, and make profane gestures with. It's all you could ever want from a vegan sausage!

½ cup cooked pinto beans, rinsed and drained
1 cup vegetable broth
1 tablespoon olive oil
2 tablespoons soy sauce
1¼ cups vital wheat gluten
¼ cup nutritional yeast flakes
1 teaspoon granulated garlic
1½ teaspoons fennel seeds, crushed
2 teaspoons smoked paprika
½ teaspoon dried thyme
Several pinches of freshly ground black pepper

Before mixing your ingredients, get your steaming apparatus ready, bringing the water to a full boil. The rest of the recipe comes together very quickly.

Have ready 4 square sheets of aluminum foil. In a large bowl, mash the beans until no whole beans are left. Mix in the vegetable broth, olive oil, and soy sauce. Throw in all the other ingredients in the order listed and mix with a fork, then knead lightly with your hands.

Divide the dough into 4 equal pieces. Place one quarter of the dough into a piece of the foil and mold into about a 5-inch log. Wrap the dough in the foil, like a Tootsie Roll. Don't worry too much about shaping it, as it will snap into shape while it's steaming because this recipe is awesome.

Place the wrapped sausages in the steamer and steam for 40 minutes. That's it! You can unwrap and enjoy immediately or refrigerate, wrapped in plastic wrap, until ready to use (for up to 5 days).

NOTES:

• These freeze well, so if you'd like to make up a double batch to use anytime, then go for it. To freeze, allow the sausages to cool. Unwrap them from the foil and place in an airtight freezer bag. They will keep for up to 1 month in the freezer. For best results, thaw before using.

• If you don't have smoked paprika, sweet paprika is a good sub, but you'll lose that smoky flavor. You can sub in 2 teaspoons of liquid smoke if you've got it, but otherwise, don't worry. They will still be delish!

CLASSIC
BAKED TOFU

makes 8 slabs · total time: 30 mins (plus 1 hour to marinate) ·
active time: 5 mins

1 (14-ounce) block extra-firm tofu,
   sliced into 8 slabs

Marinade:

3 tablespoons soy sauce (or Bragg
   Liquid Aminos)

1 tablespoon prepared yellow mustard

1 tablespoon olive oil

¾ cup vegetable broth

2 teaspoons garlic powder

NOTE:

I don't call for Bragg Liquid Aminos
anywhere else in the book, but I'm
going to suggest using it here instead
of soy sauce or tamari if you can get
your hands on it. Perhaps it's my hippie
vegan sensibilities, but sometimes
Bragg's really hits the spot. It's similar
to soy sauce, but with a slightly acidic
smoky flavor that works perfectly here.

You need this tofu in your life. It's the tofu you keep in the fridge,
at the ready for sandwiches or slicing up over salads. It's the tofu
you serve warm, with a pile of greens and lots of tahini sauce. It's
the tofu that you spike with a fork right out of the oven and wolf
down before serving everyone else. It's chewy and succulent, with
just enough flavor to be delicious without being overpowering,
letting it slide stealthily into any meal at any time.

In a bowl big enough to accommodate the tofu, mix together all the marinade
ingredients. Add the tofu and marinate for an hour (or overnight), flipping at
least once.

Preheat oven to 425°F. Line a rimmed baking sheet with parchment paper.

Place the tofu in a single layer on the baking sheet, cover with tin foil, and
bake for 15 minutes. Remove the tin foil, flip the tofu, and spoon on more
marinade. Then bake (uncovered) for another 12 to 15 minutes. The tofu
should be browned at the edges.

Serve immediately, or let cool and keep refrigerated in a well-sealed container
for up to 5 days.

SESAME TOFU

serves 4 · total time: 15 mins · active time: 5 mins

This is the easiest thing in the world! It's embarrassing even to call it a recipe. It's more like intuition. Make it once and you won't ever have to measure again. There are only three ingredients and it's still super flavorful and great to top off bowls or salads or to tuck into sandwiches. You can broil or grill it. Life is good.

3 tablespoons soy sauce or tamari

1 tablespoon toasted sesame oil

14 ounces extra-firm tofu, pressed (if you have time, but okay if not), sliced widthwise into 8 slabs

Measure out the soy sauce and sesame oil onto a dinner plate. Dredge the tofu into the mixture to get it coated on both sides.

TO GRILL:

Preheat a cast-iron grill pan over medium-high heat. Spray with oil. Cook the tofu for 3 to 5 minutes on each side, flipping with a metal spatula.

TO BROIL:

Preheat the broiler. Place the tofu on a baking sheet and position about 6 inches from the heat. Broil for 3 to 5 minutes on each side, keeping a close eye so that it doesn't burn.

Serve in slabs or cut into strips, depending on what you're serving it with.

SIMMERED SEITAN

makes about 2 pounds · total time: 1 hour · active time: 10 mins

8 cups vegetable broth

6 cloves garlic, smashed

2 cups vital wheat gluten

5 tablespoons nutritional yeast flakes

1 cup cold water

½ cup soy sauce

2 tablespoons tomato paste

1 scant teaspoon grated lemon zest

NOTES:

- Make sure that your broth is strongly flavored and salty enough, since that is where most of the flavor in the seitan will be coming from.

- The key here is to make sure that your seitan is simmering, not boiling. Keep an eye on it, especially in the first 15 minutes, to make sure that it isn't at a rapid boil but at a low and steady simmer. Adjust the heat as needed.

- To ready your seitan for any recipe, just give it a little squeeze over the sink to get some of the liquid out. This way, it will brown more easily when you cook it.

- Seitan freezes wonderfully! Squeeze most of the liquid out and store in an airtight bag in the freezer for up to 1 month.

Dubbed "wheat meat" for its chewy texture and meaty appearance, seitan is not just the king of fake meats, but it's also a savory delicacy in its own right. Its precise origin isn't exactly known, but it was popularized in the '60s by Buddhist monks and has been gaining ground ever since.

The artisan way of creating perfect seitan involves an intensive process of washing and kneading flour until all that's left is a delicious glob of wheat protein. But there's a much easier and foolproof way that will have you sauté-ready in about an hour, and the secret is vital wheat gluten. It's a high-gluten flour available in natural-foods stores, and it's becoming more and more common on the grocery shelf.

Of course you can buy seitan ready-made, but the homemade method is easy: Make a savory dough, drop into boiling water, and simmer for an hour. Totally easy, totally yummy.

Fill a stockpot with the broth and smashed garlic, cover, and bring to a boil.

In the meantime, in a large bowl, mix together the gluten and nutritional yeast. Make a well in the center and add the water, soy sauce, tomato paste, and lemon zest. Mix with a fork, and then use your hands to knead for about 3 minutes, until it's an elastic dough and everything looks well incorporated. Form into a log and divide into thirds with a knife. Let rest until the broth has come to a full boil.

Once boiling, lower the heat to a simmer. This is important: The broth should not be at a rolling boil or you risk the seitan getting waterlogged (aka turning into brains). Add the gluten pieces and partially cover the pot so that steam can escape. Let simmer for 45 minutes, turning occasionally. Make sure to keep an eye on the heat because it may start to boil again, in which case, just turn it down a notch to keep at a low, steady simmer.

When the seitan is done, you can let it cool in the broth, or remove a portion to use right away. Once cooled, refrigerate in a tightly covered container submerged in the broth for up to 5 days.

STEAMED CHICKY SEITAN

makes 4 cutlets · total time: 50 mins · active time: 10 mins

Here it is! Seitan cutlets made with chickpeas that are great for recipes where others might use chicken. I really love 'em. They're totally steamed and totally easy; like seitan sausages, only folded into parcels, so you can cut them into long strips if you like, or grill them whole to top Caesar salad. If you don't have powdered sage, you can use dried rubbed sage; just be careful to rub it between your fingers to get it as fine as possible. And I do recommend finding powdered sage, even if only for this recipe, because I promise you'll be making it often enough! Also, if you've got a strong, salty, chicken-style broth, there couldn't be a more appropriate place to use it.

2/3 of a 15-ounce can chickpeas, rinsed and drained (1 cup)

1 cup strong, salty vegetable broth

1 tablespoon olive oil

3 tablespoons soy sauce

1 1/3 cups vital wheat gluten

1/3 cup nutritional yeast flakes

2 teaspoons onion powder

1 teaspoon granulated garlic

1 teaspoon dried powdered sage

1/2 teaspoon salt

Several pinches of freshly ground black pepper

Before mixing your ingredients, get your steaming apparatus ready, bringing the water to a full boil. The rest of the recipe comes together very quickly.

Have ready 4 square sheets of aluminum foil. In a large bowl, mash the chickpeas well, until no whole ones are left. Mix in the broth, olive oil, and soy sauce. Throw in all the other ingredients in the order listed. Mix well, using a fork, and then lightly knead with your hands.

Divide the dough into 4 equal pieces. Form each piece into a patty that is 4 to 5 inches wide. Place each patty in the center of a foil square and fold the foil up into a parcel. Don't wrap the foil too tight, because the seitan will expand.

Place the wrapped patties in the steamer and steam for 40 minutes. That's it! You can unwrap and enjoy immediately or refrigerate until ready to use. They'll keep in the fridge (tightly wrapped in plastic wrap) for up to 5 days. They also freeze nicely for up to 3 months.

Grilled Seitan

Grilling is my favorite way to enjoy seitan, and it doesn't have to be complicated. The charred bits give it great depth and smokiness, and the quick cooking ensures that it remains juicy and doesn't dry out.

TO GRILL: Preheat a grill pan over medium-high heat. Thinly slice into long strips (about 1/4 inch thick). Place the strips in a bowl, drizzle with a little olive oil, sprinkle with salt and freshly ground black pepper, and toss to coat. Spray the grill pan with oil and cook the seitan on each side for 3 to 5 minutes, until grill marks appear. These slices are perfect over salads or in sandwiches (try hummus, avocado, lettuce, tomato, and seitan), or perhaps with mashed potatoes and some gravy.

BREAKFAST, BRUNCH & BAKES

for the Morning

For me,
BREAKFAST
most days

is a bowl of oatmeal with maple syrup, bananas, and nuts. You don't need a recipe for that, do you? Instead, I'm going to provide a few savory ideas that are quick enough to prepare on any morning, and then a few recipes that will make for a relatively easy and very satisfying brunch. Of course, morning would not exist without muffins and scones, so there are a few of those recipes thrown in for good measure, too!

MEDITERRANEAN
OVERNIGHT SCRAMBLE

serves 4 · total time: 20 mins · active time: 20 mins

14 ounces extra-firm tofu

¼ cup kalamata olives, chopped

1 roasted red pepper (store-bought or homemade; see page 118)

2 tablespoons fresh lemon juice

2 tablespoons nutritional yeast flakes

½ teaspoon dried thyme

2 tablespoons finely chopped fresh basil leaves

2 cloves garlic, minced

¼ teaspoon ground turmeric

¼ teaspoon crushed red pepper flakes (optional)

¼ teaspoon salt

Several pinches of freshly ground black pepper

1 tablespoon olive oil

If you can take 10 minutes to mash a bunch of stuff up in a bowl the night before, you can have scrambled tofu in 7 minutes the next morning. This scramble is perfect for tucking into an on-the-go wrap, with things like avocado, hummus, and lettuce, or try a big scoop on your bagel. Of course, you can also serve it with roasted potatoes, like a civilized human being. What's so great is how effortless it is. There's a little chopping, but nothing you can't handle before bed, and the rest is just like playing in the sandbox, mushing the tofu up with your hands and adding a host of flavorful ingredients that season your tofu as you sleep. A quick sauté the next morning and you're done.

Naturally, if you want to make this right away and eat it, that is totally cool, too. No need to let it sit overnight.

Crumble the tofu into a mixing bowl. Now mash it with your hands until it's very crumbly and only pea-size pieces remain. You don't want it to be completely mushy. Add the olives, red pepper, lemon juice, nutritional yeast, thyme, basil, garlic, turmeric, crushed red pepper flakes, salt, and black pepper, and mix well with your hands. Cover with plastic wrap and refrigerate overnight.

In the morning, preheat a large, heavy-bottomed pan over medium-high heat and add the oil. Cook the tofu for 5 to 7 minutes, stirring occasionally, until heated through and lightly browned. Serve.

MY THAI OVERNIGHT SCRAMBLE

serves 4 · total time: 20 mins · active time: 20 mins

14 ounces extra-firm tofu

2 tablespoons fresh lime juice

1 tablespoon Thai red curry paste (or to taste)

½ cup thinly sliced shiitake mushrooms

½ cup thinly sliced scallions

2 tablespoons panko bread crumbs

½ teaspoon dried thyme

2 tablespoons finely chopped fresh Thai basil leaves (regular basil may be used)

2 tablespoons finely chopped fresh cilantro

2 cloves garlic, minced

2 teaspoons minced fresh ginger

¼ teaspoon ground turmeric

¼ teaspoon crushed red pepper flakes (optional)

1 tablespoon soy sauce or tamari

1 tablespoon olive oil

This is another overnight scramble, this time with a quick stop in Thailand via (as usual) Brooklyn. The panko bread crumbs help absorb the flavors, but if you're gluten-free you can leave them out. Since Thai curry pastes vary from brand to brand, start with a tablespoon. If it tastes like it needs more, mix a teaspoon or so extra with a tablespoon of water and add it at the end. This makes a great wrap with some avocado and bean sprouts if you've got them!

Crumble the tofu into a mixing bowl. Now mash it with your hands until it's very crumbly and only pea-size pieces remain. You don't want it to be completely mushy. In a tiny cup or ramekin, mix the lime juice with the curry paste, just to get it dissolved. Add the mixture to the tofu, along with the mushrooms, scallions, bread crumbs, thyme, basil, cilantro, garlic, ginger, turmeric, crushed red pepper flakes, and soy sauce, and mix well with your hands. Cover with plastic wrap and refrigerate overnight.

In the morning, preheat a large, heavy-bottomed pan over medium-high heat and add the oil. Cook the tofu for 5 to 7 minutes, stirring occasionally, until heated through and lightly browned. Taste for seasoning, and serve.

MUFFIN PAN
MINI OMELETS

makes 12 mini omelets · total time: 45 mins · active time: 10 mins

Maybe you already know my omelet recipe—it's been on my Web site for years. But are you ever, like, "I want to make tofu omelets, but I don't want to have to cook in batches in a skillet, I want them all to cook at once. And I want to be able to do stuff while they're cooking, so it would be rad if they could be baked. And I want them to be tiny, so I can stuff them into, say, English muffins for breakfast. And I want the whole process to be adorable." Well then, this is the recipe for you! All of the ingredients are whizzed up in a food processor, scooped into a muffin tin, and baked away. The result is a pint-size omelet, perfect for sandwiches, or to use to sandwich a filling, or just to be served alongside potatoes for a brunch. I keep extras in the fridge just to snack on, since I even love how they taste cold.

2 cloves garlic, peeled

1 (14-ounce) package soft (silken) tofu

½ cup water

2 tablespoons nutritional yeast flakes

1 tablespoon olive oil

½ teaspoon ground turmeric

1 teaspoon salt

½ cup chickpea flour

1 tablespoon arrowroot or organic cornstarch

Preheat the oven to 350°F.

Chop the garlic in a food processor. Add the tofu, water, nutritional yeast, olive oil, turmeric, and salt. Purée until smooth. Add the chickpea flour and arrowroot and purée again for about 10 seconds, until combined. Make sure to scrape down the sides so that everything is well incorporated.

Brush a 12-cup muffin pan lightly with oil. Pour the batter into each well until a little over halfway full. Bake for 25 minutes, or until the edges have pulled away from the sides a bit and the top is firm to the touch.

For the best results, let cool for at least 10 minutes. Then flip the pan onto a cooling rack and enjoy! They taste great at room temperature, too.

CHIPOTLE SAUSAGE HASH

serves 4 · total time: 45 mins · active time: 20 mins

Here's the beauty of a hash: Everything comes together in one big pan, there are plenty of textures to keep you interested, and it's such a casual, spur-of-the-moment meal that you can make the seasonings work with almost anything you've got on hand. Here I combined two of my fave brunch flavors, chipotle and curry, and pretty traditional hash ingredients: Yukon Gold potatoes, sausages (well, maybe vegan sausages aren't traditional, but you get my drift), and onion. There's a lot of smoky and spicy flavor going on, and a hint of lime juice at the end brightens everything up. I like this for dinner, too, so feel free to enjoy any time of day.

Often hash is served with a poached egg on top, and I completely understand why. It can get pretty dry, and it's awesome to have something fatty, saucy, and delicious cutting through the flavors. To that end, I serve this with a mild tahini sauce and chopped avocado. They add creaminess and a nice flavor contrast, and the dressing is super easy to put together. I also serve it over steamed kale, because I do that with everything and because it sops up the sauce and because I enjoy the chewy texture. But a nice bed of fresh salad greens or raw spinach would be a fine touch, too.

PREPARE THE HASH:

Preheat a large skillet over medium-high heat and add 1 tablespoon of the oil. Cook the potatoes in the oil with the salt for about 12 minutes, keeping the pan covered and flipping the potatoes every few minutes. The potatoes should be edible, but still very firm at this point, and lightly browned on a few sides. You can make the dressing while the potatoes are cooking (see directions below).

Add the onion and the remaining 1 tablespoon oil and cook for about 5 minutes, tossing frequently, until the onions are softened (no need to keep covered anymore).

Now add the sausages, cilantro, oregano, and curry, and cook for about 2 more minutes, just to brown and cook it through a bit. Add the chipotles and cook just to integrate the flavors and make sure the potato is tender enough to eat. Toss with the lime juice and taste for salt and seasonings.

PREPARE THE DRESSING:

Add all of the ingredients to a small blender or food processor and purée until smooth. Start with ½ cup of the water and see if more is necessary. Keep refrigerated until ready to use.

Pour the dressing over the top of the hash and sprinkle with the chopped avocado and cilantro.

For the hash:

2 tablespoons olive oil

1 pound Yukon Gold potatoes, diced into ½-inch pieces

½ teaspoon salt

1 small yellow onion, finely diced

2 vegan sausages (store-bought or homemade; see page 237), cut into ½-inch pieces (see Notes)

¼ cup chopped fresh cilantro

1 teaspoon dried oregano

1 teaspoon mild curry powder

⅓ cup chipotles in adobo sauce, seeded, finely chopped

2 tablespoons fresh lime juice

For the Tahini Dressing:

1 clove garlic, peeled

¼ cup tahini

2 tablespoons nutritional yeast flakes

2 tablespoons mellow white miso

½ cup to ¾ cup water

For serving:

1 ripe avocado, pitted, peeled, and chopped into chunks

Chopped fresh cilantro or scallions

NOTES:

- It's worth it to take the time to chop the potatoes small enough, because that way they cook through quickly and integrate with the other ingredients.

- If using homemade sausages, only 2 are necessary. If using store-bought, I would recommend the Field Roast or Tofurky brands (any flavor) and use 3, since they're a bit smaller.

- I remove the seeds from the chipotles as best I can; that way you get the smokiness and spice without the unbearable heat of too many seeds. It is still spicy, so if you're a spice wimp, start with half the amount of chipotles and go from there.

SCRAMBLED CHICKPEAS

serves 4 · total time: 20 mins · active time: 20 mins

2 tablespoons olive oil

1 medium red onion, quartered and thinly sliced

½ teaspoon salt, plus a pinch

2 (15-ounce) cans chickpeas, rinsed and drained (3 cups)

½ teaspoon ground turmeric

Several pinches of freshly ground black pepper

3 cloves garlic, minced

3 tablespoons chopped fresh dill, plus extra for garnish (optional)

2 tablespoons fresh lemon juice

Because sometimes you don't feel like scrambling tofu. This stuff is simple yet slamming. Charred garlicky chickpeas and caramelized onions with hints of fresh dill and a splash of lemon are perfect breakfast elements. I love it alongside breakfast potatoes, or with biscuits and gravy, or simply on toast with tomato and maybe some avocado. If you'd like to be decadent, Miso-Tahini Dressing (page 192) makes a great topping, too.

I want to make sure you get the texture right, so lemme explain: You want to mash the chickpeas so that there are few whole pieces left but not so much that you've made hummus. If I had to break the texture down into percentages, I'd say the chickpeas should be about 25 percent mush so that the flavors have something to cling to, and the rest should be slightly mashed.

Preheat a large pan over medium-high heat and add 2 teaspoons of the oil. Sauté the onion in the oil with a pinch of salt for about 7 minutes, until browned. Add the chickpeas and toss them to warm them up a bit. Use a potato masher or sturdy fork to partially mash the chickpeas, just so that few whole pieces are left (see headnote).

Add 1 tablespoon of the oil and cook the chickpeas for about 7 more minutes, tossing only occasionally, so that they get a little charred. Add the remaining ½ teaspoon salt, turmeric, and black pepper, along with a splash of water (a tablespoon or two) to keep everything from getting too dry. Mix well.

Push the chickpeas over to the side and, in a clear spot in the pan, sauté the garlic in the remaining 1 teaspoon oil for only about 15 seconds. Then toss everything together and add the dill and lemon juice.

At this point it is pretty much done, but you may need to add a few more splashes of water if it seems dry. Taste for seasoning, and serve. You may garnish with a little extra dill, if you like.

PUFFY PILLOW PANCAKES

makes 6 pancakes · total time: 30 mins · active time: 20 mins

These pancakes were inspired by the movie *Dan in Real Life*. Honestly, I don't remember much about the film except for one thing: the pivotal pancake scene. Juliette Binoche was flipping these magnificent golden brown creatures on a griddle. I think she was pissed off about something in the scene, but all I could concentrate on were those puffy pillows of pancakes, perfectly golden brown, lined up like jewel cushions on display. I fussed and fussed with my pancake batter until I achieved these perfect results!

1½ cups all-purpose flour

3½ teaspoons baking powder

1 teaspoon salt

2 tablespoons granulated sugar

1 cup almond milk (or your favorite non-dairy milk)

2 teaspoons apple cider vinegar

1 tablespoon ground flaxseed

½ cup water

3 tablespoons canola oil

½ teaspoon pure vanilla extract

In a large bowl, sift together the flour, baking powder, salt, and sugar. Make a well in the center.

Measure the milk into a large measuring cup or small bowl. Add the vinegar and ground flaxseed, and use a fork to vigorously mix the ingredients until foamy. This will take a minute or so.

Pour the milk mixture into the center of the dry ingredients. Add the water, canola oil, and vanilla and use a fork to mix until a thick, lumpy batter forms. That should take about a minute. It doesn't need to be smooth; just make sure you get all the ingredients incorporated.

Preheat a pan or griddle over medium-low heat and let the batter rest for 10 minutes.

Lightly coat the griddle with oil. Add ⅓ cup batter to the griddle for each pancake, and cook for about 4 minutes, until puffy. Flip the pancakes, adding a new coat of oil to the pan if needed, and cook for another 3 minutes or so. The pancakes should be a little under an inch thick and golden brown. Let the pancakes rest on a cooling rack covered with aluminum foil until ready to serve. To reheat, place pancakes on a baking sheet covered with foil in a 300°F degree oven for 5 minutes or so.

NOTES:

- Don't use an electric mixer for the batter. Overmixing tends to result in a dense pancake. I simply use a dinner fork to get everything mixed.

- You have to let the batter rest for 10 minutes or so before cooking. The vinegar and baking powder need time to react with each other, and the gluten needs to settle in and rest.

- Don't crowd the pan. Even in my big cast-iron pan, I don't make more than two pancakes at once. If you have a large pancake griddle, then use it! (Just for the record, I don't have one.)

- Don't use too much oil in the pan. It will result in a tough exterior. A very thin layer of oil is what you want; a spray can of organic canola oil works perfectly for this.

- Preheat the pan for a good 10 minutes. I use cast iron and put it over moderately low heat (right around 3 on my stovetop), but you will probably need to adjust a little to get it just right. Remember, the temp is not set in stone. Lower and raise in tiny increments as needed. Even turning the dial ¼ inch can result in big changes.

- Use a measuring cup (with a rounded bottom if possible) to scoop out the batter for uniformly sized pancakes. And remember to spray the cup with oil between scoops to prevent sticking.

CARROT CAKE PANCAKES

makes 6 pancakes • total time: 30 mins • active time: 20 mins

2 tablespoons ground flaxseed

1 cup almond milk (or your favorite non-dairy milk)

1 teaspoon apple cider vinegar

¼ cup water

¼ cup pure maple syrup, plus more for serving

2 tablespoons canola oil

1 teaspoon pure vanilla extract

1¼ cups all-purpose flour

2 teaspoons baking powder

½ teaspoon salt

1 teaspoon ground cinnamon

½ teaspoon ground ginger

½ teaspoon ground nutmeg

¼ teaspoon ground allspice

1 cup peeled and grated carrot (about 6 ounces; see Note)

NOTE:

A note about the grated carrot: I do mean *grated*, not just shredded. Since the cooking time on these is so short, the smaller you can get the carrot pieces, the better. If you don't feel like grating the carrots by hand, use the shredding attachment on your food processor. Then remove that attachment and put in your metal blade. Pulse until the carrots look grated (but not puréed!).

When you want carrot cake but it's way too early in the day to eat cake and retain your dignity—Carrot Cake Pancakes to the rescue! These are moist and homey with hints of spice, just like their cakey inspiration. You can also add pecans or walnuts (½ cup or so), if that's your thing.

In a small bowl, using a fork, beat the ground flaxseed together with the milk for about a minute. Add the vinegar, water, maple syrup, oil, and vanilla. Mix well.

In a large bowl, sift together the flour, baking powder, salt, cinnamon, ginger, nutmeg, and allspice. Make a well in the center and add the wet ingredients. Mix with a wooden spoon just until combined. Fold in the grated carrot. Let the batter rest for 10 minutes or so.

Preheat a large nonstick pan or griddle over medium heat. Lightly coat the pan with oil. Add the batter in scant ⅓-cup scoops. Cook for about 4 minutes (or until the tops look mostly cooked), then flip and cook until lightly browned, 4 more minutes.

Stack on a plate covered with aluminum foil until ready to eat. Serve with maple syrup.

COCONUT FRENCH TOAST

makes 6 toasts · total time: 25 mins · active time: 25 mins

If you love the taste of toasted coconut, then this is the breakfast for you. It tastes so special, and yet it's so easy. Serve with your usual French toast accoutrements, like maple syrup and bananas. Something tropical, like mango, would be great as a topping, too. And I never met a plate of French toast that couldn't benefit from blueberries. Use your favorite sandwich bread. I like to use seven-grain bread, but whole wheat, sourdough, or even white would be just dandy. It's essential that you use a spatula thin enough to get under the toast and keep the coconut coating intact. You don't want to lose all that deliciousness!

¼ cup all-purpose flour

1 tablespoon organic cornstarch

⅛ teaspoon salt

1 cup almond milk (or your favorite non-dairy milk)

1 teaspoon coconut extract or pure vanilla extract

¾ cup unsweetened shredded coconut

6 slices of your favorite bread

Refined coconut oil, for the pan

Preheat a large nonstick pan or griddle over medium heat.

In a wide bowl, mix together the flour, cornstarch, and salt. Whisk in the milk until relatively few lumps are left. Mix in the extract.

Spread the shredded coconut onto a dinner plate. Dip each slice of bread into the batter and let the excess drip off. Then, press each side of the bread into the shredded coconut, to coat.

When the pan is hot enough, add a thin layer of coconut oil (about a tablespoon) and use a spatula to evenly coat the bottom of the pan. Cook the coated bread for 4 minutes on each side, until brown and toasty. Add extra oil when you flip the toast. Serve hot.

SINFULLY WHOLESOME WAFFLES

makes eight 6-inch waffles · total time: 45 mins ·
active time: 45 mins

2 cups almond milk (or your favorite
  non-dairy milk)

1 tablespoon apple cider vinegar

1 ¾ cups whole-wheat pastry flour
  (all-purpose flour works, too)

1 tablespoon baking powder

½ teaspoon salt

2 tablespoons ground flaxseed

½ cup water

3 tablespoons olive oil

3 tablespoons pure maple syrup

1 teaspoon pure vanilla extract

½ cup rolled oats

¼ cup wheat germ

For serving:

Fresh berries

Pure maple syrup

NOTE:

If wheat germ isn't a staple in your
kitchen, then another ¼ cup rolled
oats will do!

VARIATION:

Add one cup fresh blueberries to the
batter (as pictured).

There's a time and a place for dessert waffles, but let's face
it, Tuesday morning is probably not it. Still, these waffles are
somehow an indulgence when topped with berries and maple syrup.
But made with flaxseed, oats, wheat germ, and whole-wheat
flour, the ingredients will have you feeling like an angel!

You can (and should) freeze these and pop 'em into the toaster
whenever you want. To freeze, simply let them cool and then slice
into whatever size will fit in your toaster. Seal in an airtight
freezer bag and freeze for up to 1 month. They usually take around
4 minutes in a standard toaster.

In a medium bowl, combine the milk and apple cider vinegar. Set aside to let
curdle.

In the meantime, in a large bowl, combine the flour, baking powder, and salt.

Add the ground flaxseed to the milk and mix vigorously until frothy, 30
seconds to 1 minute. Add the mixture to the flour along with the water,
olive oil, maple syrup, and vanilla. Mix with a wooden spoon until mostly
combined, and then fold in the oats and wheat germ.

Preheat a waffle iron and let the batter rest. Cook the waffles according to
your waffle-iron directions, spraying or brushing the waffle iron with oil
between each waffle. Serve with fresh berries and maple syrup.

BLUEBERRY-MAPLE-BRAN MUFFINS

makes 12 muffins · total time: 40 mins · active time: 10 mins

This is my favorite kind of muffin: deliciously wheaty with a bit of sweetness and juicy fruit inside. I use only maple extract here rather than a larger amount of maple syrup because I don't want a million-dollar muffin and maple syrup is expensive, plus so much of the flavor bakes out anyway. Extract works perfectly and a little bit goes a long way. It's a good ingredient to have on hand for oatmeal, so it's probably worth it to invest in a bottle.

Cooking spray
1 cup almond milk (or your favorite non-dairy milk)
1 tablespoon apple cider vinegar
1½ cups wheat bran
1 cup all-purpose flour or whole-wheat pastry flour
½ cup granulated sugar
1½ teaspoons baking powder
½ teaspoon baking soda
½ teaspoon salt
¼ cup canola oil
¼ cup unsweetened applesauce
2 tablespoons light molasses
1 tablespoon maple extract
1 teaspoon pure vanilla extract
1 cup blueberries (fresh or frozen)

Preheat the oven to 350°F. Lightly spray a 12-cup muffin pan with cooking spray.

In a medium bowl, combine the milk and the apple cider vinegar and set aside to let curdle.

In another medium bowl, mix together the wheat bran, flour, sugar, baking powder, baking soda, and salt. Make a well in the center and add the curdled milk, oil, applesauce, molasses, and both extracts. Stir together the wet ingredients in the well. Then mix the wet and dry ingredients together just until the dry ingredients are moistened, being careful not to overmix. Fold in the blueberries.

Fill each muffin well most of the way full with batter. Bake for 22 to 28 minutes; if your blueberries were frozen, then use the longer baking time. The tops should feel firm to the touch. A toothpick test won't necessarily work here because the blueberries are wet, but if you stick a toothpick or knife in, no batter should appear.

Remove from the oven, and when cool enough to handle (usually 10 minutes or so), transfer the muffins to a cooling rack to let cool the rest of the way.

NOTE:

If made as 12 muffins, these will just peek out of the top of the tins. If you'd like larger muffins, then just fill up 10 muffin cups. The batter will come very close to the top, but it will be OK.

BANANA-NUT
MUFFINS

makes 12 muffins · total time: 40 mins · active time: 10 mins

Cooking spray

3 large very ripe bananas

¼ cup almond milk (or your favorite non-dairy milk)

¼ cup unsweetened applesauce

2 tablespoons refined coconut oil, melted, or canola oil

1 tablespoon ground flaxseed

1 teaspoon pure vanilla extract

1½ cups all-purpose flour or whole-wheat pastry flour

1 teaspoon baking soda

1 teaspoon baking powder

½ teaspoon salt

½ teaspoon ground cinnamon

¼ teaspoon ground allspice

½ cup granulated sugar

¾ cup chopped pecans

¾ cup chopped walnuts

I bet I make these muffins more often than any other baked good, because bananas are always on my kitchen counter in various stages of ripeness. The fact that I make them so often should speak for itself, because other than that, I don't have *that* much to say about them: They're a solid banana muffin! Not too sweet and fairly low in oil. This version is studded with just the right amount of nuts (read: lots), and I like to get wild and mix it up with pecans and walnuts. Of course, you can use just one kind of nut. Other changes you might want to make: Use a cup of berries instead, if they're in season; or if you're feeling more like dessert, replace ½ cup of the walnuts with chocolate chips.

Preheat the oven to 375°F. Lightly spray a 12-cup muffin pan with cooking spray.

In a medium bowl, mash the bananas until they look puréed, with only a few small chunks left. Add the milk, applesauce, oil, ground flaxseed, and vanilla and stir vigorously with a fork.

Sift in the flour, baking soda, baking powder, salt, cinnamon, and allspice, and then add the sugar, too. Mix just until the wet and dry ingredients are incorporated, being careful not to overmix. Fold in the nuts.

Fill each muffin well most of the way full with batter. Bake for 18 to 20 minutes. The tops should be lightly browned and a knife inserted through the center should come out clean (although sometimes it can appear steamy if you hit a chunk of banana).

Remove from the oven and, when cool enough to handle (usually 10 minutes or so), transfer the muffins to a cooling rack to let cool the rest of the way.

CORNBREAD MUFFINS

makes 12 muffins · total time: 40 mins · active time: 10 mins

Cooking spray

1 cup almond milk (or your favorite non-dairy milk)

2 teaspoons apple cider vinegar

1 cup all-purpose flour or whole-wheat pastry flour

1 cup medium-ground cornmeal

1/3 cup granulated sugar

2 teaspoons baking powder

1/2 teaspoon baking soda

1/2 teaspoon salt

2 tablespoons refined coconut oil, melted

2 tablespoons unsweetened applesauce

1 cup corn kernels (thawed if using frozen)

These are what I consider the perfect cornbread muffin, whether for breakfast or for chili. Beautifully golden, not too sweet, plenty of corn flavor, and lots of great texture, too, thanks to fresh corn kernels baked right in. As usual, fresh kernels cut right from the cob are best. But frozen is perfectly fine, too. Just make sure they are thawed first.

If you'd like to turn this into a berry corn muffin, feel free to add 1 teaspoon of vanilla extract and 1 teaspoon grated lemon zest along with the wet ingredients, then fold in 1 cup of berries.

Preheat the oven to 350°F. Lightly spray a 12-cup muffin pan with cooking spray.

In a medium bowl, combine the milk and the apple cider vinegar, then set aside to let curdle.

In another medium bowl, mix together the flour, cornmeal, sugar, baking powder, baking soda, and salt. Make a well in the center and add the curdled milk, oil, and applesauce. Stir together the wet ingredients in the well. Then mix the wet and dry ingredients together just until the dry ingredients are moistened, being careful not to overmix. Fold in the corn kernels.

Fill each muffin well most of the way full with batter. Bake for 18 to 22 minutes. The tops should feel firm to the touch and a knife inserted through the center should come out clean.

Remove from the oven and, when cool enough to handle (usually 10 minutes or so), transfer the muffins to a cooling rack to let cool the rest of the way.

LEMON-BLUEBERRY LOAF

makes one 8-inch loaf · total time: 1 hour 10 mins ·
active time: 15 mins

This loaf is a great reason to turn your oven on during the summer—beautiful cakey slices laced with lemon and studded with blueberries. Sweet perfection! If you want lemon that makes you pucker, you can add the optional lemon glaze, but it's wonderful buck naked as well.

Preheat the oven to 350°F and lightly grease a 4 x 8–inch loaf pan.

In a large bowl, stir together the milk, lemon juice, and lemon zest. Add the oil, applesauce, and granulated sugar and mix vigorously. Stir in the vanilla.

Sift in the flour, baking powder, and salt, and stir until smooth. The batter will be thick! Fold in the blueberries, and then transfer the batter to the prepared loaf pan using a rubber spatula.

Bake for 50 minutes to 1 hour. The top should be lightly browned and firm to the touch. A knife inserted through the center should come out mostly clean.

Let cool in the pan for 15 minutes or so, then invert onto a cooling rack and let cool completely. It may take an hour or so!

If using the glaze, mix the glaze ingredients together in a medium bowl until smooth. It should be a thick but pourable consistency. Place the cooling rack over the sink, then pour the glaze over the top of the loaf, letting the excess drip off. Allow the glaze to set in a cool place, then slice and serve.

½ cup almond milk (or your favorite non-dairy milk)

3 tablespoons fresh lemon juice

1 tablespoon finely grated lemon zest

¼ cup canola oil

2 tablespoons unsweetened applesauce

¾ cup granulated sugar

1 teaspoon pure vanilla extract

2 cups all-purpose flour

2½ teaspoons baking powder

½ teaspoon salt

1 cup blueberries (fresh or frozen; see Note)

For the glaze (optional):

½ cup confectioners' sugar, sifted

2 tablespoons fresh lemon juice

¼ teaspoon pure vanilla extract

NOTE:

If using frozen blueberries, the baking time will be on the longer side. I recommend using wild blueberries if you can find them because they're smaller and hold together nicely during the long baking time.

BANANA-BERRY SCONES

makes 12 scones · total time: 40 mins · active time: 15 mins

These are big, beautiful scones, studded with ruby red raspberries. Coconut oil gives them that perfect shortbread texture, and the banana adds a sweet backdrop of flavor. Make sure that the ones you pick are overripe, with lots of brown spots, and when you mash them, they should appear almost puréed, with no large lumps. Instead of being mixed into the batter, the raspberries are scattered over the tops of the scones and pressed in, so that the scone centers retain their texture. It also has the added benefit of making the scones look super cool.

2 average-size overripe bananas

¾ cup non-dairy milk

1 teaspoon pure vanilla extract

3 cups all-purpose flour

2 tablespoons baking powder

½ cup granulated sugar

½ teaspoon salt

½ cup refined coconut oil, chilled

1 cup fresh raspberries

Turbinado sugar, for sprinkling the tops (optional)

Preheat the oven to 400°F. Line a large baking sheet with parchment paper.

Using a small masher or a fork, mash the banana in a small bowl until it's relatively smooth, with no large lumps. Mix in the milk and vanilla and set aside.

In a large bowl, sift together the flour and baking powder, and then mix in the granulated sugar and salt.

Add the coconut oil in small chunks and cut it into the flour using two kitchen knives so that it resembles coarse crumbs. Now add the banana-milk mixture and lightly knead with your hands until everything comes together. Be careful not to overmix. It should be very stiff.

Use a ½-cup dry measuring cup to scoop dough out onto a large baking sheet. Scatter the raspberries onto the tops of the scones, pushing lightly with your finger to get them to stay. Sprinkle lightly with turbinado sugar, if you like.

Bake for 18 minutes, until the bottoms are golden. Transfer to a cooling rack to let cool completely.

MARBLED
BANANA BREAD

makes one 8-inch loaf · total time: 1 hour 10 mins · active time: 15 mins

1 cup well-mashed very ripe banana (about 3 average-size)

¾ cup granulated sugar

2 tablespoons canola oil

⅓ cup almond milk (or your favorite non-dairy milk)

1 teaspoon pure vanilla extract

1½ cups all-purpose flour

¾ teaspoon baking soda

¾ teaspoon salt

3 tablespoons unsweetened cocoa powder

6 tablespoons boiling water

Here we've got something that reminds me of pressing my face against the glass dessert case at my neighborhood Jewish bakery. Marbled treats were a childhood fascination, and they still hold some of that "How did you do that?" wonder. What can I say—swirls of cocoa are an impressive trick!

It takes a little extra work and a few extra bowls, but isn't it worth it to reawaken that childhood intrigue? This banana bread is perfectly banana-y and not too sweet. The outside of the loaf is a little crunchy after being baked, but if you leave it in Tupperware or plastic wrap at room temp overnight, it gets very moist. It tastes great both ways!

Preheat the oven to 350°F.

In a large bowl, combine the banana with the sugar, oil, milk, and vanilla, whisking until smooth.

Now add the flour, baking soda, and salt, and gently mix just to incorporate. It's okay if there is some flour still visible; be careful not to overmix at this point.

Scoop out 1 cup of the batter and transfer it to a small bowl. Now, in a small heatproof cup, mix the cocoa powder with 3 tablespoons boiling water and stir vigorously with a fork until the chocolate is dissolved. Add this chocolate mixture to the 1 cup batter and mix until the chocolate is thoroughly smooth and incorporated.

Now, back to the plain banana batter in the large bowl. Add 3 tablespoons of boiling water and mix that batter until relatively smooth.

Here comes the fun part—it's time to marble! Lightly grease a 4 x 8–inch loaf pan. Scoop alternate ½ cupfuls of chocolate batter and plain batter into the loaf pan. Nothing has to be precise here; in fact, the more random, the better. Once all of the batter is in the pan, take a butter knife and swirl it through the batter in circular directions for about 10 seconds.

Bake for 55 minutes. Use a butter knife to test for doneness. It might appear a little steamy or sticky from the bananas, but so long as it's not coated in batter, the bread is done. Let cool on a cooling rack, and enjoy!

Rosemary–Chocolate Chip Cookies 272 • Jumbo Oatmeal–
Raisin Cookies 275 • Chai Spice Snickerdoodles 276 •
Kitchen Sink Chocolate Cookies 279 • Chocolate Gingerbread
Cookies with White Chocolate Chips 280 • Norah's Lemon–
Lemon Cookies 283 • Peanut Butter–Chocolate Chip Bars
285 • Chewy Coconut-Date Bars 286 • Just Chocolate
Cake with Gooey Ganache 287 • Sugar & Spice Pineapple
Upside-Down Cake 288 • Orange–Chocolate Chip Bundt
Cake 291 • Chocolate-Zucchini Bundt Cake 292 • Cherry–
Chocolate Chunk Mini Loaves 294 • Almondine Cookies
295 • Strawberries & Cream Bread Pudding 297 • Peachy
Raspberry Cobbler 298

DESSERTS

CHAPTER
11

Who doesn't need a SWEET TREAT

after a long, hard day? Sure, most nights you can reach for some fresh fruit or a carton of coconut-based ice cream, but it really doesn't take much effort to have some warm cookies, or a beautiful Bundt cake that you can feel really proud of. The recipes here are, for the most part, "dump and bake." All you need are a mixing bowl and a fork and you're good to go. (And an oven. And a baking dish. But you get the idea.) There are some icing options that are easy as well, and they can make your dessert a bit fancier if that's how you're feeling. I've also tried to keep the ingredients pretty pantry friendly. Because the last thing you want between you and that cookie fix is a trip to Timbuktu.

ROSEMARY-CHOCOLATE CHIP COOKIES

makes 24 cookies · total time: 30 mins · active time: 15 mins

½ cup refined coconut oil, softened

2 tablespoons loosely packed chopped fresh rosemary

⅓ cup light brown sugar

¼ cup granulated sugar

¼ cup almond milk (or your favorite non-dairy milk)

1 tablespoon ground flaxseed (golden preferred)

2 teaspoons pure vanilla extract

1⅓ cups all-purpose flour

½ teaspoon salt

½ teaspoon baking soda

½ cup semisweet chocolate chips

NOTES:

- I simply use a fork to mix most of the cookie recipes in this book. True, it takes a little more elbow grease and time to beat the oils and sugars adequately, but for me it's somehow worth it not to have to break out the handheld mixer. If you don't see the logic in this (because there really isn't any), then feel free to use your handheld mixer!

- I also use a cookie disher, which is a small ice cream scoop. But for years I relied on nothing but a tablespoon and my eyeballs to make sure my cookies were the same size, so you can do that, too.

- Make sure that your coconut oil is at room temperature. It shouldn't be clear and melted, just somewhat creamy without any large lumps.

There is something otherworldly about the rosemary-chocolate combination, and it makes these my favorite cookies in this world. Did I already say that about another cookie? It was a lie. These are buttery, golden, sublime, and just slightly exotic. If you haven't tried the rosemary-chocolate combo, be prepared to fall in love.

Preheat the oven to 350°F. Lightly grease two large baking sheets.

In a large bowl, use a fork to beat together the coconut oil and rosemary until relatively smooth. Add both sugars and beat for about 1 minute.

Add the milk and ground flaxseed and beat once again, for 30 seconds or so. Mix in the vanilla.

Add about half of the flour, as well as the salt and baking soda, and mix well. Add the remainder of the flour, along with the chocolate chips, and mix well until it looks like, well, cookie dough.

Scoop rounded spoonfuls of dough (about 2 tablespoons per cookie) onto the baking sheets about 2 inches apart. Flatten gently with your hands. Bake for 10 to 12 minutes, until the bottoms are golden brown.

Let cool on the sheets for 3 minutes or so, then transfer to cooling racks to let cool the rest of the way.

Rosemary Chocolate Chip Cookies

serves: 24   name: anya

from the kitchen of: lisa

instructions:
Preheat oven to 350°
Beat together rosemary
& coconut oil
Add almond milk, mix in
vanilla

ingredients:
1 1/2 cup coconut oil
2 T rosemary
1/4 c white sugar
1/3 c brown sugar
1/2 c almond milk
1/2 t vanilla
1/2 c chocolate chips

JUMBO OATMEAL-RAISIN COOKIES

makes about 10 big cookies · total time: 30 mins · active time: 15 mins

These are big bakery-style oatmeal cookies, loaded with raisins and just a touch of cinnamon. They're perfect for an after-school treat. Or during school. Or during work. Or, well, anytime.

Preheat the oven to 350°F. Line two large baking sheets with parchment paper.

In a large bowl, use a strong fork or whisk to vigorously stir together the oil, both sugars, applesauce, and ground flaxseed. Stir for about 1 minute, until very well combined. Mix in the vanilla.

Sift in the flour, baking soda, cinnamon, and salt and mix to combine. Add the oats and raisins, and use your hands to form a dough.

Scoop onto the baking sheets, using about ¼ cup dough per cookie. Flatten a little with your hands. Since you're using two sheets, put 5 cookies on each sheet. Bake for 12 to 14 minutes, until the edges are lightly browned.

Let cool on the sheets for about 5 minutes, then transfer to a cooling rack to let cool completely.

¼ cup canola oil

⅓ cup packed light brown sugar

¼ cup granulated sugar

¼ cup unsweetened applesauce

1 tablespoon ground flaxseed (golden preferred)

1 teaspoon pure vanilla extract

½ cup all-purpose flour

½ teaspoon baking soda

½ teaspoon ground cinnamon

½ teaspoon salt

1½ cups rolled oats

¾ cup raisins

CHAI SPICE
SNICKERDOODLES

makes 24 cookies • total time: 30 mins • active time: 15 mins

For the topping:

¼ cup granulated sugar

¾ teaspoon ground cardamom

¼ teaspoon ground ginger

¼ teaspoon ground cinnamon

Pinch of ground cloves

For the cookies:

½ cup canola oil

1 cup granulated sugar

¼ cup pure maple syrup

3 tablespoons almond milk (or your favorite non-dairy milk)

2 teaspoons pure vanilla extract

2 cups all-purpose flour

1 teaspoon baking soda

¼ teaspoon salt

½ teaspoon ground cinnamon

These are an enticing spin on classic cinnamon snickerdoodles, livened up with Indian chai spices: ginger, cardamom, and a hint of cloves. Of course cookies are always fun to eat, but the crunchy, sugary tops on these make them even more so.

Preheat the oven to 350°F. Line two large baking sheets with parchment paper.

PREPARE THE TOPPING:

Mix all of the topping ingredients together on a dinner plate. Set aside.

PREPARE THE COOKIES:

In a medium bowl, use a fork to vigorously mix together the oil, sugar, maple syrup, and milk. Mix for at least 1 minute, until it resembles applesauce. Then mix in the vanilla.

Sift in the flour, baking soda, salt, and cinnamon, stirring as you add them. Once all the ingredients are added, mix until you've got a pliable dough. Get in there with your hands to mix; it's the easiest way to get the dough to come together.

Roll the dough into walnut-size balls. Pat into the sugar topping to flatten into roughly 2-inch disks. Transfer to the baking sheets, sugar side up, at least 2 inches apart (they do spread a little). This should be easy, as the bottom of the cookies should just stick to your fingers, so you can flip them over onto the baking sheet. Bake for 10 to 12 minutes. They should be a bit browned on the bottoms.

Let cool on the sheets for 5 minutes, then transfer to a cooling rack to let cool completely.

KITCHEN SINK
CHOCOLATE COOKIES

makes 24 cookies · total time: 30 mins · active time: 15 mins

Gorp! Good old raisins and peanuts round out this chunky chocolate-oatmeal cookie. It's the perfect bite for chocolate lovers. And raisin lovers. And peanut lovers. And for all lovers of delicious treats.

Preheat the oven to 350°F. Line two baking sheets with parchment paper.

In a large bowl, beat together the sugar, oil, ground flaxseed, and applesauce until well incorporated, about 2 minutes. Mix in the vanilla.

Sift in the flour, cocoa powder, baking powder, and salt and mix well, then fold in the oats, chocolate chips, raisins, and peanuts and mix until well incorporated.

Drop heaping tablespoonfuls of the dough onto the baking sheets, about 2 inches apart. Pat the tops down with your fingers a bit. Bake for 10 to 12 minutes, until the bottoms appear a few shades darker.

Let cool on the sheets for 5 minutes, then transfer to a cooling rack to let cool the rest of the way.

¾ cup granulated sugar

¼ cup canola oil

1 tablespoon ground flaxseed

⅓ cup unsweetened applesauce

1 teaspoon pure vanilla extract

¾ cup all-purpose flour

⅓ cup unsweetened cocoa powder

½ teaspoon baking powder

½ teaspoon salt

1 cup rolled oats

½ cup semisweet chocolate chips

½ cup raisins

½ cup dry-roasted peanuts

CHOCOLATE GINGERBREAD COOKIES
with White Chocolate Chips

makes 24 cookies · total time: 35 mins · active time: 15 mins

½ cup canola oil

¾ cup granulated sugar

¼ cup light molasses

¼ cup non-dairy milk (any kind)

1 teaspoon pure vanilla extract

1 teaspoon chocolate extract (optional; extra vanilla extract is okay, too)

1⅔ cups all-purpose flour

⅓ cup unsweetened cocoa powder

½ teaspoon baking soda

½ teaspoon baking powder

¼ teaspoon salt

1 tablespoon ground ginger

¼ teaspoon ground cloves

¾ cup white chocolate chips

I love to put chocolate where it doesn't belong! I'm a double offender here, first with cocoa in the gingerbread cookies and second with the white chocolate chips. The result is a spicy, rich molasses cookie with sultry chocolate undertones and ooey-gooey chips. Vegan white chocolate can be hard to find. My favorite is the VeganSweets brand sold at Pangea (www.veganstore.com). But if you can't get your hands on white chocolate chips, then semisweet is a nice treat, as well!

Preheat the oven to 350°F. Line two large baking sheets with parchment paper.

In a medium bowl, use a fork to vigorously mix together the oil, sugar, molasses, and milk. Mix for at least 1 minute, until it resembles a dark caramel. Then mix in the vanilla and chocolate extracts.

Sift in 1 cup of the flour, cocoa powder, baking soda, baking powder, salt, ginger, and cloves. Stir until well combined. Add the white chocolate chips and the remaining ⅔ cup flour and stir briefly, then get in there with your hands to mix. It's the easiest way to get the dough to come together.

Roll the dough into walnut-size balls and flatten into roughly 2-inch disks. Place 2 inches apart on the baking sheet and bake for 10 to 12 minutes, until the bottoms appear a few shades darker.

Let cool on the sheets for 5 minutes, then transfer to a cooling rack to let cool the rest of the way.

NORAH'S LEMON-LEMON COOKIES

makes 24 cookies · total time: 40 mins · active time: 15 mins

First, a Yiddish lesson. *Tante*/TAHN-tah (n): aunt. *Shana*/SHAY-nah (adj): Pretty. *Punim*/POO-nim (n): face. *Keekhl*/KEE-kuhl (n): cookie. *Ferkakte*/fur-KOCKTA (adj): for the purpose of this entry, let's just say that it means "rustic." OK, on to the recipe!

These are a super-lemony sweet treat! I created them for my niece Norah, who asked Grammo (my mom) to ask Tante Isa to make her some lemon cookies with lemon icing. Who can refuse a *keekhl* to that *shana punim!* They're shortbread-ish lemony cookies with a pucker-up lemon glaze. I think they look and taste best when left a little *ferkakte,* so don't be too careful about making them into perfect disks.

For the cookies:

½ cup refined coconut oil, melted

¾ cup granulated sugar

3 tablespoons almond milk

2 tablespoons finely grated lemon zest (from about 2 lemons), plus more for sprinkling (optional)

1 teaspoon pure vanilla extract

1½ cups all-purpose flour

1 teaspoon organic cornstarch

½ teaspoon baking powder

½ teaspoon salt

For the glaze:

2 cups confectioners' sugar

3 tablespoons fresh lemon juice

½ teaspoon pure vanilla extract

1 tablespoon refined coconut oil, melted

Preheat the oven to 350°F. Line two large baking sheets with parchment paper.

In a large bowl, use a fork to beat together the coconut oil and sugar for about 1 minute. Add the almond milk, lemon zest, and vanilla, and beat for 1 more minute, until it resembles applesauce.

Add about half of the flour, as well as the cornstarch, baking powder, and salt, and mix well. Add the remainder of the flour and mix until a soft dough forms.

Scoop the dough onto the baking sheets in rounded spoonfuls (about 2 tablespoons per cookie). Flatten the tops gently with your hands. Bake for 10 to 12 minutes, until the bottoms are golden brown.

Let cool on the sheets for 3 minutes or so, then transfer to cooling racks to let cool the rest of the way.

For the glaze, place the confectioners' sugar in a large bowl. If it is very hard and clumpy, you'll need to sift it, but if it's relatively soft and the clumps easily turn to powder when pinched, then no need. Add the lemon juice, vanilla, and coconut oil and stir vigorously, until a thick and smooth but pourable icing forms. If it seems way too thick, add warm water by the teaspoon until the desired texture is achieved.

While the cookies are on the cooling racks, spoon a tablespoon of icing over each one, letting it drip down the sides. This will make your counter messy, so if that's a problem, you can do it over your sink or place some parchment paper underneath. If you like, zest some extra lemon over each one for pretty yellow flecks. Let the glaze set (10 to 20 minutes depending on the temperature of your room), and serve.

NOTE:

When pressing the dough tops down with your fingers, it's not a bad idea to leave crevices, so that even more of the luscious glaze can settle into the cookies.

PEANUT BUTTER– CHOCOLATE CHIP BARS

makes 8 bars · total time: 50 mins · active time: 10 mins

These are kind of a chewy granola bar. Perfect for a lunch box treat, a picnic, or hey, since there's cereal and oatmeal in there, why not breakfast? These are so easy and so much yummier than packaged granola bars that there is no reason not to give 'em a go. If you love a salty-sweet combo, you can use roasted salted peanuts here, or increase the amount of salt by a big pinch.

Cooking spray
½ cup smooth natural peanut butter
⅓ cup pure maple syrup
⅓ cup brown rice syrup
1 tablespoon canola oil
1 teaspoon pure vanilla extract
½ teaspoon salt
2 cups rolled oats
1 cup crisp rice cereal (like Rice Krispies)
½ cup roasted peanuts, chopped
⅓ cup semisweet chocolate chips

Preheat the oven to 350°F. Line an 8-inch square baking pan with parchment paper, letting the ends overhang a little, and spray lightly with cooking spray.

In a large bowl, stir together the peanut butter, maple syrup, and brown rice syrup until smooth. A strong fork usually gets the job done pretty well. Mix in the oil, vanilla, and salt.

Starting with the fork and then wetting your hands and kneading together well, mix in the oats and crisp rice cereal. Be very firm; the cereal should even crunch up a bit as you're kneading, and you should have a compact, slightly crumbly mixture. Add the peanuts and chocolate chips and, once again, knead until well distributed.

Transfer the mixture to the prepared pan and press in very firmly and as evenly as you can. Bake for 22 to 25 minutes, until the edges appear golden.

Let cool completely in the pan. Remove from the pan by pulling up the sides of the parchment. The best way to slice the bars is to use a chef's knife and press down in one firm motion. Do not saw through the bars. Store in the fridge individually wrapped in plastic wrap and they should keep for at least 5 days.

CHEWY COCONUT-DATE BARS

makes 8 bars · total time: 50 mins · active time: 10 mins

Cooking spray

½ cup smooth natural almond butter

⅓ cup pure maple syrup

⅓ cup brown rice syrup

1 tablespoon refined coconut oil, melted

1 teaspoon coconut extract or pure vanilla extract

½ teaspoon salt

2 cups rolled oats

1 cup crisp rice cereal (like Rice Krispies)

¾ cup unsweetened shredded coconut

½ cup dates, coarsely chopped

Another granola-y bar! This time with coconut and dates. The coconut gets all toasty and tropical as the bar bakes. If you have coconut extract around, then it adds a little more coconutty flavor, but vanilla works, too. To measure the dates, pack them tightly in the measuring cup and then chop.

Preheat the oven to 350°F. Line an 8-inch square baking pan with parchment paper, letting the ends overhang a little, and spray lightly with cooking spray.

In a large bowl, stir together the almond butter, maple syrup, and brown rice syrup until smooth. A strong fork usually gets the job done pretty well. Mix in the oil, extract, and salt.

Starting with the fork and then wetting your hands and kneading together well, mix in the oats and crisp rice cereal. Be very firm; the cereal should even crunch up a bit as you're kneading, and you should have a compact, slightly crumbly mixture. Add the coconut and dates and, once again, knead until well distributed.

Transfer the mixture to the prepared pan and press in very firmly and as evenly as you can.

Bake for 22 to 25 minutes. The sides should be golden.

Let cool completely in the pan. Remove from the pan by pulling up the sides of the parchment. The best way to slice the bars is to use a chef's knife and press down in one firm motion. Do not saw through the bars. Store bars in the fridge individually wrapped in plastic wrap and they should keep for at least 5 days.

JUST CHOCOLATE CAKE

with Gooey Ganache

makes one 8-inch round cake · total time: 1 hour ·
active time: 20 mins

Chocolate cake. Sometimes that's all you need—a nice slab of it, nothing fancy, no fruit or mint nor hint of citrus. They say that chocolate mimics the euphoria of being in love, but how do they know that love isn't mimicking chocolate? It could choose a worse role model. If you don't have a round springform pan, you can line an 8-inch square pan with parchment and have a cute little square cake instead.

1 cup almond milk (or your favorite non-dairy milk)

1 teaspoon apple cider vinegar

¾ cup granulated sugar

⅓ cup canola oil

1½ teaspoons pure vanilla extract

1 cup all-purpose flour

⅓ cup unsweetened cocoa powder

¾ teaspoon baking soda

½ teaspoon baking powder

¼ teaspoon salt

For the ganache:

⅔ cup almond milk (or your favorite non-dairy milk)

8 ounces semisweet chocolate, chopped, or chocolate chips

3 tablespoons pure maple syrup

Preheat the oven to 350°F. Lightly grease an 8-inch springform pan.

Whisk together the milk and vinegar in a large bowl and set aside for a few minutes to let curdle. Then add the sugar, oil, and vanilla, and mix well.

In another bowl, sift together the flour, cocoa powder, baking soda, baking powder, and salt. Add to the wet ingredients in two batches and beat until no large lumps remain (a few tiny lumps are okay).

Pour the batter into the prepared pan and bake for 32 to 35 minutes, until a toothpick inserted through the center comes out clean.

Place on a cooling rack to let cool completely, then release from the pan.

PREPARE THE GANACHE:

In a small saucepan, bring the milk to a boil, then lower the heat to a simmer. Add the chocolate chips and maple syrup and mix with a fork. Turn off the heat and mix until thoroughly melted. Let cool for about 15 minutes before using.

Pour the ganache over the cooled cake and gently tilt the cake at all angles to get the ganache to drip down the sides. Let set, and then dig in!

PINEAPPLE UPSIDE-DOWN CAKE

serves 9 · total time: 1 hour · active time: 20 mins

¾ cup almond milk (or your favorite non-dairy milk)

1 teaspoon apple cider vinegar

¼ cup plus 2 teaspoons canola oil

½ cup light brown sugar

6 to 9 pineapple rings (fresh or canned)

¼ cup granulated sugar

¼ cup unsweetened applesauce

2 teaspoons pure vanilla extract

1¼ cups all-purpose flour

1½ teaspoons baking powder

1 teaspoon cinnamon

½ teaspoon allspice

½ teaspoon salt

Maraschino cherries or fresh raspberries (optional)

This cake is just plain fun. I love to invert the baked cake and peel away the parchment, revealing the lovely caramelized pineapples. Try to gather a crowd to watch the excitement! It's a great way to make something a little fancy that still comes together in one pan. I prefer to use fresh pineapple, which I can get in the produce aisle at the supermarket, but canned is just fine, too. Make sure the canned rings are packed only in their own juice, though, not heavy syrup. If using an 8-inch pan, the baking time will be on the longer side and you'll probably need to use 6 rings instead of 9. You can use a deep round pan as well, if you prefer. Serve slightly warm with a little vegan vanilla ice cream, if you like.

Preheat the oven to 375°F. Lightly grease a 9-inch square baking pan and line it with parchment. Pour the milk into a small bowl and add the apple cider vinegar; set aside to let curdle.

Grease the parchment paper with 2 teaspoons of the oil. Sprinkle ¼ cup of the brown sugar in a relatively even layer over the oil. Layer in the pineapple rings, and set the pan aside.

Now make the batter. In a large bowl, whisk together the curdled milk, remaining ¼ cup brown sugar, granulated sugar, remaining ¼ cup canola oil, applesauce, and vanilla. Sift in the flour, baking powder, cinnamon, allspice, and salt and whisk until smooth.

Pour the cake batter over the pineapple rings. Bake for 40 to 45 minutes, or until a knife inserted through the center comes out clean.

Let cool for 15 minutes or so. Now invert the cake onto a plate and peel away the parchment. Continue to let cool, although it tastes great slightly warm, too. Top with cherries or berries (if desired), slice, and serve.

ORANGE-CHOCOLATE CHIP
BUNDT CAKE

serves 12 · total time: 1 hour 10 mins · active time: 15 mins

There's something about Bundt cake that makes me want a cup of coffee and a gossipy conversation. This one is bright with orange and studded with chocolate chips, and it's so easy to make that you'll definitely want to gossip about it.

Preheat the oven to 350°F. Lightly grease a 12-cup Bundt pan and set aside.

In a large bowl, vigorously whisk together the milk, orange juice, canola oil, applesauce, ground flaxseed, and cornstarch. The mixture should become foamy. Mix in the sugar and whisk until well combined, 30 seconds or so. Mix in the orange zest and vanilla.

Use a fine-mesh strainer to sift in about half of the flour, all of the baking powder, the baking soda, and salt. Mix until well combined, and then add in the rest of the flour and mix until smooth. Fold in the chocolate chips.

Pour the batter into the prepared pan. Bake for 50 to 55 minutes. The top should be browned and puffed and firm to the touch. Stick a knife through the center to test for doneness.

Let cool for 10 minutes, then invert on a cooling rack to let cool completely. Slice and serve! Tightly wrap leftovers in plastic wrap. You can slice the cake into individual portions and freeze those as well.

1 cup almond milk (or your favorite non-dairy milk)

½ cup fresh orange juice

⅓ cup canola oil

⅓ cup unsweetened applesauce

2 tablespoons ground flaxseed (golden preferred)

1 tablespoon organic cornstarch

1 cup granulated sugar

1 tablespoon grated orange zest

1 tablespoon pure vanilla extract

2 ⅔ cups all-purpose flour

1 teaspoon baking powder

½ teaspoon baking soda

¾ teaspoon salt

1 cup semisweet chocolate chips

CHOCOLATE-ZUCCHINI BUNDT CAKE

serves 12 · total time: 1 hour 15 mins · active time: 20 mins

3 cups all-purpose flour

½ cup unsweetened cocoa powder

2 teaspoons baking powder

1 teaspoon baking soda

½ teaspoon salt

1 cup granulated sugar

1 cup unsweetened applesauce

¾ cup almond milk (or your favorite non-dairy milk)

½ cup canola oil

1 tablespoon pure vanilla extract

2 cups shredded zucchini

For the ganache:

½ cup almond milk (or your favorite non-dairy milk)

2 tablespoons pure maple syrup

6 ounces semisweet chocolate, chopped, or chocolate chips

This was one of my favorite cakes at my favorite bakery in Portland, Oregon, Back To Eden. No matter how many foofy cupcakes there were on display, I always went for a big hunk of this humble but delicious cake! It's moist and chocolaty and somehow those little bits of zucchini are like rays of sunshine even on the grayest of Portland days. The ganache is totally optional. If you've got no one to impress and simply want a yummy chocolate cake to slip into your lunch box all week, then feel free to leave it off.

Preheat the oven to 350°F. Lightly grease a 12-cup Bundt pan and set aside.

In a large bowl, sift together the flour, cocoa powder, baking powder, baking soda, and salt. Mix in the sugar.

Make a well in the center and add the applesauce, milk, oil, and vanilla. Use a whisk to mix the wet ingredients together in the well, and then incorporate the wet and dry ingredients until well combined. Fold in the zucchini.

Pour into the prepared pan. Bake for about 50 minutes (a butter knife inserted into the center should come out clean).

Let cool for 10 minutes or so, then invert onto a cooling rack to let cool completely.

PREPARE THE GANACHE:

Bring the almond milk to a roaring boil in a small saucepan. Add the maple syrup. Turn off the heat and whisk in the chocolate chips until totally melted and smooth.

Place the cooling rack over the sink so that excess ganache falls into the sink and not all over the counter. Pour the ganache over the cake, and let it set before slicing and serving.

CHERRY-CHOCOLATE CHUNK MINI LOAVES

makes 8 mini loaves · total time: 45 mins · active time: 15 mins

Cooking spray

½ cup unsweetened applesauce

¼ cup natural almond butter

⅓ cup almond milk (or your favorite non-dairy milk)

⅓ cup unsweetened cocoa powder

⅓ cup plus 2 tablespoons boiling water

¾ cup granulated sugar

1 teaspoon pure vanilla extract

1 teaspoon chocolate extract (optional; extra vanilla extract is okay, too)

⅛ teaspoon almond extract

1½ cups all-purpose flour

¾ teaspoon baking soda

¾ teaspoon salt

4 ounces chocolate, chopped into approximately ½-inch chunks

1 cup chopped sweet cherries (thawed if using frozen)

Nothing says "fun" more than oozy chocolate and sweet, jubilant cherries. Mini loaves are really cute, and I hope that is reason enough to convince you to purchase a mini loaf pan. If not, a muffin tin will work instead! I use chocolate chunks here to achieve the aforementioned ooziness. But you can sub chocolate chips, of course.

I love this method of mixing applesauce with nut butter as your fat. It gives you fiber and protein and nutrients that oil or straight-up applesauce in baked goods wouldn't, and it's also great for structure, crumb, and flavor.

Preheat the oven to 350°F. Lightly spray an 8-loaf mini loaf pan with cooking spray.

Put the applesauce, almond butter, milk, and cocoa powder in a mixing bowl. Pour the ⅓ cup boiling water into the bowl with the chocolate mixture, mixing quickly with a fork to make a thick chocolate sauce. Add the sugar and extracts and mix well.

Sift about half of the flour, along with the baking soda and salt, into the chocolate mixture, and gently stir just to incorporate. Then measure out 1 tablespoon of boiling water and stir again. Now add the rest of the flour and the remaining 1 tablespoon boiling water and stir just until smooth. Take care not to overmix. Fold in the chocolate chunks and the cherries.

Spoon the batter into the prepared pan, filling the wells about three-quarters full.

Bake for 26 to 28 minutes. The tops should be puffy and firm. Stick a knife into the center of a loaf to check for doneness. A little bit of wetness is okay since it could be from a chocolate chunk or a cherry, but the knife should come out mostly dry.

Let cool for 10 minutes, then invert the pan and place the loaves on a cooling rack to let cool some of the way. They're yummy when still a bit warm, with the chocolate chunks oozy and melty. When fully cooled, wrap in plastic wrap to keep them from drying out. If not serving within a day, refrigerate the wrapped loaves.

ALMONDINE COOKIES

makes 24 cookies · total time: 35 mins · active time: 15 mins

These cookies look like little aardvarks! They are rich and buttery and full of almond flavor, with a ground almond base and toasted slivered almonds on top. It's important that the almond paste and coconut oil are both at room temp in order to get the dough to come together beautifully.

7 ounces almond paste, at room temperature

½ cup refined coconut oil, softened

⅔ cup granulated sugar

½ teaspoon almond extract

½ teaspoon pure vanilla extract

1 cup all-purpose flour

½ teaspoon baking powder

½ cup slivered almonds

2 to 3 tablespoons almond milk

Preheat the oven to 325°F. Line two medium baking sheets with parchment paper.

In a food processor, pulse together the almond paste and coconut oil. Once smooth, pulse in the sugar. Transfer to a large bowl and mix in the extracts.

Now use a handheld mixer to mix in the flour and baking powder. The dough should form a soft mass when pressed together.

Place the almonds on a plate and pour the milk into a teacup. For each cookie, scoop 1 tablespoon of dough, roll in your palms to form into a ball, dip one end into the almond milk, and press the moistened end into the nuts. If necessary, press the nuts into the surface of the ball. Place the dough balls, nut side up, on the baking sheets, at least 2 inches apart. Bake for 14 minutes, until the cookies have puffed and spread a little and the nuts are just slightly toasted.

Let cool on the baking sheet for 5 minutes to firm up before carefully transferring to a cooling rack to let cool the rest of the way.

STRAWBERRIES & CREAM
BREAD PUDDING

serves 8 · total time: 1 hour · active time: 20 mins

Sometimes I stare at my bakery-fresh bread with laser eyes, trying to make it a little bit stale so that I can make bread pudding. It doesn't usually work. But there is no better use for day-old bread than bread pudding! This version is rich with coconut milk and juicy sweet strawberries bleeding into the batter. It's so creamy and berrylicious. Serve warm with a little coconut-based vanilla ice cream for added decadence.

6 cups 1-inch-cubed day-old bread (about 1 pound)

1 cup almond milk (or your favorite non-dairy milk)

3 tablespoons organic cornstarch

1 cup coconut milk

½ cup granulated sugar

2 tablespoons fresh lemon juice

1 teaspoon pure vanilla extract

½ teaspoon ground cinnamon

2 cups strawberries, sliced ¼ inch thick

Optional glaze:

1 cup confectioners' sugar

1 tablespoon almond milk

½ teaspoon pure vanilla extract

1 tablespoon refined coconut oil, melted

Preheat the oven to 350°F. Lightly grease an 8-inch square pan.

Place the cubed bread in a large bowl. In another bowl, whisk together the almond milk with the cornstarch to dissolve. Mix in the coconut milk, sugar, lemon juice, vanilla, and cinnamon. Pour over the cubed bread and stir to coat. Let sit for at least 15 minutes to let the liquid soak into the bread.

Fold in the strawberries, then pour into the pan and spread so that it's relatively even.

Bake for 30 to 35 minutes, until the top is lightly browned and feels firm to the touch. Allow to cool a bit on a cooling rack, then serve warm. Drizzle with glaze, if using.

PREPARE THE GLAZE:
Sift the confectioners' sugar into a large bowl. Add the almond milk, vanilla, and coconut oil and stir until smooth.

PEACHY RASPBERRY COBBLER

serves 6 · total time: 1 hour · active time: 20 mins

For the filling:
2½ cups sliced frozen peaches
2½ cups frozen raspberries
2 tablespoons fresh lemon juice
½ cup granulated sugar
2 tablespoons organic cornstarch
2 tablespoons all-purpose flour
⅛ teaspoon salt

For the biscuit topping:
3 tablespoons almond milk (or your favorite non-dairy milk)
2 teaspoons apple cider vinegar
1½ cups all-purpose flour
1½ teaspoons baking powder
¼ teaspoon salt
3 tablespoons granulated sugar
¼ cup refined coconut oil

For sprinkling:
½ teaspoon ground cinnamon
1 tablespoon granulated sugar

There's no reason you can't have cobbler on a weeknight! With all of the organic frozen fruit on the market these days, the fruit tastes like it just fell off the tree. Or vine. Or wherever fruit grows. This one is a twist on peach melba. Peaches and raspberries burst into a thick, juicy, bubbly mess, peeking out from cinnamon-sugar-topped biscuits. Serve warm with vegan vanilla ice cream for a taste of summer any time of year.

PREPARE THE FILLING:

Preheat the oven to 425°F. Mix all of the filling ingredients together in an 8-inch square baking dish. Cover with aluminum foil and bake for 20 minutes.

PREPARE THE BISCUIT TOPPING:

Combine the milk and vinegar in a measuring cup and set aside to let curdle. In a large bowl, sift together the flour, baking powder, and salt. Stir in the sugar. Add the coconut oil by the tablespoonful, cutting it into the flour with your fingertips or two kitchen knives until large crumbs form. Add the milk-vinegar mixture and gently stir a few times to combine.

On a separate plate, mix together the cinnamon and sugar. Remove the pan from the oven, discard the foil, and top the filling with tablespoon-size dollops of biscuit batter. Sprinkle with the cinnamon-sugar mixture.

Bake, uncovered, for 20 more minutes. The fruit should be very bubbly and the biscuits on top sunken in but firm where peeking out from the fruit. Spoon into dishes and serve warm.

ACKNOWLEDGMENTS

First and foremost, I thank my recipe testers, who soaked the cashews, microplaned the garlic, breaded the tofu, and steamed the seitan like total champs. Thank you, guys! You dried my tears and made me smile throughout this entire process.

Lucy Allbaugh
Nikki Benecke Brandt
Michelle Cavigliano
Loz Corona
Lisa Coulson
Nadine D. Doupe
Kelly Dyer
Heather Galaxy
Annemarie Gasthuis
Erin Goddard

Paula Simone Gross
Cara Heberling
Eryn Hiscock
Holly Hutcheson
Angelina Kelly
Allison Nordahl
Lyndsay Orwig
Thalia C. Palmer
Alexandra Penn
Gabrielle Pope

Stephanie Roy
Dayna Rozental
Amanda Sacco
Jess Scone
Garrick Stegner
Claudia Weber
Angela White
Shanell Dawn Williams
Liz Wyman

Thank you to my boyfriend, John McDevitt, for his valuable feedback and support, and for always understanding why there had to be a pile of food magazines in the living room at all times.

Thank you to my mom, Marlene Schifter Stewart, for testing recipes and texting me questions from the aisles of the supermarket. And my sis and family, Michelle, Aaron, Norah, and Max.

Omaha thank-yous:

For prepping and cleaning and going to Whole Foods with me:
Leigh Ellis, Daniel Ocanto

And my Teal Cat crew: Aaron Markley and Nate Welker

For coming over and eating and making Omaha feel like home:
Laura Burhenn, Tessa Wedberg, Megan Hunt, Dave Homan, James "Z" Walmsley, John Henry Muller, and, most important, Denise Muller

For being kitty cats: Kirby, Fizzle, and Avocado

And everyone in Vegan Omaha!

NYC thank-yous:

Terry Hope Romero, for being my everything,
including but not limited to cast-iron-grill carrier and hand model

For the amazing photos, the immensely talented Vanessa Rees

For food styling and specifically snap pea styling, Lauren LaPenna

For food styling and specifically maple syrup pouring, Kate Lewis

For the oodles of doodles, Erica Rose Levine

For moral support, Marshall the cat.

For being eye candy, or at least in the same room as us, Roy Rogers.

My amazing agent, Marc Gerald, thank you for being there from the beginning and maybe even being the beginning.

Little, Brown thank-yous:

My editor, Michael Sand, for believing in the book, even after The Breadbowl Incident.

Mario Pulice and Julianna Lee, for directing the art and making sure my cleavage was in place.

Peggy Freudenthal, for being the best copyeditor ever and totally getting it.

Laura Palese for making everything come together with the beautiful design.

INDEX

WEIGHT

Formulas

OUNCES TO GRAMS
multiply ounces by 28.35

POUNDS TO GRAMS
multiply pounds by 453.5

POUNDS TO KILOS
multiply pounds by .45

Exact Equivalents

1 ounce = 28.35 grams

1 pound = 453.59 grams
.45 kilograms

Approximate Equivalents

$\frac{1}{4}$ ounce	7 grams
$\frac{1}{2}$ ounce	14 grams
1 ounce	28 grams
$1\frac{1}{4}$ ounces	35 grams
$1\frac{1}{2}$ ounces	40 grams
$1\frac{2}{3}$ ounces	45 grams
2 ounces	55 grams
$2\frac{1}{2}$ ounces	70 grams
4 ounces	112 grams
5 ounces	140 grams
8 ounces	228 grams
10 ounces	280 grams
15 ounces	425 grams
16 ounces (1 pound)	454 grams

VOLUME

Formulas

CUPS TO MILLILITERS
   multiply cups by 2.4

CUPS TO LITERS
   multiply cups by .24

Exact Equivalents

1 teaspoon = 4.9 milliliters

1 tablespoon = 14.8 milliliters

1 ounce = 29.57 milliliters

1 cup = 236.6 milliliters

1 pint = 473.2 milliliters

Approximate Equivalents

¼ cup	60 milliliters
⅓ cup	80 milliliters
½ cup	120 milliliters
⅔ cup	160 milliliters
¾ cup	177 milliliters
1 cup	230 milliliters
1¼ cups	300 milliliters
1½ cups	360 milliliters
1⅔ cups	400 milliliters
2 cups	460 milliliters
2½ cups	600 milliliters
3 cups	700 milliliters
4 cups (1 quart)	.95 liter
4 quarts (1 gallon)	3.8 liters

LENGTH

Formula: INCHES TO CENTIMETERS
multiply inches by 2.54

TEMPERATURE

Formula

FAHRENHEIT TO CENTIGRADE
   subtract 32 from Fahrenheit,
   multiply by 5, then divide by 9

(F−32) x 5⁄9

Approximate Equivalents

250°F	120°C
275°F	135°C
300°F	150°C
325°F	160°C
350°F	180°C
375°F	190°C
400°F	200°C
450°F	230°C